D1600804

Coherence in Thought and Action

Life and Mind: Philosophical Issues in Biology and Psychology
Kim Sterelny and Robert A. Wilson, editors

Cycles of Contingency: Developmental Systems and Evolution, Susan Oyama, Paul E. Griffiths, and Russell D. Gray, editors, 2000

Coherence in Thought and Action, Paul Thagard, 2000

Coherence in Thought and Action

Paul Thagard

A Bradford Book

MIT Press

Cambridge, Massachusetts

London, England

This book was set Sabon by Best-set Typesetter Ltd., Hong Kong, and was printed and bound in the United States of America.

First printing, 2000

Library of Congress Cataloging-in-Publication Data

$ 39.95
Thagard, Paul.
  Coherence in thought and action / Paul Thagard.
    p. cm.—(Life and mind)
  "A Bradford book."
  Includes bibliographical references and index.
  ISBN 0-262-20131-3 (alk. paper)
  1. Truth—Coherence theory. I. Title. II. Series.

BD 171 .T45 2000
121—dc21   00-035503

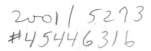

2001 / 5273
#45446316

This book is dedicated to all my coherence collaborators, especially Cam, Chris, Claire, Karsten, Keith, Lije, Michael, and Ziva.

Contents

Preface

This book is an essay on how people make sense of each other and the world they live in. Making sense is the activity of fitting something puzzling into a coherent pattern of mental representations that include concepts, beliefs, goals, and actions. I propose a general theory of coherence as the satisfaction of multiple interacting constraints and show that the theory has numerous psychological and philosophical applications. Much of human cognition can be understood in terms of constraint satisfaction as coherence, and many of the central problems of philosophy can be given coherence-based solutions.

Chapter 1 outlines the importance of the concept of coherence for philosophy and psychology and proposes *cognitive naturalism* as a unified approach to answering philosophical and psychological questions. Chapter 2 develops the cognitive theory of constraint satisfaction as coherence. Chapters 3 and 4 address important philosophical problems concerning the nature of knowledge and reality. Justification of our claims to knowledge is based on five kinds of coherence: explanatory, conceptual, analogical, deductive, and perceptual. These also provide the means to evaluate claims about the nature of reality, for example concerning the existence of the external world, other minds, and God.

Chapter 5 shows the relevance of coherence to philosophical and psychological problems in ethics and politics, arguing that ethical and political judgments are appraisals based on deliberative coherence as well as on the kinds of coherence described in chapter 3. Such appraisals concern not only what to believe, but also what to do, and hence address coherence in action as well as thought. Chapter 6 proposes a new theory of emotional coherence, according to which our appraisals of people, things, and actions emerge from judgments of coherence. It also contends that beauty in science and art is a matter of emotional coherence. Chapter 7 discusses how people who disagree about scientific and other issues can form a consensus on the basis of coherence and communication. Chapter 8 contrasts the coherentist approach to causal inference with probabilistic approaches, particularly Bayesian networks. Finally, chapter 9 suggests some directions for future research on how ideas if about coherence can contribute to progress in philosophy and psychology.

The result, I hope, is a highly coherent theory of coherence. Here briefly is what the book aims to do:

• Provide a far more general and precise account of coherence than has previously been available.

• Increase understanding of how human minds make sense of the way the world is and what to do in it.

• Develop coherence-based answers to central problems in epistemology, metaphysics, ethics, politics, and aesthetics.

• Use ideas about coherence to unify philosophical and psychological problems and to integrate cognition and emotion.

• Understand how consensus can be reached, and identify why it is often difficult to achieve.

• Explain the relation between coherence and probabilistic reasoning.

I hope it all makes sense.

Acknowledgments

For research support I am very grateful to the Killam Fellowship program of the Canada Council and the Natural Sciences and Engineering Research Council of Canada. I am also indebted to the many people who have helped me develop ideas about coherence, including Toby Donaldson, Chris Eliasmith, Nina Gandhi, David Gochfeld, Gilbert Harman, Keith Holyoak, Kim Honeyford, Steve Kimbrough, Walter Kintsch, Ziva Kunda, Elijah Millgram, Greg Nelson, Josef Nerb, Greg Nowak, Claire O'Loughlin, Michael Ranney, Steve Roehrig, Paul Rusnock, Patricia Schank, Cameron Shelley, Miriam Solomon, and Karsten Verbeurgt. I am particularly grateful to Keith Holyoak, Elijah Millgram, Michael Ranney, and Cameron Shelley for valuable comments on a previous draft of the whole book. Thanks to Alan Thwaits for editorial assistance.

For various chapters of this book, I have adapted parts of the following articles:

Thagard, P. (1998). Ethical coherence. *Philosophical psychology* 11: 405–422. Reprinted with permission of Carfax Publishing Company. Appears in chap. 5.

Thagard, P. (2000). Probabilistic networks and explanatory coherence. *Cognitive Science Quarterly* 1: 91–114. Reprinted with permission of Hermes Science Publishing. Appears in chap. 8.

Thagard, P., Eliasmith, C., Rusnock, P., and Shelley, C. P. (forthcoming). Knowledge and coherence. In R. Elio (ed.), *Common sense, reasoning, and rationality* (vol. 11). New York: Oxford University Press. Appears in chap. 3.

Thagard, P., and Kunda, Z. (1998). Making sense of people: coherence mechanisms. In S. J. Read and L. C. Miller (eds.), *Connectionist models of social reasoning and social behavior* (pp. 3–26). Hillsdale, N.J.: Erlbaum. Reprinted with permission of Lawrence Erlbaum Associates. Appears in chap. 4.

Thagard, P., and Verbeurgt, K. (1998). Coherence as constraint satisfaction. *Cognitive Science* 22: 1–24. Reprinted with permission of the Cognitive Science Society. Appears in chaps. 2, 3.

Coherence in Thought and Action

Coherence in Philosophy and Psychology

At the start of the twentieth century, the disciplines of psychology and philosophy were beginning to separate from each other. Originating in the laboratories of Wilhelm Wundt and William James in the 1870s, experimental psychology had grown rapidly in Germany and the United States. Whereas physics became an experimental subject in the 1600s, it took several more centuries before the investigation of mind also became experimental. The nature and operation of mind had been a central concern of philosophers since Plato, and philosophers should have been excited by the eruption of empirical information. Instead, philosophy went its own way, distancing itself from experimental studies of mind and denying their relevance to traditional problems such as the nature of inference and knowledge.

The two main movements of twentieth century philosophy, analytic philosophy and phenomenology, were explicitly antipsychological. Analytic philosophy became dominant in English-speaking countries, establishing a methodology that emphasized logical or linguistic conceptual analysis as central to philosophical investigation and pushing the study of mind into the background. In Germany and later in France, the philosophical approach of phenomenology, originated by Husserl, set itself the task of describing phenomena of conscious experience in order to grasp their ideal meaning. Both analytic philosophy and phenomenology clearly separate philosophy from empirical psychology, establishing philosophy as a conceptual, nonempirical enterprise.

Although analytic philosophy and phenomenology are still widely practiced and taught, intellectually they have fallen on hard times in recent decades. Both have declined into focusing on internal puzzles and historical retrospectives. In contrast, philosophy of mind and allied areas have been reenergized by regaining contact with empirical psychology, particularly with cognitive psychology, which began to supersede behaviorism in the mid 1950s. Cognitive science has emerged as the interdisciplinary study of mind and intelligence, embracing artificial intelligence, linguistics, anthropology, and neuroscience, as well as psychology and philosophy. Now, at the beginning of a new century, it is clear that psychology and philosophy have many fruitful interconnections.

This book explores one such interconnection involving the role of coherence in thought. I use a computational theory of coherence to illuminate both the psychological task of understanding human thinking and the philosophical task of evaluating how people ought to think. The purpose of this introductory chapter is to explain why coherence is a crucial concept for both philosophy and psychology, and to outline the view I call *cognitive naturalism*, which embraces the symbiosis of psychology and philosophy.

1   COHERENCE IN PSYCHOLOGY

People frequently make inferences about what to believe and what to do. Suppose you are trying to decide whether to buy a used car from someone. You need to be able to infer whether the car is in good condition, partly by relying on your own observations and partly by relying on what the seller says about the car's history, maintenance, and repair records. Whether you believe the seller depends on how trustworthy he or she seems to be, which depends on the inferences you make concerning what kind of person the seller is and whether he or she is telling the truth in this instance. On the traditional account of inference that has been with us since Aristotle, your inferences are a series of steps, each with a conclusion following from a set of premises. Part of your chain of inference might be something like this: The seller looks honest. So the seller is honest. So what the seller says is true. So the car is reliable. So I will buy it.

Another view of inference understands it differently, not as the sort of serial, conscious process just described, but as a largely unconscious process in which many pieces of information are combined in parallel into a coherent whole. On this view, your inference about the car and its seller is the result of mentally balancing many complementary and conflicting pieces of information until they all fit together in a satisfying way. The result is a holistic judgment about the nature of the car, the nature of the seller, and whether to buy the car. Such judgments are the result of integrating the diverse information you have to deal with into a coherent total package. Whether you believe what the seller says about the car will depend in part on what you can infer about the car and vice versa.

Talk of holism and coherence might sound rather mystical, but I am not proposing a kind of New Age cognitive psychology. As chapter 2 describes, coherence-based inference can be characterized just as rigorously as traditional, logic-based inference. Moreover, much of human thinking is naturally understood as coherence-based, in domains as diverse as social impression formation, scientific-theory choice, discourse comprehension, visual perception, and decision making. Later chapters will show how these and other kinds of human thinking can be understood in terms of coherence processes. A precise and psychologically plausible theory of coherence has much to contribute to cognitive, social, and developmental psychology. One benefit, described in chapter 6, is a unified account of cognition and emotion.

2 COHERENCE IN PHILOSOPHY

Philosophy differs from psychology in that it is traditionally concerned with normative questions about how people should think, not just descriptive questions about how they do think. At the center of this normative concern is justification: are we justified in having the beliefs that we have acquired, and how can we justify the acquisition of new beliefs? For many philosophers, justification is a matter of finding the right foundation consisting of a set of indubitable beliefs from which other beliefs can be inferred. Two sources of certainty have been pursued: reason and sense experience. Rationalists such as Plato and Descartes attempted to use reason alone to achieve foundations of knowledge that could provide sources of justification for other beliefs. In contrast, empiricists such as Locke, Berkeley, and Hume took sense experience as the foundation for all knowledge.

Today, it is generally recognized that both of these foundational approaches to justification are failures. There are no indubitable truths of reason of the sort that Plato and Descartes sought, and even if there were, they would be too trivial to provide a basis for all the other things we think we know. Similarly, there are no indubitable truths of sense experience, and sense experience alone is too meager a foundation for the rich theoretical knowledge we achieve in science and everyday life. Rationalism and empiricism are both defective theories of knowledge.

The failure of foundational epistemologies has impelled many philosophers, including Hegel (1967), Bradley (1914), Bosanquet (1920), Neurath (1959), Quine (1963), BonJour (1985), and Harman (1986), to pursue an account of justification in terms of coherence. Our knowledge is not like a house that sits on a foundation of bricks that have to be solid, but more like a raft that floats on the sea with all the pieces of the raft fitting together and supporting each other. A belief is justified not because it is indubitable or is derived from some other indubitable beliefs, but because it coheres with other beliefs that jointly support each other. Coherentist justification applies not only to particular beliefs, but also to the justification of particular kinds of deductive and inductive inference (Goodman 1965), and to the justification of ethical principles on the basis of how well they fit with ethical judgments and background knowledge (Rawls 1971). To justify a belief, inferential practice, or ethical principle, we do not have to build up from an indubitable foundation; rather we merely have to adjust our whole set of beliefs, practices, and principles until we reach a coherent state that Rawls calls *reflective equilibrium.*

Coherentist justification of this sort is much more promising than the foundationalist approach, but there is also something philosophically unsatisfying about it. In contrast to the neat Euclidean picture of foundational axioms yielding a set of fully justified axioms, we have vague talk of everything fitting together. What does it mean for a belief or practice or principle to be part of the maximally coherent set? How is coherence maximized? The term "reflective equilibrium" is apt for describing a state in which the maximally coherent state has been achieved, but it provides no insight on how to achieve it.

Chapter 2 provides a much more precise account of coherence as constraint satisfaction, along with algorithms for computing coherence. Later chapters show how different kinds of coherence, employing different kinds of representations and constraints, cover the most important areas of philosophical thought. My aim, however, is not just to describe the logic of coherence, but to give a psychologically plausible account of how coherence mechanisms operate in the human mind. A computational and naturalistic account of coherence can help not only with traditional philosophical problems of justification, but also with psychological concerns about how the mind works. Before undertaking that task, however, some preliminary remarks about the relation of philosophy and psychology are in order.

3   WHY PHILOSOPHY ABANDONED PSYCHOLOGY

It is commonly believed that in the nineteenth century psychology emerged from philosophy, just as physics, chemistry, and biology had earlier used experimental methods to develop beyond philosophical speculation. In contrast, Reed (1997) argues that it is more accurate to say that philosophy emerged from psychology. The history of philosophy before 1900 is dominated by figures who approached epistemological and metaphysical issues in tandem with questions concerning the nature of mind: Plato, Aristotle, Descartes, Hobbes, Locke, Berkeley, Hume, Kant, and Mill, to name just a few. For these thinkers, philosophy and psychology clearly were not separate disciplines. Similarly for the founders of experimental psychology such as Wundt and James, philosophy and psychology were intimately connected. The connection was broken by the development of schools of philosophy that were explicitly antagonistic to any influence of empirical psychology on philosophy.

The two most influential approaches to philosophy in the twentieth century, analytic philosophy and phenomenology, were both formed in reaction to a view disparaged as *psychologism*. Through the influence of Frege and Russell, formal logic became established as a philosophical tool viewed as much superior to psychology for the understanding of inference and the structure of knowledge. Husserl, the founder of phenomenology, began his career discussing the nature of mathematical knowledge in the philosophical/psychological tradition of Brentano, but quickly shifted, partly as a result of Frege's criticisms, to an a priori, nonexperimental investigation of consciousness. Thus the emergence of antipsychologism in twentieth-century philosophy was actually a break with much of the previous history of the subject.

Why did philosophers make this break? It would be superficial to give a purely sociological explanation, although there certainly were concerns among philosophers that their power and influence were waning in comparison to the emerging psychologists. In the United States, the American Philosophical Association was formed *after* the American Psychological Association, and specialty philosophical journals such as *Philosophical Review* were started years after the *American Journal of Psychology* (Wilson 1990). Philosophers in German universities circulated a petition in 1913 to urge that the growing practice of appointing psychologists to philosophy professorships be stopped (Ash 1995, Kusch 1995). Institutionally, philosophers were undoubtedly threatened by the growth of experimental psychology, but there are deeper, more conceptual explanations of why philosophy became antipsychological. For both Frege and Husserl, avoiding psychology was essential for establishing objective truths. Frege's *Basic Laws of Arithmetic*, published in 1893, began with a diatribe against what he called the "psychological logicians," whom he accused of writing logic books that are "bloated with unhealthy psychological fat that conceals all more delicate forms" (Frege 1964, 24). On his view, "the laws of truth are not psychological laws: they are boundary stones set in an eternal foundation, which our thought can overflow, but never displace" (1964, 13). Knowledge of arithmetic has nothing to do with psychology, Frege claimed, but is purely a matter of logic. Similarly, Husserl in 1913 made a sharp distinction between psychology and his enterprise of "pure phenomenology," which he intended to establish "not as a science of facts, but as a science of essential Being," leading the way to "Absolute Knowledge" (Husserl 1962, 40–41). Logical and phenomenological approaches both promised to provide philosophy with a priori knowledge, which no work tainted with empirical psychology could achieve.

The decades have not been kind to either of these ambitious enterprises. Gödel showed in 1931 that logic was insufficient for the foundations of arithmetic, and indubitable a priori truths of the sort sought by Frege, Husserl, and many other philosophers have been elusive. At best, the only defensible a priori truths are trivialities such as "Not every statement is both true and false" (Putnam 1983). The search for solid foundations for knowledge has undoubtedly failed, and this failure has cast some philosophers into the desperate postmodern conclusion that philosophy is dead and that nothing survives but discourse about discourse. Such despair is unwarranted if one adopts a perspective that is coherentist and naturalistic.

Analytic philosophy and phenomenology attracted followers not only because they offered certainty, but also because they offered methods for making philosophical progress. Logical analysis and phenomenological reflection gave philosophers ways of pursuing foundational goals that sharply demarcated their methods from those of empirical psychologists. Along the way, acute philosophers in both traditions often made interesting and important observations about language, meaning, and life in general, although the results of the core methods of logical analysis and phenomenological reduction have been meager. In recent decades, however, naturalistic approaches have undergone a dramatic revival.

4 COGNITIVE NATURALISM

Naturalistic approaches to philosophy that tie it closely to empirical science are as old as philosophy itself. Precursors of contemporary naturalism include Thales, Aristotle, Bacon, Hume, Mill, Peirce, and countless others. Philosophical naturalists see philosophy as continuous with science in both subject matter and method, rejecting supernatural entities. Naturalism need not, however, reduce philosophy to empirical science, which is highly relevant to normative issues in logic, ethics, and aesthetics but does not fully suffice to settle those issues (see chapter 5).

What distinguishes the movement I call *cognitive naturalism* is its close ties with cognitive science, an interdisciplinary amalgam of psychology, artificial intelligence, neuroscience, and linguistics that originated in the mid 1950s (Gardner 1985). The central hypothesis of cognitive science is that thought can be understood in terms of computational procedures on mental representations. This hypothesis has had enormous empirical success, providing explanations of numerous phenomena of human problem solving, learning, and language use. Although there is considerable dispute within cognitive science concerning what kinds of procedures and representations are most important for understanding mental phenomena, the computational/representational approach is common to current work on how mind can be understood in terms of rules, concepts, analogies, images, and neural networks (see Thagard 1996 for a concise survey).

Mirroring the diversity of approaches to cognitive science, philosophers within the cognitive-naturalist movement draw on different aspects of contemporary psychology, linguistics, artificial intelligence, and neuroscience. But the differences should not obscure the commonalities among philosophers who agree that many traditional philosophical problems are intimately tied with results in the cognitive sciences that have implications for issues in epistemology, metaphysics, and ethics (see, for example, P. S. Churchland 1986; P. M. Churchland 1995; Giere 1988; Goldman 1986; Harman 1986; May, Friedman, and Clark 1996).

Cognitive naturalism contrasts with philosophical approaches that predate the rise of the computational/representational view of mind. Quine is an influential twentieth-century naturalist whose epistemological views display the impact of behaviorist psychology, seen especially in his concern with observable stimuli. Quine's major work, *Word and Object*, was published in 1960 and was strongly influenced by his association with his behaviorist colleague B. F. Skinner, but it ignored the emerging approach of George Miller and Jerome Bruner, who were also at Harvard and who started the Center for Cognitive

Studies in 1960. Quine's naturalistic epistemology is a behaviorist naturalism rather than a cognitive naturalism. Another naturalistic movement in the twentieth century was the "scientific philosophy" of the logical positivists. However, its leaders, such as Carnap and Reichenbach, followed Frege in rejecting the relevance of empirical psychology to epistemological issues and in basing their theories on formal logic. If human thinking employed the apparatus of symbolic logic, then there would be little difference between logical naturalism and cognitive naturalism. But there is abundant evidence that thought requires mental representations such as concepts and images, and computational procedures such as spreading activation and pattern matching, that go beyond the kinds of structures and inference allowed in the logical framework. Frege would have said, so much the worse for psychology, but the failure of the logicist approach to epistemology does not permit such arrogance.

A third kind of naturalistic epistemology is found in the writings of sociologists such as Latour and Woolgar (1986), who claim to explain the development of science exclusively in terms of social relations such as power. Social naturalism, however, is compatible with cognitive naturalism if it more reasonably offers social explanations as complementary to cognitive explanations of science rather than as alternatives. Examples of how cognitive and social naturalism can be combined can be found in Goldman's (1992) discussion of epistemic standards for social practices, Bloor's (1992) acceptance of a cognitive background to social relations, and my own discussion of cognitive and social explanation schemas for scientific change (Thagard 1999).

Unlike the monolithic social naturalism of Latour and Woolgar, cognitive naturalism is nonexclusionary.

Applying the cognitive sciences to philosophical problems is completely compatible with also applying other sciences as appropriate. Metaphysical questions concerning space and time, for example, are more heavily tied with contemporary physics such as the general theory of relativity. Cognitive naturalism is compatible with physicalism, the thesis that all natural phenomena are physical, so long as it is recognized that physics is not the only science relevant to philosophical issues. In sum, cognitive naturalism is intended to supersede behavioral and logical naturalism, but it is compatible with nonexclusionary social and physical naturalisms.

This book is an extended exercise in cognitive naturalism, combining psychology and philosophy in ways that are intended to illuminate both fields. Philosophical ideas about coherence turn out to be highly relevant to understanding important psychological phenomena, while computational ideas greatly enrich understanding of coherence. Cognitive naturalism supersedes analytic philosophy and phenomenology and points the way to ongoing cooperation and coevolution of philosophy and psychology. This book pursues a cognitive-naturalist approach not only to epistemology (chaps. 3, 7) and metaphysics (chap. 4), but also ethics (chap. 5), political philosophy (chap. 5), and aesthetics (chap. 6). Let me emphasize that tying philosophy closely to the cognitive sciences does not mean the death of philosophy, because cognitive naturalism only enriches the philosophical enterprise in both content and method.

5 SUMMARY

Philosophy and psychology went their separate ways in the twentieth century, but the separation has been costly.

Cognitive naturalism is the rising approach to philosophy that finds close ties between philosophy and the cognitive sciences, including psychology, neuroscience, linguistics, and artificial intelligence. A computational approach to coherence has the potential to provide both a powerful theory of important cognitive mechanisms and a non-foundational solution to philosophical problems about justification.

2

Coherence as Constraint Satisfaction

As chapter 1 described, the concept of coherence has been important in many areas of philosophy and psychology. But what is coherence? Given a large number of elements (propositions, concepts, or whatever) that are coherent or incoherent with each other in various ways, how can we accept some of these elements and reject others in a way that maximizes coherence? How can coherence be computed? Answers to these questions are important not only for philosophical understanding and the development of machine intelligence, but also for developing a cognitive theory of the role of coherence in human thinking.

Section 1 of this chapter offers a simple characterization of coherence problems that is general enough to apply to a wide range of current philosophical and psychological applications summarized in section 2. Maximizing coherence is a matter of maximizing satisfaction of a set of positive and negative constraints. Section 3 describes five algorithms for computing coherence, including a connectionist method from which my characterization of coherence was abstracted. Coherence problems are inherently intractable computationally, in the sense that, under widely held assumptions of computational complexity theory, there are no efficient (polynomial-time) procedures for solving them. There exist, however, several effective approximation algorithms for maximizing-coherence problems, including one using connectionist (neural network) techniques. Different algorithms yield different methods for measuring coherence, and this is discussed in section 4.

This chapter presents a characterization of coherence that is as mathematically precise as the tools of deductive logic and probability theory more commonly used in philosophy. The psychological contribution of this chapter is that it provides an abstract formal characterization that unifies numerous psychological theories with a mathematical framework that encompasses constraint-satisfaction theories of hypothesis evaluation, analogical mapping, discourse comprehension, impression formation, and so on. Previously these theories shared an informal characterization of cognition as parallel constraint satisfaction, along with the use of connectionist algorithms to perform constraint satisfaction. The new precise account of coherence makes clear what these theories have in common besides connectionist implementations. Moreover, the mathematical characterization generates results of considerable computational interest, including a proof that the coherence problem is NP-hard (nondeterministic-polynomial-hard) and the development of algorithms that provide nonconnectionist means of computing coherence.

1   CONSTRAINT SATISFACTION

When we make sense of a text, picture, person, or event, we need to construct an interpretation that fits with the available information better than alternative interpretations. The best interpretation is one that provides the most coherent account of what we want to understand, considering both pieces of information that fit with each other and pieces of information that do not fit with each other.

For example, when we meet unusual people, we may consider different combinations of concepts and hypotheses that fit together to make sense of their behavior. Coherence can be understood in terms of maximal satisfaction of multiple constraints in a manner informally summarized as follows:

• The elements are representations, such as concepts, propositions, parts of images, goals, actions, and so on.

• The elements can cohere (fit together) or incohere (resist fitting together). Coherence relations include explanation, deduction, facilitation, association, and so on. Incoherence relations include inconsistency, incompatibility, and negative association.

• If two elements cohere, there is a positive constraint between them. If two elements incohere, there is a negative constraint between them.

• The elements are to be divided into ones that are accepted and ones that are rejected.

• A positive constraint between two elements can be satisfied either by accepting both elements or by rejecting both elements.

• A negative constraint between two elements can be satisfied only by accepting one element and rejecting the other.

• The coherence problem consists of dividing a set of elements into accepted and rejected sets in a way that satisfies the most constraints.

Examples of coherence problems are given in section 2.

More precisely, consider a set E of elements, which may be propositions or other representations. Two members of E, e_1 and e_2, may cohere with each other because of some relation between them, or they may resist cohering with each other because of some other relation.

We need to understand how to make E into as coherent a whole as possible by taking into account the coherence and incoherence relations that hold between pairs of members of E. To do this, we partition E into two disjoint subsets, A and R, where A contains the accepted elements of E, and R contains the rejected elements of E. We want to perform this partition in a way that takes into account the local coherence and incoherence relations. For example, if E is a set of propositions and e_1 explains e_2, we want to ensure that if e_1 is accepted into A, then so is e_2. On the other hand, if e_1 is inconsistent with e_3, we want to ensure that if e_1 is accepted into A, then e_3 is rejected and put into R. The relations of explanation and inconsistency provide constraints on how we decide what can be accepted and rejected.

More formally, we can define a *coherence problem* as follows. Let E be a finite set of elements $\{e_i\}$ and C be a set of constraints on E understood as a set $\{(e_i, e_j)\}$ of pairs of elements of E. C divides into C+, the positive constraints on E, and C–, the negative constraints on E. With each constraint is associated a number w, which is the weight (strength) of the constraint. The problem is to partition E into two sets, A and R, in a way that maximizes compliance with the following two *coherence conditions*:

· If (e_i, e_j) is in C+, then e_i is in A if and only if e_j is in A.

· If (e_i, e_j) is in C–, then e_i is in A if and only if e_j is in R.

Let W be the weight of the partition, that is, the sum of the weights of the satisfied constraints. The coherence problem is then to partition E into A and R in a way that maximizes W. Because *a coheres with b* is a symmetric relation, the order of the elements in the constraints does not matter.

Intuitively, if two elements are positively constrained, we want them either to be both accepted or both rejected.

On the other hand, if two elements are negatively constrained, we want one to be accepted and the other rejected. Note that these two conditions are intended as desirable results, not as strict requisites of coherence: the partition is intended to maximize compliance with them, not necessarily to ensure that *all* the constraints are simultaneously satisfied, since simultaneous satisfaction may be impossible. The partition is coherent to the extent that A includes elements that cohere with each other while excluding ones that do not cohere with those elements. We can define the *coherence* of a partition of E into A and R as W, the sum of the weights of the constraints on E that satisfy the above two conditions. Coherence is maximized if there is no other partition that has greater total weight.

This abstract characterization applies to the main philosophical and psychological discussions of coherence. It will not handle nonpairwise inconsistencies or incompatibilities, for example, when there is a joint inconsistency among the three propositions "Al is taller than Bob," "Bob is taller than Cary," and "Cary is taller than Al." However, there are computational methods for converting constraint satisfaction problems whose constraints involve more than two elements into binary problems (Bacchus and van Beek 1998). Hence my characterization of coherence in terms of constraints between two elements suffices in principle for dealing with more complex coherence problems with nonbinary constraints.

An unrelated notion of coherence is used in probabilistic accounts of belief, where degrees of belief in a set of propositions are called coherent if they satisfy the axioms of probability (see chapter 8 for a discussion of the relation between coherence and probability). The characterization of coherence as constraint satisfaction does not by itself furnish a way of understanding degrees of acceptance, but the connectionist algorithm discussed below in section 4 indicates how such degrees can be computed. To show that a given problem is a coherence problem in the sense of this chapter, it is necessary to specify the elements and constraints, provide an interpretation of acceptance and rejection, and show that solutions to the given problem do in fact involve satisfaction of the specified constraints.

2 COHERENCE PROBLEMS

In coherence theories of truth, the elements are propositions, and accepted propositions are interpreted as true, while rejected propositions are interpreted as false. Advocates of coherence theories of truth have often been vague about the constraints, but entailment is one relation that furnishes a positive constraint and inconsistency is a relation that furnishes a negative constraint (Blanshard 1939). Whereas coherence theories of justification interpret "accepted" as "judged to be true," coherence theories of truth interpret "accepted" as "true." A coherence theory of truth may require that the second coherence condition be made more rigid, since two inconsistent propositions can never both be true, but chapter 4 argues against such a theory.

Epistemic justification is naturally described as a coherence problem as specified above. Here the elements in E are propositions, and the positive constraints can be a variety of relations among propositions, including entailment and also more complex relations such as explanation. The negative constraints can include inconsistency, but also weaker constraints such as competition. Some propositions are to be accepted as justified, while others rejected.

The theory of explanatory coherence shows how constraints can be specified for evaluating hypotheses and other propositions (see Thagard 1989, 1992b, and chap. 3 below). In that theory, positive constraints arise from relations of explanation and analogy that hold between propositions, and negative constraints arise either because two hypotheses contradict each other or because they compete with each other to explain the same evidence.

Russell has argued that the justification of mathematical axioms is similarly a matter of coherence (Russell 1973, see also Kitcher 1983, and chapter 3). Axioms are accepted not because they are a priori true, but because they serve to generate and systematize interesting theorems, which are themselves justified in part because they follow from the axioms.

Goodman contended that the process of justification of logical rules is a matter of making mutual adjustments between rules and accepted inferences, bringing them into conformity with each other (Goodman 1965, Thagard 1988, chap. 7). Logical justification can then be seen as a coherence problem: the elements are logical rules and accepted inferences; the positive constraints derive from justification relations that hold between particular rules and accepted inferences; and the negative constraints arise because some rules and inferences are inconsistent with each other.

Similarly, Rawls (1971) argued that ethical principles can be revised and accepted on the basis of their fit with particular ethical judgments. Determining fit is achieved by adjusting principles and judgments until a balance between them, reflective equilibrium, is achieved. Daniels (1979) advocated that *wide* reflective equilibrium should also require taking into account relevant empirical background theories. Brink (1989) defended a theory of ethical justification based on coherence between moral theories and considered moral beliefs. Swanton (1992) proposed a coherence theory of freedom based on reflective equilibrium considerations. As in Goodman's view of logical justification, the acceptance of ethical principles and ethical judgments depends on their coherence with each other. Coherence theories of law have also been proposed, holding the law to be the set of principles that makes the most coherent sense of court decisions and legislative and regulatory acts (Raz 1992).

Thagard and Millgram (1995, Millgram and Thagard 1996) have argued that practical reasoning also involves coherence judgments about how to fit together various possible actions and goals. On this account, the elements are actions and goals, the positive constraints are based on facilitation relations (action a facilitates goal g), and the negative constraints are based on incompatibility relations (you cannot go to Paris and London at the same time). Deciding what to do is based on inference to the most coherent plan, where coherence involves evaluating goals as well as deciding what to do. Hurley (1989) has also advocated a coherence account of practical reasoning, as well as ethical and legal reasoning.

In psychology, various perceptual processes such as stereoscopic vision and interpreting ambiguous figures are naturally interpreted in terms of coherence and constraint satisfaction (Marr and Poggio 1976, Feldman 1981). Here the elements are hypotheses about what is being seen, and positive constraints concern various ways in which images can be put together. Negative constraints concern incompatible ways of combining images, for example, seeing the same part of an object as both its front and its back. Word perception can be viewed as a coherence problem in which hypotheses about how letters form words can be evaluated against each other on the basis of constraints on the shapes and interrelations of letters (McClelland and Rumelhart

1981). Kintsch (1988) described discourse comprehension as a problem of simultaneously assigning complementary meanings to different words in a way that forms a coherent whole. For example, the sentence "The pen is in the bank" can mean that the writing implement is in the financial institution, but in a different context it can mean that the animal containment is in the side of the river. In this coherence problem, the elements are different meanings of words, and the positive constraints are given by meaning connections between words like "bank" and "river." Other discussions of natural-language processing in terms of parallel constraint satisfaction include St. John and McClelland 1992 and MacDonald, Pearlmutter, and Seidenberg 1994. Analogical mapping can also be viewed as a coherence problem. Here two analogs are put into correspondence with each other on the basis of various constraints such as similarity, structure, and purpose (Holyoak and Thagard 1989, 1995).

Coherence theories are also important in recent work in social psychology. Read and Marcus-Newhall (1993) have experimental results concerning interpersonal relations that they interpret in terms of explanatory coherence. Shultz and Lepper (1996) have reinterpreted old experiments about cognitive dissonance in terms of parallel constraint satisfaction. The elements in their coherence problem are beliefs and attitudes, and dissonance reduction is a matter of satisfying various positive and negative constraints. Kunda and Thagard (1996) have shown how impression formation, in which people make judgments about other people based on information about stereotypes, traits, and behaviors, can also be viewed as a kind of coherence problem. The elements in impression formation are the various characteristics that can be applied to people; the positive constraints come from correlations among the characteristics; and the negative constraints come from negative correlations. For example, if you are told that someone is a Mafia nun, you have to reconcile the incompatible expectations that she is moral (nun) and immoral (Mafia). Thagard and Kunda (1998) argue that understanding other people involves a combination of conceptual, explanatory, and analogical coherence.

Important political and economic problems can also be reconceived in terms of parallel constraint satisfaction. Arrow (1963) showed that standard assumptions used in economic models of social welfare are jointly inconsistent. Gerry Mackie (personal communication) has suggested that deliberative democracy should not be thought of in terms of the idealization of complete consensus, but in terms of a group process of satisfying numerous positive and negative constraints. Details remain to be worked out, but democratic political decision appears to be a matter of both explanatory and deliberative coherence. Explanatory coherence is required for judgments of fact that are relevant to decisions, and multiagent deliberative coherence is required for choosing what is optimal for the group as a whole. See the end of chapter 5 for further discussion of coherence in politics.

Table 2.1 summarizes the various coherence problems that have been described in this section. Although much of human thinking can be described in terms of coherence, I do not mean to suggest that cognition is one big coherence problem. For example, the formation of elements such as propositions and concepts and the construction of constraint relations between elements depend on processes to which coherence is only indirectly relevant. Similarly, serial step-by-step problem solving such as finding a route to get from Waterloo to Toronto is not best understood as a coherence problem, unlike choosing between alternative routes that have been previously identified. The claim that much of human inference is a matter of coherence in the

Table 2.1
Kinds of coherence problems

	Elements	Positive constraints	Negative constraints	Accepted as
Truth	Propositions	Entailment, etc.	Inconsistency	True
Epistemic justification	Propositions	Entailment, explanation, etc.	Inconsistency, competition	Known
Mathematics	Axioms, theorems	Deduction	Inconsistency	Known
Logical justification	Principles, practices	Justification	Inconsistency	Justified
Ethical justification	Principles, judgments	Justification	Inconsistency	Justified
Legal justification	Principles, court decisions	Justification	Inconsistency	Justified
Practical reasoning	Actions, goals	Facilitation	Incompatibility	Desirable
Perception	Images	Connectedness, parts	Inconsistency	Seen
Discourse comprehension	Meanings	Semantic relatedness	Inconsistency	Understood
Analogy	Mapping hypotheses	Similarity, structure, purpose	1-1 mappings	Corresponding
Cognitive dissonance	Beliefs, attitudes	Consistency	Inconsistency	Believed
Impression formation	Stereotypes, traits	Association	Negative association	Believed
Democratic deliberation	Actions, goals, propositions	Facilitation, explanation	Incompatible actions and beliefs	Joint action

sense of constraint satisfaction is nontrivial; chapter 8 discusses the alternative claim that inference should be understood probabilistically.

3   COMPUTING COHERENCE

If coherence can indeed be generally characterized in terms of satisfaction of multiple positive and negative constraints, we can precisely address the question of how coherence can be computed, i.e., how elements can be selectively accepted or rejected in a way that maximizes compliance with the two coherence conditions on constraint satisfaction. This section describes five algorithms for maximizing coherence:

- An *exhaustive* search algorithm that considers all possible solutions

- An *incremental* algorithm that considers elements in arbitrary order

- A *connectionist* algorithm that uses an artificial neural network to assess coherence

- A *greedy* algorithm that uses locally optimal choices to approximate a globally optimal solution

- A *semidefinite programming* (SDP) algorithm that is guaranteed to satisfy a high proportion of the maximum satisfiable constraints

The first two algorithms are of limited use, but the others provide effective means of computing coherence.

Algorithm 1: Exhaustive

The obvious way to maximize coherence is to consider all the different ways of accepting and rejecting elements. Here is the exhaustive algorithm:

1. Generate all possible ways of partitioning elements into accepted and rejected.

2. Evaluate each of these for the extent to which it achieves coherence.

3. Pick the one with highest value of W.

The problem with this approach is that for n elements, there are 2^n possible acceptance sets. A small coherence problem involving only 100 propositions would require considering 2^{100} = 1,267,650,600,228,229,401,496,703, 205,376 different solutions. No computer, and presumably no mind, can be expected to compute coherence in this way except for trivially small cases.

In computer science, a problem is said to be intractable if there is no deterministic polynomial-time solution to it, i.e., if the amount of time required to solve it increases at a faster-than-polynomial rate as the problem grows in size. For intractable problems, the amount of time and memory space required to solve the problem increases rapidly as the problem size grows. Consider, for example, the problem of using a truth table to check whether a compound proposition is consistent. A proposition with n connectives requires a truth table with 2^n rows. If n is small, there is no difficulty, but an exponentially increasing number of rows is required as n gets larger. Problems in the class NP include ones that can be solved in polynomial time by a *nondeterministic* algorithm that allows guessing.

Members of an important class of problems called NP-complete are equivalent to each other in the sense that if one of them has a polynomial-time solution, then so do all the others. A new problem can be shown to be NP-complete by showing (a) that it can be solved in polynomial time by a nondeterministic algorithm, and (b) that a problem already known to be NP-complete can be transformed into it, so that a polynomial-time solution to the new problem would serve to generate a polynomial-time solution to all the other problems. If only (b) is satisfied, then the problem is said to be NP-hard, i.e., at least as hard as the NP-complete problems. In the past two decades, many problems have been shown to be NP-complete, and deterministic polynomial-time solutions have been found for none of them, so it is widely believed that the NP-complete problems are inherently intractable. (For a review of NP-completeness, see Garey and Johnson 1979; for an account of why computer scientists believe that P ≠ NP, see Thagard 1993.)

Millgram (1991) noticed that the problem of computing coherence appears similar to other problems known to be intractable and conjectured that the coherence problem is also intractable. He was right: Karsten Verbeurgt proved that MAX CUT, a problem in graph theory known to be NP-complete, can be transformed to the coherence problem (Thagard and Verbeurgt 1998, appendix). If there were a polynomial-time solution to coherence maximization, there would also be a polynomial-time solution to MAX CUT and all the other NP-complete problems. So, on the widely held assumption that P ≠ NP (i.e., that the class of problems solvable in polynomial time is not equal to NP), we can conclude that the general problem of computing coherence is computationally intractable. As the number of elements increases, a general solution to the problem of maximizing coherence will presumably require an exponentially increasing amount of time.

For epistemic coherence and any other kind of problem that involves large numbers of elements, this result is potentially disturbing. Each person has thousands or millions of beliefs. Epistemic coherentism requires that justified beliefs must be shown to be coherent with other beliefs. But the transformation of MAX CUT to the coherence problem shows, on the assumption that P ≠ NP, that computing coherence will be an exponentially increasing function of the number of beliefs.

Algorithm 2: Incremental

Here is a simple, efficient serial algorithm for computing coherence:

i. Take an arbitrary ordering of the elements $e_1, \ldots, e_n$ of E.

ii. Let A and R, the accepted and rejected elements, be empty.

iii. For each element e_i in the ordering, if adding e_i to A increases the total weight of satisfied constraints more than adding it to R, then add e_i to A; otherwise, add e_i to R.

The problem with this algorithm is that it is seriously dependent on the ordering of the elements. Suppose that we have just 4 elements with a negative constraint between e_1 and e_2 and positive constraints between e_1 and e_3, e_1 and e_4, and e_2 and e_4. In terms of explanatory coherence, e_1 and e_2 could be thought of as competing hypotheses, with e_1 explaining more than e_2, as shown in figure 2.1. The three other algorithms for computing coherence discussed in this section accept e_1, e_3, and e_4, while rejecting e_2. But the serial algorithm will accept e_2 if it happens to come first in the ordering. In general, the serial algorithm does not do as well as the other algorithms at satisfying constraints and accepting the appropriate elements.

Although the serial algorithm is not prescriptively attractive as an account of how coherence should be

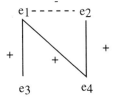

Figure 2.1
A simple coherence problem. Positive constraints are represented by solid lines, and the negative constraint is represented by a dashed line.

computed, it may well describe to some extent people's limited rationality. Ideally, a coherence inference should be nonmonotonic in that maximizing coherence can lead to rejecting elements that were previously accepted. In practice, however, limitations of attention and memory may lead people to adopt local, suboptimal methods for calculating coherence (Hoadley, Ranney, and Schank 1994). Psychological experiments are needed to determine the extent to which people do coherence calculations suboptimally. In general, coherence theories are intended to be both descriptive and prescriptive, in that they describe how people make inferences when they are in accord with the best practices compatible with their cognitive capacities (Thagard 1992b, 97).

Algorithm 3: Connectionist

A more effective method for computing coherence uses connectionist (neural network) algorithms. This method is a generalization of methods that have been successfully applied in computational models of explanatory coherence, deliberative coherence, and elsewhere.

Here is how to translate a coherence problem into a problem that can be solved in a connectionist network:

1. For every element e_i of E, construct a unit u_i that is a node in a network of units U. Such networks are very roughly analogous to networks of neurons.

2. For every positive constraint in C+ on elements e_i and e_j, construct a symmetric excitatory link between the corresponding units u_i and u_j. Elements whose acceptance is favored can be positively linked to a special unit whose activation is clamped at the maximum value. Reasons for favoring some classes of elements are discussed in section 7 of chapter 3.

3. For every negative constraint in C– on elements e_i and e_j, construct a symmetric inhibitory link between the corresponding units u_i and u_j.

4. Assign each unit u_i an equal initial activation (say 0.01), then update the activation of all the units in parallel. The updated activation of unit is calculated on the basis of its current activation, the weights on links to other units, and the activation of the units to which it is linked. A number of equations are available for specifying how this updating is done (McClelland and Rumelhart 1989). For example, on each cycle the activation of unit j, a_j, can be updated according to the following equation:

$$a_j(t+1) = a_j(t)(1-d) + \text{net}_j(\max - a_j(t)) \text{ if net}_j > 0,$$
$$\text{otherwise net}_j(a_j(t) - \min)$$

Here d is a decay parameter (say 0.05) that decrements each unit at every cycle, min is a minimum activation (−1), max is maximum activation (1). Based on weight w_{ij} between each unit i and j, we can calculate net_j, the net input to a unit, by $\text{net}_j = \Sigma_i w_{ij} a_i(t)$. Although all links in coherence networks are symmetrical, the flow of activation is not, because a special unit with activation clamped at the maximum value spreads activation to favored units linked to it, such as units representing evidence in the explanatory coherence model ECHO. Typically, activation is constrained to remain between a minimum (e.g., −1) and a maximum (e.g., 1).

5. Continue the updating of activation until all units have settled, that is, achieved unchanging activation values. If a unit u_i has final activation above a specified threshold (e.g., 0), then the element e_i represented by u_i is deemed to be accepted. Otherwise, e_i is rejected.

We thus get a partitioning of elements of E into accepted and rejected sets by virtue of the network U set-

Table 2.2
Comparison of coherence problems and connectionist networks

Coherence	Connectionist network
Element	Unit
Positive constraint	Excitatory link
Negative constraint	Inhibitory link
Conditions on coherence	Parallel updating of activation
Element accepted	Unit activated
Element rejected	Unit deactivated

tling in such a way that some units are activated and others deactivated. Intuitively, this solution is a natural one for coherence problems. Just as we want two coherent elements to be accepted or rejected together, so two units connected by an excitatory link will tend to be activated or deactivated together. Just as we want two incoherent elements to have one that is accepted and the other rejected, so two units connected by an inhibitory link will tend to suppress each other's activation, with one activated and the other deactivated. A solution that enforces the two conditions on maximizing coherence is provided by the parallel update algorithm that adjusts the activation of all units at once on the basis of their links and previous activation values. Table 2.2 compares coherence problems and connectionist networks.

Connectionist algorithms can be thought of as maximizing the "goodness of fit" or "harmony" of the network, defined by $\Sigma_i\Sigma_j w_{ij}a_i(t)a_j(t)$, where w_{ij} is the weight on the link between two units, and a_i is the activation of a unit (Rumelhart, Smolensky, Hinton, and McClelland 1986, 13). The characterization of coherence given in section 1 is an abstraction from the notion of goodness of fit. The value of this abstraction is that it provides a general account of coherence independent of neural network implementations and makes possible investigation of alternative algorithmic solutions to coherence problems. (See section 4 for discussion of various measures of coherence.)

Despite the natural alignment between coherence problems and connectionist networks, the connectionist algorithms do not provide a universal, guaranteed way of maximizing coherence. We cannot prove in general that connectionist updating maximizes the two conditions on satisfying positive and negative constraints, since settling may achieve only a local maximum. Moreover, there is no guarantee that a given network will settle at all, let alone that it will settle in a number of cycles that is a polynomial function of the number of units.

While there are no mathematical guarantees on the quality of solutions produced by neural networks, empirical results for numerous connectionist models of coherence yield excellent results. ECHO is a computational model of explanatory coherence that has been applied to many cases from the history of science and legal reasoning, including cases with more than 150 propositions (Thagard 1989, 1991, 1992a, 1992b, Nowak and Thagard 1992a, 1992b, Eliasmith and Thagard 1997). Computational experiments have revealed that the number of cycles of activation updating required for settling does not increase as networks become larger: fewer than 200 cycles suffice for all ECHO networks tried so far. ARCS is a computational model of analog retrieval that selects a stored analog from memory on the basis of its having the most coherent match with a given analog (Thagard, Holyoak, Nelson, and Gochfeld 1990). ARCS networks tend to be much larger than ECHO networks—up to more than 400 units and more than 10,000 links—but they still settle in fewer than 200 cycles, and the number of cycles for settling barely increases with network size. Thus, quantitatively these networks are very well behaved, and they also produce the results that one would expect for coherence maximization. For example, when ARCS is used to retrieve an analog for a representation of *West Side Story* from a data base of representations of 25 of Shakespeare's plays, it retrieves *Romeo and Juliet*.

The dozen coherence problems summarized in table 2.1 might give the impression that the different kinds of inference involved in all the problems occur in isolation from each other. But any general theory of coherence must be able to say how different kinds of coherence can interact. For example, the problem of other minds can be understood as involving both explanatory coherence and analogical coherence: the plausibility of my hypothesis that you have a mind is based both on it being the best explanation of your behavior and on the analogy between your behavior and my behavior (chapter 4, section 4). The interconnections between different kinds of coherence can be effectively modeled by introducing new kinds of constraints between the elements of the different coherence problems. In the problem of other minds, the explanatory-coherence element representing the hypothesis that you have a mind can be connected by a positive constraint with the analogical-coherence element representing the mapping hypothesis that you are similar to me. Choosing the best explanation and the best analogy can then occur simultaneously as interconnected coherence processes. Similarly, ethical justification and epistemic justification can be intertwined through constraints that connect ethical principles and empirical beliefs, for example, about human nature (chap. 5). A full, applied coherence theory would specify the kinds of connecting constraints that interrelate the different kinds of coherence problems. The parallel connectionist algorithm for maximizing coherence has no difficulty in performing the simultaneous evaluation of interconnected coherence problems.

Algorithm 4: Greedy

Other algorithms are also available for solving coherence problems efficiently. I owe to Toby Donaldson an algorithm that starts with a randomly generated solution and then improves it by repeatedly flipping elements from the accepted set to the rejected set or vice versa. In computer science, a *greedy* algorithm is one that solves an optimization problem by making a locally optimal choice intended to lead to a globally optimal solution. Selman, Levesque, and Mitchell (1992) presented a greedy algorithm for solving satisfiability problems, and a similar technique produces the following coherence algorithm:

1. Randomly assign the elements of E into A or R.

2. For each element e in E, calculate the gain (or loss) in the weight of satisfied constraints that would result from flipping e, i.e., moving it from A to R if it is in A or moving it from R to A otherwise.

3. Produce a new solution by flipping the element that most increases coherence, i.e., move it from A to R or from R to A. In case of ties, choose randomly.

4. Repeat (2) and (3) until either a maximum number of tries have taken place or until there is no flip that increases coherence.

On the examples on which it has been tested, this algorithm usually produces the same acceptances and rejections as the connectionist algorithm; exceptions arise from the random character of the initial assignment in step 1 and from the greedy algorithm's breaking ties randomly.

Although the greedy algorithm largely replicates the performance of ECHO and DECO on the examples on which we have tried it, it does not replicate the performance of ACME, which does analogical mapping not simply by accepting and rejecting hypotheses that represent the best mappings, but by choosing as the best mappings hypotheses represented by units with higher activations than alternative hypotheses. In general, the output of the greedy algorithm, dividing elements into accepted or rejected, is less informative than the output of the connectionist algorithm, which produces activations that indicate *degrees* of acceptance and rejection. Empirical tests of coherence theories have found strong correlations between experimental measurements of people's confidence about explanations and stereotypes and the activation levels produced by connectionist models (Read and Marcus-Newhall 1993, Kunda and Thagard 1996, Schank and Ranney 1992). Hence the connectionist algorithm is much more suitable than the greedy algorithm for modeling psychological data. Moreover, with its use of random solutions and a great many coherence calculations, the greedy algorithm seems less psychologically plausible than the connectionist algorithm.

Algorithm 5: Semidefinite programming

The proof that the graph-theory problem MAX CUT can be transformed to the coherence problem shows a close relation between them (see the appendix to Thagard and Verbeurgt 1998). MAX CUT is a difficult problem in graph theory that until recently had no good approximation: for twenty years the only known approximation technique was one similar to the incremental algorithm for coherence described above. This technique only guarantees an expected value of 0.5 times the optimal value. Recently, however, Goemans and Williamson (1995) discovered an approximation algorithm for MAX CUT that delivers an expected value of at least 0.87856 times the optimal value. Their algorithm depends on rounding a solution to a relaxation of a nonlinear optimization problem, which can be formulated as a semidefinite programming (SDP) problem, a generalization of linear programming to semidefinite matrices. Mathematical details and proofs are provided in the appendix to Thagard and Verbeurgt 1998.

From the perspective of coherence, two results are important, one theoretical and the other experimental. Verbeurgt proved that the semidefinite programming technique applied to MAX CUT can also be used for the coherence problem, with the same 0.878 performance guarantee: using this technique guarantees that the weight of the constraints satisfied by a partition into accepted and rejected will be at least 0.878 of the optimal weight. But where does this leave the connectionist algorithm, which has no similar performance guarantee? We have run computational experiments to compare the results of the SDP algorithm to those produced by the connectionist algorithms used in existing programs for explanatory and deliberative coherence. Like the greedy algorithm, the semidefinite-programming solution handles ties between equally coherent partitions differently from the connectionist algorithm, but otherwise it yields equivalent results.

4   MEASURING COHERENCE

The formal constraint-satisfaction characterization of coherence and the various algorithms for computing coherence suggest various means by which coherence can be measured. Such measurement is useful for both philosophical and psychological purposes. Philosophers concerned with normative judgments about the justification of belief systems naturally ask questions about the degree of coherence of a belief or set of beliefs. Psychologists can use the degree of coherence as a variable to correlate with experimental measures of mental performance, such as expressed confidence of judgments.

There are three sorts of measurement of coherence that are potentially useful:

- The degree of coherence of an entire set of elements
- The degree of coherence of a subset of the elements
- The degree of coherence of a particular element

The goodness-of-fit (harmony) measure of a neural network defined in section 3, $\Sum_{ij} w_{ij} a_i(t) a_j(t)$, can be interpreted as the coherence of an entire set of elements, and the assigned activation values as representing their acceptance and rejection. This measure is of limited use, however, since it is very sensitive to the number of elements, as well as to the particular equations used to update activation in the networks. Sensitivity to the sizes of networks can be overcome by dividing goodness-of-fit by the number of elements or by the number of links or constraints (see Shultz and Lepper 1996). Holyoak and Thagard (1989) found that goodness-of-fit did not give a reliable metric of the degree of difficulty of analogical mapping, which they instead measured in terms of the number of cycles required for a network to settle.

Network-independent measures of coherence can be stated in terms of the definition of a coherence problem given in section 1. For any partition of the set of elements into accepted and rejected, there is a measure W of the sum of the weights of the satisfied constraints. Let W_opt be the coherence of the optimal solution. The ideal measure of coherence achieved by a particular solution would be W/W_opt, the ratio of the coherence W of the solution to the coherence W_opt of the optimal solution; thus the best solution would have measure one. This measure is difficult to obtain, however, since the value of the optimal solution is not generally known. Another possible measure of coherence is the ratio W/W^*, where W^* is the sum of the weights of all constraints. This ratio does not necessarily indicate the closeness to the optimal solution as W/W_opt would, but it does have the property that the higher the ratio, the closer the solution is to optimal. Thus it gives a size-independent measure of coherence. In addition, when there is a solution where all constraints are satisfied, W/W^* is equal to W/W_opt.

Neither goodness-of-fit nor W/W^* provides a way of defining the degree of coherence of a subset of elements. This is unfortunate, since we would like be able to quantify judgments such as "Darwin's theory of evolution is more coherent than creationism," where Darwin's theory consists of a number of hypotheses. The connectionist algorithm does provide a useful way to measure the degree of coherence of a particular element, since the activation of a unit represents the degree of acceptability of the element. The coherence of a set of elements can then be roughly measured as the mean activation of those elements. It would be desirable to define, within the abstract model of coherence as constraint satisfaction, a measure of the degree of coherence of a particular element or of a subset of elements, but it is not clear how to do so. Such coherence is highly nonlinear, since the coherence of an element depends on the coherence of all the elements that constrain it, including elements with which it competes. The coherence of a set of elements is not simply the sum of the weights of the constraints satisfied by accepting them, but depends also on the comparative degree of constraint satisfaction of other elements that negatively constrain them.

Unlike most of the rest of the book, this chapter has been rather technical, in order to provide a rigorous account of coherence. Computing coherence is a matter of maximizing constraint satisfaction and can be accomplished approximately by several different algorithms. The most psychologically appealing models of coherence optimization are provided by connectionist algorithms. These use neuronlike units to represent elements, and excitatory and inhibitory links to represent positive and negative constraints. Settling a connectionist network by spreading activation results in the activation (acceptance) of some units and the deactivation (rejection) of others. Coherence can be measured in terms of the degree of constraint satisfaction accomplished by the various algorithms.

3

Knowledge

Many contemporary philosophers favor coherence theories of knowledge (Bender 1989, BonJour 1985, Davidson 1986, Harman 1986, Lehrer 1990). But the nature of coherence is usually left vague, with no method provided for determining whether a belief should be accepted or rejected on the basis of its coherence or incoherence with other beliefs. Haack's (1993) explication of coherence relies largely on an analogy between epistemic justification and crossword puzzles. This chapter shows how epistemic coherence can be understood in terms of maximization of constraint satisfaction, in keeping with the computational theory presented in chapter 2. Knowledge involves at least five different kinds of coherence—explanatory, analogical, deductive, perceptual, and conceptual—each requiring different sorts of elements and constraints.

Explanatory coherence subsumes Susan Haack's recent "foundherentist" theory of knowledge. This chapter shows how her crossword-puzzle analogy for epistemic justification can be interpreted in terms of explanatory coherence and describes how her use of the analogy can be understood in terms of analogical coherence. I then give an account of deductive coherence, showing how the selection of mathematical axioms can be understood as a constraint-satisfaction problem. Moreover, visual interpretation can also be understood in terms of satisfaction of multiple constraints. After a brief account of how conceptual coherence can also be understood in terms of constraint satisfaction, I conclude with a discussion of how the "multicoherence" theory of knowledge avoids many criticisms traditionally made against coherentism.

1 HAACK'S "FOUNDHERENTISM" AND EXPLANATORY COHERENCE

Susan Haack's book *Evidence and Inquiry* (1993) presents a compelling synthesis of foundationalist and coherentist epistemologies. From coherentism, she incorporates the insights that there are no indubitable truths and that beliefs are justified by the extent to which they fit with other beliefs. From empiricist foundationalism, she incorporates the insights that not all beliefs make an equal contribution to the justification of beliefs and that sense experience deserves a special, if not completely privileged, role. She summarizes her "foundherentist" view with the following two principles (Haack 1993, 19):

(FH1) A subject's experience is relevant to the justification of his empirical beliefs, but there need be no privileged class of empirical beliefs justified exclusively by the support of experience, independently of the support of other beliefs.

(FH2) Justification is not exclusively one-directional, but involves pervasive relations of mutual support.

Haack's explication of "pervasive relations of mutual support" relies largely on an analogy with how crossword puzzles are solved by fitting together clues and possible interlocking solutions.

To show that Haack's epistemology can be subsumed within the account of coherence as constraint satisfaction,

I will reinterpret her principles in terms of the theory of explanatory coherence (TEC) and describe how crossword puzzles can be solved as a constraint-satisfaction problem by the computational model (ECHO) that instantiates TEC. TEC is informally stated in the following principles (Thagard 1989, 1992a, 1992b):

Principle E1: Symmetry   Explanatory coherence is a symmetric relation, unlike, say, conditional probability. That is, two propositions p and q cohere with each other equally.

Principle E2: Explanation   (a) A hypothesis coheres with what it explains, which can either be evidence or another hypothesis. (b) Hypotheses that together explain some other proposition cohere with each other. (c) The more hypotheses it takes to explain something, the lower the degree of coherence.

Principle E3: Analogy   Similar hypotheses that explain similar pieces of evidence cohere.

Principle E4: Data Priority   Propositions that describe the results of observations have a degree of acceptability on their own.

Principle E5: Contradiction   Contradictory propositions are incoherent with each other.

Principle E6: Competition   If p and q both explain a proposition, and if p and q are not explanatorily connected, then p and q are incoherent with each other (p and q are explanatorily connected if one explains the other or if together they explain something).

Principle E7: Acceptance   The acceptability of a proposition in a system of propositions depends on its coherence with them.

The last principle, Acceptance, states the fundamental assumption of coherence theories that propositions are accepted on the basis of how well they cohere with other propositions. It corresponds to Haack's principle FH2 that acceptance depends not on any deductive derivation but on relations of mutual support. Principle E4, Data Priority, makes it clear that TEC is not a pure coherence theory that treats all propositions equally in the assessment of coherence but, like Haack's principle FH1, gives a certain priority to experience. Like Haack's theory, TEC does not treat sense experience as the source of given, indubitable beliefs, but allows the results of observation and experiment to be overridden on the basis of coherence considerations. For this reason, it is preferable to treat TEC as affirming a kind of discriminating coherentism rather than as a hybrid of coherentism and foundationalism (see the discussion of indiscriminateness in section 7).

TEC goes beyond Haack's foundherentism in specifying more fully the nature of the coherence relations. Principle E2, Explanation, describes how coherence arises from explanatory relations: when hypotheses explain a piece of evidence, the hypotheses cohere with the evidence and with each other. These coherence relations establish the positive constraints required for the global assessment of coherence in line with the characterization of coherence in chapter 2. When a hypothesis explains evidence, this establishes a positive constraint that tends to make them either accepted together or rejected together. In some cases, evidence can also contribute to the explanation, as when a hypothesis in conjunction with observations explains some other observation. Then the hypothesis and the evidence used in the explanation cohere on the basis of statement (b) of principle E2 rather than statement (a).

Principle E3, Analogy, establishes positive constraints between hypotheses that accomplish similar explanations. The negative constraints required for a global assessment of coherence are established by principles E5 and E6, Contradiction and Competition. When two propositions are incoherent with each other because they are contradictory or in explanatory competition, there is a negative constraint between them that will tend to make one of them accepted and the other rejected. Principle E4, Data Priority, can also be interpreted in terms of constraints, by positing a special element EVIDENCE that is always accepted and that has positive constraints with all evidence derived from sense experience. The requirement to satisfy as many constraints as possible will tend to lead to the acceptance of all elements that have positive constraints with EVIDENCE, but their acceptance is not guaranteed. Constraints are *soft*, in that coherence maximizing will tend to satisfy them, but not all constraints will be satisfied simultaneously.

As chapter 2 showed, the idea of maximizing constraint satisfaction is sufficiently precise that it can be computed using a variety of algorithms. The theory of explanatory coherence (TEC) is instantiated by a computer program (ECHO) that uses input about explanatory relations and contradiction to create a constraint network that performs the acceptance and rejection of propositions on the basis of their coherence relations. ECHO can be used to simulate the solution of Haack's crossword-puzzle analogy for foundherentism. Figure 3.1 is the example that Haack uses to illustrate how foundherentism envisages mutual support. In the crossword puzzle, the clues are analogous to sense experience and provide a basis for filling in the letters. But the clues are vague and do not themselves establish the entries, which must fit with the other entries. Filling in each entry depends not only on the clue for it but also on how the entries fit with each other. In terms of coherence as constraint satisfaction, we can say that there are positive constraints connecting particular letters with each other and with the clues. For example, in 1 across the hypothesis that the first letter is H coheres with the hypotheses that the second letter is I and the third letter is P. Together, these hypotheses provide an explanation of the clue, since "hip" is the start of the cheerful expression "Hip hip hooray!" Moreover, the hypothesis that I is the

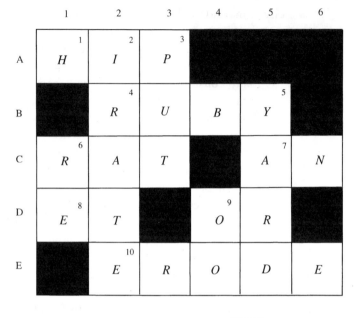

Figure 3.1
Crossword puzzle used to illustrate coherence relations, adapted from Haack 1993 (p. 85).

second letter of 1 across must cohere with the hypothesis that I is the first letter of 2 down, which, along with other hypotheses about the word for 2 down, provides an answer for the clue for 2 down. These coherence relations are positive constraints that a computation of the maximally coherent interpretation of the crossword puzzle should satisfy. Contradictions can establish incoherence relations: only one letter can fill each square, so if the first letter of 1 across is H, it cannot be another letter.

Chris Eliasmith simulated a solution to the crossword puzzle, using the program ECHO, that takes input of the following form:

(explain (hypothesis 1 hypothesis 2 ...) evidence)

For the crossword puzzle, we can identify each square using a system of letters A to E down the left side and numbers 1 to 6 along the top, so that location of the first letter of 1 across is A1. Then we can write A1 = H to represent the hypothesis that the letter H fills this square. Writing C1a for the clue for 1 across, ECHO can be given the following input:

(explain (A1=H A2=I A3=P) C1a)

This input establishes positive constraints among all pairs of the four elements listed, so that the hypotheses that the letters are H, I, and P tend to be accepted or rejected together in company with the clue C1a. Since the clue is given, it is treated as data, and therefore the element C1a has a positive constraint with the special EVIDENCE element, which is accepted. For real crossword puzzles, explanation is not quite the appropriate relation to describe the connection between entries and clues, but it is appropriate here because Haack uses the crossword-puzzle example to illuminate explanatory reasoning. (A full statement of the input to ECHO to handle the crossword-puzzle example can be found in the appendix to Thagard, Eliasmith, Rusnock, and Shelley, forthcoming, available on the Web at http://cogsci.uwaterloo.ca/articles/pages/epistemic.html.) ECHO does not model how people solve the crossword puzzle by working out clues one at a time, but it does serve to evaluate a full solution as one that is generally coherent.

The crossword-puzzle analogy is useful in showing how beliefs can be accepted or rejected on the basis of how well they fit together. But TEC and ECHO go well beyond the analogy, since they demonstrate how coherence can be computed. ECHO not only has been used to simulate the crossword-puzzle example; it has been applied to many of the most important cases of theory choice in the history of science, as well as to examples from legal reasoning and everyday life (Eliasmith and Thagard 1997; Nowak and Thagard 1992a, 1992b; Thagard 1989, 1992b, 1999). Moreover, ECHO has provided simulations of the results of a variety of experiments in social and educational psychology, so it meshes with a naturalistic approach to epistemology tied with human cognitive processes (Read and Marcus-Newhall 1993, Schank and Ranney 1992, Byrne 1995). Thus the construal of coherence as constraint satisfaction, as manifested in the theory of explanatory coherence and the computational model ECHO, subsumes Haack's foundherentism.

2 ANALOGICAL COHERENCE

Although explanatory coherence is the most important contributor to epistemic justification, it is not the only kind of coherence. While the crossword-puzzle analogy plays a central role in her presentation of foundherentism, Haack nowhere acknowledges the important contributions of analogies to epistemic justification. TEC's principle E3 allows such a contribution, since it establishes coherence (and hence positive constraints) among analogous hypotheses. This principle was based on the frequent use of analogies by scientists, for example, Darwin's use of the

Table 3.1
Analogical mapping between epistemic justification and crossword puzzle completion

Epistemic justification	Crossword puzzles
Observations	Clues
Explanatory hypotheses	Words
Explanatory coherence	Words fitting with clues and each other

analogy between artificial and natural selection in support of his theory of evolution.

Using analogies, as Haack does when she compares epistemic justification to crossword puzzles, requires the ability to map between two analogs, the target problem to be solved and the source that is intended to provide a solution. Mapping between source and target is a difficult computational task, but in recent years a number of computational models have been developed that perform it effectively. Haack's analogy between epistemic justification and crossword puzzles uses the mapping shown in table 3.1.

Analogical mapping can be understood in terms of coherence and multiple constraint satisfaction, where the elements are hypotheses concerning what maps to what and the main constraints are similarity, structure, and purpose (Holyoak and Thagard 1995). To highlight the similarities and differences with explanatory coherence, here are comparable principles of analogical coherence:

Principle A1: Symmetry Analogical coherence is a symmetric relation among mapping hypotheses.

Principle A2: Structure A mapping hypothesis that connects two propositions, $R(a, b)$ and $S(c, d)$, coheres with mapping hypotheses that connect R with S, a with c, and b with d. And all those mapping hypotheses cohere with each other.

Principle A3: Similarity Mapping hypotheses that connect elements that are semantically or visually similar have a degree of acceptability on their own.

Principle A4: Purpose Mapping hypotheses that provide possible contributions to the purpose of the analogy have a degree of acceptability on their own.

Principle A5: Competition Mapping hypotheses that offer different mappings for the same object or concept are incoherent with each other.

Principle A6: Acceptance The acceptability of a mapping hypothesis in a system of mapping hypotheses depends on its coherence with them.

In analogical mapping, the coherence elements are hypotheses concerning which objects and concepts correspond to each other. Initially, mapping favors hypotheses that relate similar objects and concepts (A3). Depending on whether analogs are represented verbally or visually, the relevant kind of similarity is either semantic or visual. For example, when Darwin drew an analogy between natural and artificial selection, both analogs had verbal representations of selection, which had similar meaning. In visual analogies, perceptual similarity can suggest possible correspondences, for example, when the atom with its electrons circling the nucleus is pictorially compared to the solar system with its planets revolving around the sun. We then get the positive constraint that if two objects or concepts in an analogy are visually or semantically similar to each other, then an analogical mapping that puts them in correspondence with each other should tend to be accepted. This kind of similarity is much more local and direct than the more general overall similarity that is found between two analogs. Another positive constraint is pragmatic: we want to encourage mappings that can accomplish the purposes of the analogy such as problem solving or explanation (A4).

Additional positive constraints arise because of the need for structural consistency (A2). In the verbal representations (CIRCLE (ELECTRON NUCLEUS)) and (REVOLVE (PLANET SUN)), maintaining structure (i.e., keeping the mapping as isomorphic as possible) requires that if we map CIRCLE to REVOLVE, then we must map ELECTRON to PLANET and NUCLEUS to SUN. The need to maintain structure establishes positive constraints, so that, for example, the hypothesis that CIRCLE corresponds to REVOLVE will tend to be accepted with or rejected with the hypothesis that ELECTRON corresponds to PLANET. Negative constraints occur between hypotheses representing incompatible mappings, for example, between, the hypothesis that the atom corresponds to the sun and the hypothesis that the atom corresponds to a planet (A5). Principles A2 and A5 together incline, but do not require, analogical mappings to be isomorphisms. Analogical coherence is a matter of accepting the mapping hypotheses that satisfy the most constraints.

The multiconstraint theory of analogy just sketched has been applied computationally to a great many examples and has provided explanations for numerous psychological phenomena. Also epistemologically important is the fact that the constraint-satisfaction construal of coherence provides a way of unifying explanatory and analogical epistemic issues. Chapter 4 argues that the solution to the philosophical problem of other minds (that is, whether there are any) requires a combination of explanatory and analogical coherence. Thus metaphysics, like science, can employ a combination of explanatory and analogical coherence to defend important conclusions. Mathematical knowledge, however, is more dependent on deductive coherence.

For millennia, epistemology has been enthralled by mathematics, taking mathematical knowledge as the purest and soundest type. The Euclidean model of starting with indubitable axioms and deriving equally indubitable theorems has influenced many generations of philosophers. Surprisingly, however, Bertrand Russell, one of the giants of the axiomatic method in the foundations of mathematics, had a different view of the structure of mathematical knowledge. In an essay he presented in 1907, Russell remarked on the apparent absurdity of proceeding from recondite propositions in symbolic logic to the proof of such truisms as 2 + 2 = 4. He concluded,

> The usual mathematical method of laying down certain premises and proceeding to deduce their consequences, though it is the right method of exposition, does not, except in the more advanced portions, give the order of knowledge. This has been concealed by the fact that the propositions traditionally taken as premises are for the most part very obvious, with the fortunate exception of the axiom of parallels. But when we push the analyses farther, and get to more ultimate premises, the obviousness becomes less, and the analogy with the procedure of other sciences becomes more visible. (Russell 1973, 282)

Just as scientists discover hypotheses from which facts of the senses can be deduced, so mathematicians discover premises (axioms) from which elementary propositions (theorems) such as 2 + 2 = 4 can be derived. Unlike the logical axioms that Russell, following Frege, used to derive arithmetic, these theorems are often intuitively obvious. Russell contrasts the a priori obviousness of such mathematical propositions with the lesser obviousness of the senses, but notes that obviousness is a matter of degree and that even where there is the highest degree of obviousness, we cannot assume that the propositions are infallible, since they may be abandoned because of conflict with other propositions. Thus for Russell, adoption of a system of mathematical axioms and theorems is much like the scientific process of acceptance of explanatory hypotheses. Let us try to exploit this analogy to develop a theory of deductive coherence.

The elements are mathematical propositions—potential axioms and theorems. The positive and negative constraints can be established by coherence and incoherence relations specified by a set of principles that are adapted from the seven principles of explanatory coherence in section 1.

Principle D1: Symmetry Deductive coherence is a symmetric relation among propositions, unlike, say, deductive entailment.

Principle D2: Deduction (a) An axiom or other proposition coheres with propositions that are deducible from it. (b) Propositions that together are used to deduce some other proposition cohere with each other. (c) The more hypotheses it takes to deduce something, the less the degree of coherence.

Principle D3: Intuitive Priority Propositions that are intuitively obvious have a degree of acceptability on their own. Propositions that are obviously false have a degree of rejectability on their own.

Principle D4: Contradiction Contradictory propositions are incoherent with each other.

Principle D5: Acceptance The acceptability of a proposition in a system of propositions depends on its coherence with them.

When a theorem is deduced from an axiom, the axiom and theorem cohere symmetrically with each other, which allows the theorem to confer support on the axiom as well as vice versa, just as an explanatory hypothesis and the evidence it explains confer support on each other (principles D1, D2). Principle D2, Deduction, is just like the second principle of explanatory coherence, but with the replacement of the coherence-producing relation of explanation by the similarly coherence-producing relation of deduction. These coherence relations are the source of positive constraints: when an axiom and theorem cohere because of the deductive relation between them, there is a positive constraint between them, so that they will tend to be accepted together or rejected together. Statement (c) of the principle has the consequence that the weight of the constraint will be reduced if the deduction requires other propositions. Just as scientists prefer simpler theories, other things being equal, Russell looked for simplicity in axiom systems: "Assuming, then, that elementary arithmetic is true, we may ask for the fewest and simplest logical principles from which it can be deduced" (Russell 1973, 275–276).

Although some explanations are deductive, not all are, and not all deductions are explanatory (Kitcher and Salmon 1989). So explanatory coherence and deductive coherence cannot be assimilated to each other. The explanatory-coherence principle E4, Data Priority, discriminated in favor of the results of sensory observations and experiments, but deductive coherence in mathematics requires a different kind of intuitive obviousness. Russell remarks that the obviousness of propositions such as $2 + 2 = 4$ derives remotely from the empirical obviousness of such observations as that 2 sheep + 2 sheep = 4 sheep. Principle D3, Intuitive Priority, does not address the source of the intuitiveness of mathematical propositions, but simply takes into account that it exists. Different axioms and theorems will have different degrees of intuitive priority. D3 provides discriminating constraints that encourage the acceptance of intuitively obvious propositions such as $2 + 2 = 4$. Russell stressed the need to avoid having falsehoods as consequences of axioms, so I have included in D3 a specific mention of intuitively obvious falsehoods being rejected, even though it is redundant: a falsehood can be indirectly rejected because it contradicts an obvious truth. Principle D4, Contradiction, establishes negative constraints that prevent two contradictory propositions from being accepted simultaneously. For mathematics, these should be constraints with very high weights. Even in mathematics, however, there is sometimes the need to live with contradictions until a way around them can be found, as when Russell discovered the paradoxes of set theory. The contradiction principle is obvious, but it is much less obvious whether there is competition between mathematical axioms in the same way there is between explanatory hypotheses, so I have not included a competition principle.

Whereas there are ample scientific examples of the role of analogy in enhancing explanatory coherence, cases of an analogical contribution to deductive coherence in mathematics are rarer, so my principles of deductive coherence do not include an analogy principle, although analogy is important in mathematical discovery (Polya 1957). Moreover, analogical considerations can indirectly enter into the choice of mathematical principles by virtue of isomorphisms between areas of mathematics that allow all the theorems in one area to be translated into theorems in the other, as when geometry is translated into Cartesian algebra.

Russell does not explicitly defend a coherentist justification of axiom systems, but he does remark, "We tend to believe the premises because we can see that their consequences are true, instead of believing the consequences because we know the premises to be true" (Russell 1973, 273–274). According to Russell, there are additional noncoherence considerations such as independence and convenience that contribute to selection of an axiom set.

Philip Kitcher (1983, 220) sees the contribution of important axiomatizations by Euclid, Cayley, Zermelo, and Kolmogorov as analogous to the uncontroversial cases in which scientific theories are adopted because of their power to unify. Principle D5, Acceptance, summarizes how axioms can be accepted on the basis of the theorems they yield, while at the same time theorems are accepted on the basis of their derivation from axioms. The propositions to be accepted are just the ones that are most coherent with each other, as shown by finding a partition of propositions into accepted and rejected sets in a way that satisfies the most constraints.

This section has discussed deductive coherence in the context of mathematics, but it is also relevant to other domains such as ethics. According to Rawl's notion of reflective equilibrium, ethical principles such as "Killing is wrong" are to be accepted or rejected on the basis of how well they fit with particular ethical judgments such as "Killing Salman Rushdie is wrong" (Rawls 1971). Ethical coherence is not only deductive coherence, however, since *wide* reflective equilibrium requires finding the most coherent set of principles and particular judgments in the light of background information, which can introduce considerations of explanatory, analogical, and deliberative coherence (chapter 5). Principle D3, Intuitive Priority, is much more problematic for ethics than for mathematics, since there is much greater diversity in ethical intuitions than in mathematical intuitions. Nobody denies that $2 + 2 = 4$, but debates rage concerning such topics as the morality of abortion. (See chapter 5 for further discussion of the role of intuition in coherence-based inference.)

Just as explanatory coherence looks for a good fit between hypotheses and evidence, deductive coherence looks for a good fit between general principles and intuitive judgments. Perception can also be construed as a coherence problem.

4 PERCEPTUAL COHERENCE

Explanatory and deductive coherence both involve propositional elements, but not all knowledge is verbal. Our perceptual knowledge includes visual, auditory, olfactory, and tactile representations of what we see, hear, smell, and feel. According to most current theories, visual perception is not a matter of directly apprehending the world, but requires inference and constraint satisfaction (Rock 1983, Kosslyn 1994). Vision is not simply a matter of taking sensory inputs and transforming them directly into interpretations that form part of conscious experience, because the sensory inputs are often incomplete or ambiguous. For example, the subjective Necker cube in figure 3.2 can be seen in two

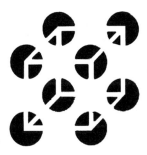

Figure 3.2
The subjective Necker cube. The perceived top edge can be seen either as being at the front or at the back of the cube. Try to make it flip back and forth by concentrating on different edges. (Source: Bradley and Petry 1977, p. 254. Copyright 1977 by Board of Trustees of the University of Illinois. Used with permission of the University of Illinois Press.)

KNOWLEDGE

different ways with different front faces. I shall not attempt here anything like a full theory of different kinds of perception, but I want to sketch how vision can be understood as a coherence problem similar to but different from the kinds of coherence so far discussed.

Visual perception begins with two-dimensional image arrays on the retina, but the visual interpretations that constitute sensory experience are much more complex than these arrays. How does the brain construct a coherent understanding of sensory inputs? In visual coherence, the elements are nonverbal representations of input images and full-blown visual interpretations, which fit together in accord with the following principles:

Principle V1: Symmetry Visual coherence is a symmetric relation between a visual interpretation and a low-level representation of sensory input.

Principle V2: Interpretation A visual interpretation coheres with a representation of sensory input if they are connected by perceptual principles such as proximity, similarity, and continuity.

Principle V3: Sensory priority Sensory input representations are acceptable on their own.

Principle V4: Incompatibility Incompatible visual interpretations are incoherent with each other.

Principle V5: Acceptance The acceptability of a visual interpretation depends on its coherence with sensory inputs, other visual interpretations, and background knowledge.

Principle V2, Interpretation, asserts that how an interpretation fits with sensory input is governed by innate perceptual principles such as ones described in the 1930s by Gestalt psychologists (Koffka 1935). According to the principle of proximity, visual parts that are near to each other join together to form patterns or groupings. Thus an interpretation that joins two visual parts together in a pattern will cohere with sensory input that has the two parts close to each other. According to the Gestalt principle of similarity, visual parts that resemble each other in respect to form size, color, or direction unite to form a homogeneous group. Hence an interpretation that combines resembling parts in a pattern will cohere with sensory input that has parts similar to each other. Other Gestalt principles encourage interpretations that find continuities and closure (lack of gaps) in sensory inputs. The visual system also has built into it assumptions that enable it to use such cues as size constancy, texture gradients, motion parallax, and retinal disparity to provide connections between visual interpretations and sensory inputs (Medin and Ross 1992, chap. 5). These assumptions establish coherence relations between visual interpretations and sensory inputs, and thereby provide positive constraints that tend to make visual interpretations accepted along with the sensory inputs with which they cohere.

Image arrays on the retina are caused by physical processes not subject to cognitive control, so we can take them as given (V3). But considerable processing begins even at the retinal level, and many layers of visual processing occur before a person has a perceptual experience. The sensory inputs may be given, but sensory experience certainly is not. Sensory inputs may fit with multiple possible visual interpretations that are incompatible with each other and are therefore incoherent and the source of negative constraints (V4).

Thus the Gestalt principles and other assumptions built into the human visual system establish coherence relations that provide positive constraints linking visual interpretations with sensory input. Negative constraints arise between incompatible visual interpretations, such as the two ways of seeing the Necker cube. Our overall visual experience arises from accepting the visual interpretation that satisfies the most positive and negative constraints.

Coherence thus produces our visual knowledge, just as it establishes our explanatory and deductive knowledge.

I cannot attempt here to sketch coherence theories of other kinds of perception: smell, sound, taste, touch. Each would have a different version of principle V2, Interpretation, involving its own kinds of coherence relations based on the innate perceptual system for that modality.

5 CONCEPTUAL COHERENCE

Given the above discussions of explanatory, deductive, analogical, and perceptual coherence, the reader might now be worried about the proliferation of kinds of coherence: just how many are there? I see the need to discuss only one additional kind of coherence, conceptual, that seems important for understanding human knowledge.

Different kinds of coherence are distinguished from each other by the different kinds of elements and constraints they involve. In explanatory coherence, the elements are propositions and the constraints are explanation-related, but in *conceptual* coherence the elements are concepts and the constraints are derived from positive and negative associations among concepts. Much work has been done in social psychology to examine how people apply stereotypes when forming impressions of other people. For example, you might be told that someone is a woman pilot who likes monster-truck rallies. Your concepts of *woman, pilot,* and *monster-truck fan* may involve a variety of concordant and discordant associations that need to be reconciled as part of the overall impression you form of this person.

Conceptual coherence can be characterized with principles similar to those already presented for other kinds of coherence:

Principle C1: Symmetry Conceptual coherence is a symmetric relation between pairs of concepts.

Principle C2: Association A concept coheres with another concept if they are positively associated, i.e., if there are objects to which they both apply.

Principle C3: Given Concepts The applicability of a concept to an object, for example, of the concept *woman* to a particular person, may be given perceptually or by some other reliable source.

Principle C4: Negative Association A concept incoheres with another concept if they are negatively associated, i.e., if an object falling under one concept tends not to fall under the other concept.

Principle C5: Acceptance The applicability of a concept to an object depends on the applicability of other concepts.

Taken together, these principles explain how people decide what complexes of concepts apply to a particular object.

The association of concepts can be understood in terms of social stereotypes. For example, the stereotypes that some Americans have of Canadians include associations with other concepts such as *polite, law-abiding, beer-drinking,* and *hockey-playing,* where these concepts have different kinds of associations each other. The stereotype that Canadians are polite (a Canadian is someone who says "Thank you" to bank machines) conflicts with the stereotype that hockey players are somewhat crude. If you are told that someone is a Canadian hockey player, what impression do you form of him? Applying stereotypes in complex situations is a matter of conceptual coherence, where the elements are concepts and the positive and negative constraints are positive and negative associations between concepts (C2, C4). Some concepts cohere with each other (e.g., law-abiding and polite), while other concepts resist cohering with each other (e.g., polite and crude). The applicability of some concepts is given, as when you can see that someone is a hockey player or are told by a reliable source that he or she is a Canadian (C3).

Many psychological phenomena concerning how people apply stereotypes can be explained in terms of conceptual-constraint satisfaction. Kunda and Thagard (1996) were able to account for most of the phenomena emerging from the literature on how people form impressions of others based on stereotypes and individuating information. Their connectionist program, IMP, successfully simulated the results of experiments that demonstrated these phenomena. For example, Kunda, Sinclair, and Griffin (1997) found that the impact of stereotypes on impressions can depend on the perceiver's judgment task and that the effects of stereotypes on trait ratings of an individual were undermined by the individual's behavior. Although construction workers are stereotyped as more aggressive than accountants, a construction worker and an accountant were viewed as equally unaggressive after having failed to react to an insult, an unaggressive behavior. But even though the stereotypes no longer affected trait ratings, they continued to influence predictions about the individual's behavior: the construction worker was still viewed as more likely than the accountant to engage in coarse aggressive behaviors such as punching and cursing.

The parallel constraint-satisfaction model predicts such a pattern when the stereotypes are associated with additional traits that are not undermined by the target's behavior and so can continue to influence behavioral predictions. In this case, even though both targets came to be viewed as equally unaggressive, the construction worker continued to be viewed as a member of the working class, and the accountant as a member of the upper middle class. Punching and cursing are positively associated with working-class status but negatively associated with upper middle-class status. Therefore, the working-class construction worker was viewed as more likely than the upper middle-class accountant to punch and curse even though the two were viewed as equally unaggressive. Conceptual coherence leads to different inferences.

There are thus five primary kinds of coherence relevant to assessing knowledge: explanatory, analogical, deductive, perceptual, and conceptual. (A sixth kind, deliberative coherence, is relevant to decision making and ethics; it is discussed in chapter 5.) Each kind of coherence involves a set of elements and positive negative constraints, including constraints that discriminate in order to favor the acceptance or rejection of some of the elements, as summarized in table 3.2. A major problem for the kind of multifaceted coherence theory of knowledge I have been presenting concerns how these different kinds of coherence relate to each other. To solve this problem, I would need

Table 3.2
Kinds of coherence and their constraints

	Elements	Positive constraints	Discriminating constraints	Negative constraints
Explanatory	Hypotheses, evidence	E2, explanation E3, analogy	E4, data priority	E5, contradiction E6, competition
Analogical	Mapping hypotheses	A2, structure	A3, similarity A4, purpose	A5, competition
Deductive	Axioms, theorems	D2, deductive entailment	D3, intuitive priority	D4, contradiction
Visual	Visual interpretations	V2, interpretation	V3, sensory priority	V4, incompatibility
Conceptual	Concepts	C2, association	C3, given concepts	C4, negative association

Names such as "E2" refer to principles stated in the text.

to describe in detail the interactions involved in each of the fifteen different pairs of kinds of coherence. Some of these pairs are straightforward. For example, explanatory and deductive coherence both involve propositional elements and very similar kinds of constraints. In addition, chapter 4 shows how explanatory and analogical coherence can interact in the problem of other minds.

The relation, however, between propositional elements (explanatory and deductive) on the one hand and visual and conceptual elements is obscure; it is not obvious, for example, how a system of explanatory coherence can interface with a system of visual coherence. One possibility is that a deeper representational level, such as the systems of vectors used in neural networks, may provided a common substratum for propositional, perceptual, and conceptual coherence.

Note that simplicity plays a role in most kinds of coherence. It is explicit in explanatory and deductive coherence, where an increase in the number of propositions required for an explanation or deduction decreases simplicity, and deliberative coherence is similar. Simplicity is implicit in analogical coherence, which encourages 1-1 mappings. Perhaps simplicity plays a role in perceptual coherence as well (Rock 1983, 146).

6 UNIFYING COHERENCE

This presentation of five kinds of coherence raises some serious questions about whether the list is exclusive and exhaustive. Are these kinds of coherence really different from each other, or are some merely variants? Are there other kinds of coherence important for cognition? How do the different kinds of coherence work together?

Some of the five kinds of coherence are indeed quite similar to each other. Explanatory and deductive coherence are alike in that both involve relations among propositions according to similar principles: compare E1–E7 with D1–D5. But I prefer to keep them distinct as separate kinds of coherence because of important differences between their fundamental coherence relations and the associated principles. Deductive coherence is based on purely deductive relations between propositions, as for example when "All cities have roads" implies "Toronto has roads." In contrast, although explanation may sometimes involve deduction, as in theories in mathematical physics, it is fundamentally a matter of there being a causal relation between what is explained and the representations that do the explaining (see Thagard 1999, chap. 7, for a defense of this view of explanation). Moreover, the source of priority is different in the two kinds of coherence. In explanatory coherence, priority is given to propositions that describe the results of experience and observation (principle E4), whereas in deductive coherence, priority accrues to propositions such as $2 + 2 = 4$, whose obviousness may rest on reasoning as well as observation (principle D3).

Conceptual coherence might seem a lot like explanatory or deductive coherence, since for inferential purposes concepts can be translated into propositions. Instead of activating the concept *pilot* to indicate that it applies to a woman Mary, we could speak instead of activating the proposition "Mary is a pilot." To do so, however, would be to obscure the direct connections of positive and negative association that exist between concepts, for example, between *pilot* and *male* and *daring*. There is abundant experimental and computational evidence that concepts are a psychologically realistic kind of mental representation not reducible to propositions (Thagard 1996, chap. 4). Moreover, the associative relations between concepts are much looser than the explanatory and deductive relations required for those kinds of coherence, so the constraints between elements in conceptual coherence deserve to be treated separately.

How many other kinds of coherence are there? Chapter 5 discusses deliberative coherence, which concerns how decisions are made on the basis of coherence among actions and goals. This sixth kind of coherence is, as far as I know, the only additional one needed to cover the main kinds of inference that people perform. Deliberative coherence concerns inferences about what to do, so it is not discussed in this chapter, which concerns inferences relevant to the development of knowledge. Chapter 6 discusses emotional coherence, which is not, however, a seventh kind of coherence along the lines so far discussed. Rather, it provides an expanded way of considering the elements and constraints of the six basic kinds of coherence, by adding emotional attitudes toward the elements.

Having six kinds of coherence might suggest that inference is a confused jumble, but they in fact suggest a unified view of coherence-based inference. All six kinds of coherence are specified in terms of elements and constraints, and we saw in chapter 2 that there are algorithms for maximizing constraint satisfaction. Hence once constraints and elements are specified, the same inference engine can work to decide which elements to accept and which to reject. The only rule of inference is this: accept a conclusion if its acceptance maximizes coherence. Different kinds of coherence furnish different kinds of elements connected by different kinds of constraints, but inference is performed by exactly the same kind of constraint-satisfaction algorithm working simultaneously with all the different elements and constraints. This makes possible a unified account of inferences based on more than one kind of coherence. Later chapters provide extended examples of complex inferences involving mixtures of explanatory, analogical, and other kinds of coherence (see chap. 4 on the problem of other minds, chap. 5 on capital punishment, and chap. 6 on trust).

Although much of cognition can be understood in terms of coherence mechanisms, there is obviously more to cognition than achieving coherence among a set of given elements. Cognition is also generative, producing new concepts, propositions, and analogies. Moreover, for coherence to be assessed, constraints among elements need to have been generated.

Generation of new elements is sometimes driven by *in*coherence. If I am trying to understand someone but fail to form a coherent impression or attribution, I may be spurred to form new elements that can add coherence to the old set of elements. To take an example from Kunda et al. 1990, if I am told that someone is a Harvard-educated carpenter, it may be difficult to reconcile the conflicting expectations associated with the two concepts. Surprise is an emotional reaction that signals that a satisfactory degree of coherence has not been achieved (see chapter 6). This reaction triggers hypothesis formation, as I ask myself how someone with a Harvard degree could end up working as a carpenter. People show ingenuity in generating explanations, for example, that the Harvard graduate was a counterculture type who preferred a non-professional career path. Hence new hypotheses and possibly also new concepts (*Ivy League laborer*) can be added to the set of elements so as to lend greater coherence to the attempt to make sense of this person. In this case, generation of elements is incoherence-driven: it is prompted by a failure to achieve an interpretation that satisfies an adequate number of the positive and negative constraints. In addition to surprise, other emotions, such as anxiety, may also signal incoherence.

Not all element generation is incoherence-driven, however. Some representations arise serendipitously, based on things we just happen to encounter. I may form a concept of Albanians as the result of meeting various immigrants from Albania, without having experienced any incoherence in my previous attempts to understand them. In other cases, new representations may arise from curiosity-driven thinking that is motivated not by any incoherence but by the desire to find out more about something that interests me. If I am interested in the Balkans, I will learn more about Serbs and Croats and may form stereotypes about them without having tried and failed to fit them together with my other social concepts. Motivation may also lead one to generate new concepts. For example, our desire to protect our stereotypes from change in the face of disconfirmation may lead us to assign individuals who threaten our stereotypes into novel subtypes that serve to isolate these individuals from their group (Kunda and Oleson 1995). Thus serendipity, curiosity, and motivation, in addition to incoherence, can spur the generation of new representations.

Where do constraints come from? Some may be innate, capturing basic conceptual relations such as that an object cannot be both red and black all over. Most constraints, however, capture empirically discovered relations between elements. For conceptual coherence, I learn that some concepts (e.g., nurse and benevolent) are positively associated, whereas other concepts (e.g., Nazi and benevolent) are negatively associated. Such associations may be learned through direct observation of nurses or Nazis as well as through cultural transmission. For explanatory coherence, the positive constraints come from understanding causal relations. The link between the hypothesis that Mary is in love and the fact to be explained that Mary is very happy depends on the causal judgment gleaned from experience that being in love can cause people to be happy. Negative constraints in explanatory coherence arise from logical contradictions (you cannot be both in love and not in love) and from competing hypotheses (maybe instead she's happy because she got a promotion at work).

Because any full account of human cognition would have to include an account of how new concepts, hypotheses, and other representations are formed, a complete cognitive architecture would have to include generation mechanisms as well as coherence mechanisms (see Thagard 1996 for a review of different kinds of learning). My goal in this book is not to propose a cognitive architecture, but merely to show how coherence mechanisms contribute to making sense of people and events.

Explanatory, analogical, deductive, visual, and conceptual coherence add up to a comprehensive, computable, naturalistic theory of epistemic coherence. Let us now see how this theory can handle some of the standard objections that have been made to coherentist epistemologies.

7   OBJECTIONS TO COHERENCE THEORIES

Vagueness

One common objection to coherence theories is *vagueness*: in contrast to fully specified theories of deductive and inductive inference, coherence theories have generally been vague about what coherence is and how coherent elements can be selected. My general characterization of coherence shows how vagueness can be overcome. First, for a particular kind of coherence, it is necessary to specify the nature of the elements and define the positive and negative constraints that hold between them. This task has been accomplished for the kinds of coherence discussed above. Second, once the elements and constraints have been specified, it is possible to use connectionist algorithms to compute coherence, accepting and rejecting elements in a way that approximately maximizes compliance with the coherence conditions (chapter 2). Computing coherence can then be as exact as deduction or probabilistic reasoning (chapter 8), and can avoid the problems of computational intractability that arise with them. Being able to do this computation does not, of course, help with the problem of generating elements and constraints, but it does show how to make a judgment of coherence with the elements and constraints on hand. Arriving at a rich, coherent set of elements—scientific theories, ethical principles, or whatever—is a very complex process that intermingles both assessment of coherence and generation of new elements; the parallel constraint-satisfaction algorithm shows only how to do the first of these. Whether a cognitive task can be construed as a coherence problem depends on the extent to which it involves evaluation of how existing elements fit together rather than generation of new elements.

Indiscriminateness

The second objection to coherence theories is *indiscriminateness*: coherence theories fail to allow that some kinds of information deserve to be treated more seriously than others. For example, in epistemic justification, it has been argued that perceptual beliefs should be taken more seriously in determining general coherence than mere speculation. The abstract characterization of coherence given in chapter 2 is indiscriminating, in that all elements are treated equally in determinations of coherence.

But all the kinds of coherence discussed above are discriminating in the sense of allowing favored elements of E to be given priority in being chosen for the set of accepted elements A. We can define a discriminating-coherence problem as one where members of a subset D of E are favored to be members of A. Favoring them does not guarantee that they will be accepted: if there were such a guarantee, the problem would be foundationalist rather than coherentist, and D would constitute the foundation for all other elements. As Audi (1993) points out, even foundationalists face a coherence problem in trying to decide what beliefs to accept in addition to the foundational ones. Explanatory coherence treats hypothesis evaluation as a discriminating-coherence problem, since it gives priority to propositions that describe observational and experimental results. That theory is not foundationalist, since evidential propositions can be rejected if they fail to cohere with the entire set of propositions. Similarly, table 3.2 makes it clear that the other five kinds of coherence are also discriminating.

Computing a solution to a discriminating-coherence problem involves only a small addition to the characterization of coherence given in chapter 2, p. 18:

For each element d in the discriminated set D, construct a positive constraint between d and a special element e_s that is assigned to the set A of accepted elements.

The effect of having a special element that constrains members of the set D is that the favored elements will tend to be accepted, without any guarantee that they will be accepted. Chapter 2 already described how the connectionist algorithm for coherence implements the discrimination condition by having an excitatory link between the unit representing d and a special unit that has a fixed, unchanging maximum activation (i.e., 1). The effect of constructing such links to a special unit is that when activation is updated, it flows directly from the activated special unit to the units representing the discriminated elements. Hence those units will more strongly tend to end up activated than nondiscriminated ones and will have a greater effect on which other units get activated. The algorithm does not, however, enforce the activation of units representing discriminated elements, which can be deactivated if they have strong inhibitory links with other activated elements. Thus a coherence computation can be discriminating while remaining coherentist.

We can thus distinguish between three kinds of coherence problems. A *pure* coherence problem is one that does not favor any elements as potentially worthy of acceptance. A *foundational* coherence problem selects a set of favored elements for acceptance as self-justified. A *discriminating* coherence problem favors a set of elements but their acceptance still depends on their coherence with all the other elements. I have shown how coherence algorithms can naturally treat problems as discriminating without being foundational.

Isolation

The *isolation* objection has been characterized as follows:

This objection states that the coherence of a theory is an inadequate justification of the theory, because by itself it doesn't supply the necessary criteria to distinguish it from illusory but consistent theories. Fairytales may sometimes be coherent as may dreams and hallucinations. Astrology may be as coherent as astronomy, Newtonian physics as coherent as Einsteinian physics. (Pojman 1993, 191)

Thus an isolated set of beliefs may be internally coherent but should not be judged to be justified.

My characterization of coherence provides two ways of overcoming the isolation objection. First, as we just saw, a coherence problem may be discriminating, giving non-absolute priority to empirical evidence or other elements that are known to make a relatively reliable contribution to solution of the kind of problem at hand. The comparative coherence of astronomy and astrology is thus in part a matter of coherence with empirical evidence, of which there is obviously far more for astronomy than astrology. Second, the existence of negative constraints such as inconsistency shows that we cannot treat astronomy and astrology as isolated bodies of beliefs. The explanations of human behavior offered by astrology often conflict with those offered by psychological science. Astrology might be taken to be coherent on its own, but once it offers explanations that compete with psychology and astronomy, it becomes a strong candidate for rejection. The isolation objection may be a problem for underspecified coherence theories that lack discrimination and negative constraints, but it is easily overcome by the constraint-satisfaction approach.

Having negative constraints, however, does not guarantee consistency in the accepted set A. The second coherence condition, which encourages dividing negatively constrained elements between A and R, is not rigid, so there may be cases where two negatively constrained elements both end up being accepted. For a correspondence theory of truth, this is a disaster, since two contradictory propositions cannot both be true. It would probably also be unappealing to most advocates of a coherence theory of truth. To overcome the consistency problem, we could revise the second coherence condition by making it rigid: a partition of elements (propositions) into accepted and rejected sets must be such that if e_i and e_j are inconsistent, then if e_i is in A then e_j *must* be in R. I do not want, however, to defend a coherence theory of truth, since there are good reasons for preferring a correspondence theory based on scientific realism (chapter 4).

For a coherence theory of epistemic justification, inconsistency in the set A of accepted propositions is also problematic, but we can leave open the possibility that coherence is temporarily maximized by adopting an inconsistent set of beliefs. We might deal with the lottery and proofreading paradoxes simply by being inconsistent, believing that a lottery is fair while believing of each ticket that it will not win, or believing that a paper must have a typographical error in it somewhere while believing of each sentence that it is flawless. A more interesting case is the relation between quantum theory and general relativity, two theories that individually possess enormous explanatory coherence. According to the eminent mathematical physicist Edward Witten, "The basic problem in modern physics is that these two pillars are incompatible. If you try to combine gravity with quantum mechanics, you find that you get nonsense from a mathematical point of view. You write down formulae which ought to be quantum gravitational formulae and you get all kinds of infinities" (Davies and Brown 1988, 90). Quantum theory and general relativity may be incompatible, but it would be folly, given their independent evidential support, to suppose that one must be rejected. Another inconsistency in current astrophysics derives from measurements that suggest that the stars are older than the universe. But astrophysics carries on, just as mathematics did when Russell discovered that Frege's axioms for arithmetic lead to contradictions.

From the perspective of formal logic, contradictions are disastrous, since from any proposition and its negation any formula can be derived: from p to p or q by addition, then from not p to q by disjunctive syllogism. Logicians who have wanted to deal with inconsistencies have been forced to resort to relevance or paraconsistent logics. But from the perspective of a coherence theory of inference, there is no need for any special logic. It may turn out at a particular time that coherence is maximized by accepting a set A that is inconsistent, but other coherence-based inferences need not be unduly influenced by the inconsistency, whose effects may be relatively isolated in the network of elements.

Conservatism

Coherence theories of justification may seem unduly conservative in that they require new elements to fit into an existing coherent structure. This charge is legitimate against serial coherence algorithms that determine for each new element whether accepting it increases coherence or not. The connectionist algorithm in chapter 2, on the other hand, allows a new element to enter into the full-blown computation of coherence maximization. If units have already settled into a stable activation, it will be difficult for a new element with no activation to dislodge the accepted ones, so the network will exhibit a modest conservatism. But if new elements are sufficiently coherent with other elements, they can dislodge previously accepted ones. Connectionist networks can be used to model the dramatic shifts in explanatory coherence that take place in scientific revolutions (Thagard 1992b).

Circularity

Another standard objection to coherence theories is that they are circular, licensing the inference of p from q and then of q from p. Logic books warn against the fallacy of begging the question, in which someone argues in a circle to infer something from itself. A typical example is someone who argues that God exists because it says so in the Bible, and that you can trust the Bible because its writing was inspired by God. Such circular arguments obviously fail to prove anything, and at first glance coherence-based inference seems circular, since many propositions may serve to support each other.

The theories of coherence and the coherence algorithms presented here make it clear that coherence-based inferences are very different from those familiar from deductive logic, where propositions are derived from other propositions in linear fashion. The characterization of coherence and the algorithms for computing it (chapter 2) involve a global, parallel, but effective means of assessing a whole set of elements simultaneously on the basis of their mutual dependencies. Inference can be seen to be holistic in a way that is nonmystical, computationally effective, and psychologically and neurologically plausible (pairs of real neurons do not excite each other symmetrically, but neuronal groups can). Deductive circular reasoning is inherently defective, but the foundational view that conceives of knowledge as building deductively on indubitable axioms is not even supportable in mathematics, as we saw in section 3. Inference based on coherence judgments is not circular in the way feared by logicians, since it effectively calculates how a whole set of elements fit together, without linear inference of p from q and then of q from p.

Coherentists such as Bosanquet (1920) and BonJour (1985) denied that the circularity evident in coherence-based justification is vicious, and the algorithms for computing coherence in chapter 2 show more precisely how a set of elements can depend on each other interactively, rather than serially. Using the connectionist algorithm, we can say that after a network of units has settled and some units are identified as being activated, then acceptance of each element represented by an activated unit is justified on the basis of its relation to all other elements. The algorithms for determining activation (acceptance) proceed fully in parallel, with each unit's activation depending on the activation of all connected units after the previous cycle. Because it is clear how the activation of each unit depends simultaneously on the activation of all other units, there need be no mystery about how acceptance can be the result of mutual dependencies. Similarly, the greedy and SDP algorithms in chapter 2 maximize constraint satisfaction globally, not by evaluating individual elements sequentially. Thus modern models of computation vindicate Bosanquet's claim that inference need not be interpreted within the confines of linear systems of logical inference.

Coherence-based inference involves no regress because it proceeds not in steps but rather by simultaneous evaluation of multiple elements. Figure 3.3a shows a viciously circular pattern of inference that starts with e_1, then infers e_2, then infers e_3, then argues in a circle back to e_1. In contrast, figure 3.3b shows the situation when a connectionist algorithm computes everything at once. Unlike entailment or conditional probability, coherence constraints are symmetric relations, which is represented by the double-headed arrows in figure 3.3b. The two-headed arrows indicate that the elements are mutually interdependent, not that one is to be inferred from the others. Activation flows mutually between the elements, but in a realistic example of inference there will also be elements that have inhibitory links with e_1 or some other elements, and some elements will be favored and given a degree of priority. The result is a pattern of inference that looks nothing at all like the circular reasoning in figure 3.3a.

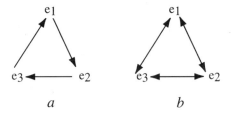

Figure 3.3
Circular versus noncircular justification. On the left (a) is a
circular series of linear inferences. On the right (b) is a set of
elements that mutually support each other.

Truth

Coherence-based reasoning is thus not circular, but it is still
legitimate to ask whether it is effective. Do inferences
based on explanatory and other kinds of coherence
produce true conclusions? Early proponents of coherence
theories of inference such as Blanshard (1939) also advocated a coherence theory of truth, according to which the
truth of a proposition is constituted by its being part of a
general coherent set of propositions. From the perspective of a coherence theory of truth, it is trivial to say that
coherence-based inference produces true (i.e., coherent)
conclusions. But a major problem arises when we try to
justify coherence-based inference with respect to a correspondence theory of truth, according to which the truth of
a proposition is constituted by its relation to an external,
mind-independent world.

Proponents of coherence theories of truth reject the
idea of such an independent world, but considerations of
explanatory coherence strongly support its existence, as I
argue in chapter 4. Hence truth is a matter also of correspondence, not coherence alone. The issue of correspondence is most acute for pure coherence problems, in which

acceptance of elements is based only on their relation to each other. But the coherence theories that have so far been computationally implemented all treat coherence problems as discriminating. For example, explanatory coherence theory gives priority (but not guaranteed acceptance) to elements representing the results of observation and experiment. Connectionist algorithms naturally implement this discrimination by spreading activation first to units representing elements that should be favored in the coherence calculation; then the activation of other units depends heavily on the activation of those initially activated units. For example, in the explanatory coherence program ECHO, activation spreads first to units representing observational elements, giving them a degree of priority even though they may eventually be rejected on the basis of the overall coherence calculation. Therefore, if we assume with the correspondence theory of truth that observation and experiment involve in part causal interaction with the world, we can have some confidence that the hypotheses adopted on the basis of explanatory coherence also correspond to the world and are not mere mental contrivances that are only internally coherent.

Given a correspondence theory of truth and the consistency of the world, a contradictory set of propositions cannot all be true. But no one ever suggested that coherentist methods guarantee the avoidance of falsehood. All that we can expect of epistemic coherence is that it is generally reliable in accepting the true and rejecting the false. Scientific thinking based on explanatory and analogical coherence has produced theories with substantial technological application, intersubjective agreement, and cumulativity. Our visual systems are subject to occasional illusions, but these are rare compared with the great preponderance of visual interpretations that enable us successfully to interact with the world. Not surprisingly, there is no foundational justification of coherentism, only the coherentist justification that coherentist principles fit well with what we believe and what we do. Temporary tolerance of contradictions may be a useful strategy in accomplishing the long-term aim of accepting many true propositions and few false ones. Hence there is no incompatibility between my account of epistemic coherence and a correspondence theory of truth.

The problem of correspondence to the world is even more serious for ethical justification, for it is not obvious how to legitimate a coherence-based ethical judgment such as "It is permissible to eat some animals but not people." Chapter 5 argues that ethical coherence involves complex interactions of deliberative, deductive, analogical, and explanatory coherence. In some cases the relative objectivity of explanatory coherence, discriminating as it does in favor of observation and experiment, can carry over to the objectivity of ethical judgments that also involve other kinds of coherence. We will see, however, that achieving rational consensus in ethics is more problematic than in epistemology.

8 LANGUAGE

My general account of coherence as constraint satisfaction and the five kinds of coherence discussed in this chapter have many potential applications for understanding people's knowledge and use of language. The topic of linguistic coherence deserves a chapter or even a volume of its own, but I have neither the expertise nor the inclination to discuss it at length. Instead, this section will merely provide pointers to some of the vast literature on coherence in language, along with brief suggestions concerning how linguistic phenomena can be viewed from the perspective of coherence as constraint satisfaction.

Part of the process of making sense of spoken and written language is dealing with syntactic ambiguities, as in the sentence "I saw her duck," in which "duck" can be either a noun or a verb. Spivey-Knowlton, Trueswell, and Tanenhaus (1993) argue for a constraint-based approach to parsing, in which syntactically relevant contextual constraints provide evidence for or against competing alternatives. Similarly, Menzel (1998) views parsing as a procedure of structural disambiguation that can be modeled by constraint-satisfaction techniques. Prince and Smolensky (1997) discuss phonological grammar in terms of optimizing the satisfaction of multiple constraints on representational well-formedness. These research programs suggest at least the possibility of construing syntactic and phonological interpretation as coherence problems of the sort defined in chapter 2.

Semantic ambiguity can also be handled by constraint-satisfaction methods. Cottrell (1988) proposes a connectionist model of lexical access in which alternative interpretations of an ambiguous word such as "deck" can be evaluated by representing alternative meanings (e.g., ship floor, pack of cards) as nodes in a constraint network. An algorithm similar to the connectionist one described in chapter 2 suffices to activate or deactivate the nodes in accord with how well they fit a given context. Similarly, as chapter 2 described, Kintsch (1988) models comprehension of ambiguous words such as "bank" in terms of associative nets, with one interpretation of the word connected to "river" and another interpretation connected to "money." Spreading excitatory and inhibitory activation enables the nets to select the most appropriate meaning for the context. Semantic disambiguation along these lines is a case of conceptual coherence as described earlier in this chapter.

In his superb book *Comprehension*, Kintsch (1998) applies his construction-integration model to many other processes involved in understanding text, including inference, memory, and problem solving. He describes the integration phase as "essentially a constraint satisfaction process that rejects inappropriate local constructions in favor of those that fit together into a coherent whole" (1998, 119). It is straightforward to interpret his account of integration in terms of the theory of coherence presented in chapter 2. Other discussions of text comprehension that can be brought within the purview of the theory of coherence as constraint satisfaction include Trabasso and Suh's (1993) account of the relevance of explanatory coherence and van den Broek's (1994) analysis of the role of causal and anaphoric relations. Analogical coherence is also relevant to comprehension of texts involving metaphor (Holyoak and Thagard 1995).

However, pursuing linguistic applications of the theory of coherence as constraint satisfaction would take me too far afield from the philosophical and psychological issues concerning inference that are my main concern. This section does not pretend to provide a theory of linguistic coherence, but should help direct anyone interested in constructing one to some of the relevant ingredients.

9   SUMMARY

This chapter has described knowledge in terms of five contributory kinds of coherence: explanatory, analogical, deductive, visual, and conceptual. By analogy to previously presented principles of explanatory coherence, it has generated new principles to capture existing theories of analogical and conceptual coherence, and it has developed new theories of deductive and visual coherence. All of these kinds of coherence can be construed in terms of constraint satisfaction and computed using connectionist and other algorithms. Haack's "foundherentist" epistemology can be subsumed within the more precise framework offered here, and many of the standard philosophical objections to coherentism can be answered within this framework. The theory of coherence also has applications to the psychological processes by which people understand discourse and other people.

4   *Reality*

According to chapter 3, inference is the process of accepting mental representations on the basis of coherence: we infer a representation if incorporating it with the rest of our representations maximizes coherence. Knowledge, in the sense used by philosophers, requires more than inferring mental representations, which constitute knowledge only if they are representations of reality. But what is reality, and what is fundamentally real? These are the basic questions of metaphysics, and this chapter uses the ideas about coherence developed in the previous two chapters to address important metaphysical questions. I begin with a discussion of the nature of truth and argue *against* a coherence theory of *truth*, as opposed to the coherence theory of *knowledge*, which was defended in chapter 3. I will argue that the coherence theory of truth fails because explanatory coherence supports the existence of a world independent of our thought of it, so that truth must be a matter of correspondence with this world. I then show how coherence as constraint satisfaction provides a new way of thinking about correspondence and approximate truth, by construing modeling the world as a coherence problem.

Explanatory coherence is also the key to fundamental questions about the nature of mind. I defend a materialist view of mind and mental processes that rejects any aspect of mind concerned with soul or spirit. Inference to the best explanation of mental phenomena does not require any dualist hypotheses that postulate nonmaterial substance. Explanatory coherence combines with analogical coherence to provide the best solution to the philosophical problem of other minds (that is, whether there are any), and it combines with other kinds of coherence to provide the best solution to the psychological problem of how we gain knowledge of other minds. Finally, I present a coherence-based answer to the question of the existence of God. A thorough discussion of this issue would require a book in itself and I do not claim to provide a definitive solution. Rather, my goal is to illustrate how coherence-based inference can be applied to metaphysical issues.

This chapter is intended to be of both philosophical and psychological interest. The metaphysical issues it addresses are some of the most basic in philosophy, but all have interesting psychological analogs. "Is there a world?" may seem like a puerile question suitable only for introductory philosophy classes and adolescent bull sessions, but the psychological and epistemological question "How do we know about the world?" is worthy of adult discussion. Thus in addressing the nature of reality I will simultaneously be discussing the nature of the mental processes that bring us knowledge of the world.

1 TRUTH AND THE WORLD

Philosophical concern with coherence arose with idealist philosophers such as Hegel (1967) and Bradley (1914). Idealism, in the metaphysical sense, is the claim that reality is fundamentally dependent on mind. It contrasts with materialism, which views reality as consisting of matter that is not mind-dependent and provides the basis for mind, which is viewed as just another function of the physical body. Idealism fits naturally with a coherence theory of truth, according to which a representation such as a proposition is true if and only if it is included in the most complete and maximally coherent set of propositions. On this view, truth just is coherence, since reality is essentially mental and there is nothing outside mind and coherence for a representation to correspond to. In contrast, the correspondence theory of truth, which dates back at least to Aristotle, says that a proposition is true if and only if the world is as the proposition says it is.

For some philosophers, talk of *the world* independent of our minds seems problematic. We have no direct access to this world, and our knowledge of it comes at best indirectly, through sensory experiences and reasoning based on them. What knowledge we may have is inescapably fallible, depending on experiences that may be illusory and reasoning that may be fallacious. All we have, the idealist says, is a complex mix of representations that must be assessed with respect to their coherence with each other, not with respect to some unattainable standard of correspondence to an unreachable and ineffable world.

But the coherence theory of truth has problems of its own. First, there are the questions about isolation from reality and indiscriminate treatment of propositions discussed in the last chapter. I argued that these problems can be overcome only by appreciating some elements as favored, but did not explain why the results of sensory observation and experiments based on it should be favored. Special status does not derive from certainty, for in a coherentist epistemology any observation can potentially be overridden on the grounds that it does not cohere with all the rest that we know. For example, my perception of a giant purple moose on skates should not immediately lead to the inference that there is a purple moose in front of me, because alternative explanations (such as that I am hallucinating) should be considered for such an unusual observation. In science, it is commonplace for physicists, psychologists, and other experimenters to reject data that they have reason to believe are faulty, for example, because the observations were based on defective instruments or were outliers with respect to other results. Nevertheless, scientists do not treat experimental results as arbitrary and fanciful: some data are thrown out for good reasons.

Observation does not provide guaranteed access to reality, but there are aspects of observation which only make sense if we understand it as being caused by an external reality rather than being a purely mental operation. Here are some aspects of observation that are difficult to explain within a purely coherentist, idealist perspective:

• People cannot observe what they want: most sensory experience is beyond conscious control.

• Different people in the same situation report very similar experiences. For example, just about everyone at a St. Louis Cardinals baseball game will see Mark McGwire hit a home run at the same time.

• Observations of rocks, fossils, and archeological sites suggest that the planet Earth has existed for billions of years, but that humans have existed only for a few million.

Thus human observation is comparatively mind-independent, intersubjective, and historically recent.

Materialism has no difficulty explaining these three facts. First, observation by an individual is largely mind-independent because it is the result of physical processes involving causal interactions between our sense organs and a material world. Second, observation is intersubjective because different individuals share very similar sensory organs and all operate in the same world. Third, the relative recency of human observation is explained by scientific theories about the development of the universe and the solar system and about the much more recent evolution of the human species.

These aspects of observation make sense within idealism only if there is some kind of collective or divine mind that determines the experiences of diverse people and that has contrived to present the appearance of a world in which people are relatively recent arrivals. But we have no independent reason to believe in such a collective or divine mind (see the discussion of God below), so the idealist explanations are lacking in simplicity. As principle E2c in the first section of chapter 3 specified, lack of simplicity deriving from introduction of additional hypotheses reduces the explanatory coherence of a theory. Leaving aside for now the issue of God, it is clear that the idealist hypothesis that the world is constituted by and dependent on mind has less explanatory coherence than the materialist hypothesis that the world consists fundamentally of molecules, atoms, subatomic particles, quarks, and the other physical entities that science has discovered.

So there is a material world independent of our minds' most coherent interpretations of it. The truth of propositions, therefore, and the verisimilitude of other mental representations, such as visual images, is not merely a matter of their coherence with other representations; rather, the truth of a proposition depends on its correspondence to the world. Of course, we have no other means but coherence to infer that a proposition *does* correspond to the world, and any particular proposition, no matter how coherent, may turn out to be false. But we have ample reason to believe that many bodies of propositions do in fact correspond to reality. People have managed to survive and reproduce for many thousands of years, and in the last few hundred they have been able to use scientific advances to gain an extraordinary physical control over the world. These advances have made possible technologies of transportation, communication, and medicine that are totally mysterious unless such scientific theories as gravity, electromagnetism, and the germ theory of disease are at least approximately true.

Socrates, Descartes, and other philosophers who have taken skepticism too seriously have unfortunately set the stage for much of the history of philosophy by asking for definitive proof for philosophical theses. Hegel and Peirce were the first philosophers to recognize that the foundational search for certainty was pointless, and that what mattered was the growth of knowledge, not its foundations. Back in 1868, Peirce urged, "Let us not pretend to doubt in philosophy what we do not doubt in our hearts" (1958, 40). What matters is how we use inferential processes to expand our knowledge and eliminate previous misconceptions. Peirce did not recognize, as Hegel did obscurely, that building inferences upon each other is based on expanding sets of coherent representations. However, Peirce's notion of abductive inference to explanatory hypotheses is the ancestor of contemporary ideas about inference to the best explanation and explanatory coherence.

2 CORRESPONDENCE AND APPROXIMATE TRUTH

But what is it for representations to correspond to the world? Philosophers of science have identified serious problems with the realist claim that scientific theories are true. Cartwright in *How the Laws of Physics Lie* (1983) considers physical laws as idealized rather than exactly true descriptions of the world. For example, Newton's law of gravitation, that two bodies exert a force between each other that varies inversely as the square of the distance between them and varies directly as the product of their masses, is not true of bodies that are electrically charged. Giere (1999) argues that the point of scientific theories is not directly to make claims about the world, but rather to define *models* that fit the world more or less well. A model, on his view, is a nonlinguistic entity that has the same relation to the world that a map has to the aspects of the world that it is intended to represent. Maps are not absolutely true or false, but can be more or less accurate and more or less detailed.

The relation between models and reality is not isomorphism, which would require there to be a one-to-one mapping between the model and the world that exactly preserves structure and behavior. Holland et al. (1986) describe the relation between a model and the world with the ugly term *quasi-homomorphism*, which means a mapping from the model to some parts of the world in which the model preserves many but not all of the structures and behaviors in the world. Assessing the relation between a model and what it represents can be viewed as a coherence problem very much like the process of analogical mapping described in chapter 3. Analogies are rarely isomorphic to each other, but can nevertheless involve correspondences between two analogs that are highly useful. Similarly, models, like maps, can provide more or less coherent representations of the world.

To show this more exactly, we need more concrete specifications of what models are. As Giere insists, theories and models are representationally heterogeneous, involving diagrams and pictures as well as equations and other propositions. So the mapping by which a theory defines a model can be complex, and the models can be entities that bear visual as well as semantic correspondences to the world. For simplicity, we can begin with the set-theoretic notion of model used in Tarskian semantics for formal languages. On this usage, a model consists of a domain D_M, which is a set of objects, and a collection R_M of relations, which are n-tuples of objects in D_M. For example, a simple domain consists of the domain {Bill, Tony, Phil} and the relation {(Bill, Tony), (Bill, Phil)} which might be interpreted as saying that Bill is taller than Tony and Phil. Properties are construed as one-place relations, corresponding to sets of the form {(o), . . .}. Similarly, we can say that the world consists of a domain of objects D_W and a set of relations R_W among the objects. The model represents the world to the extent that there is a mapping from D_M to D_W and from R_M to R_W such that the relations in R_M have corresponding relations in R_W.

Because isomorphism is too much to expect of an approximating model, we can think of the world as providing constraints on the model, without the expectation that all the constraints will be satisfied. The degree of coherence between the model and the world is then measured by the degree of constraint satisfaction, W/W^*, as defined at the end of chapter 2. In this coherence problem, the elements are set-theoretic relations, such as *(Bill, Tony) is a member of* {*(Bill, Tony), (Bill, Phil)*}, and the constraints are between model elements and world elements: a model element is to be accepted if and only if the corresponding world element is accepted. The coherence of the model with respect to the world is then measured by W/W^*, the ratio of total weight of constraints satisfied to the total weight of all constraints established by the mapping between the model and the world.

Coherence can similarly be defined using more interesting kinds of models than the Tarskian kind. For example, in physics and other mathematical fields, a dynamic system is often conceived in terms of a mathematical space with orthogonal coordinate directions representing each of the variables needed to specify the instantaneous state of the system (Baker and Gollub 1995). The *state space* of a system is the set of states it can be in as determined by the variables that are used to measure it. For example, the state of a particle moving in one dimension is specified by its position and velocity. Relations between variables are specified by equations that define a trajectory of a particle through the state space. We can think of the equations as defining a model state space that is intended to correspond to the state space of the actual world. For example, an equation with three variables generates a three-dimensional state space. A particular state of the world can be specified by a list of numbers called a vector, which contains the values of all the variables at a particular time. The model as defined by the equations specifies possible transitions from one vector to another, so that changes in the system can be specified by lists of vectors or, equivalently, by diagrams that draw a picture of the relations between vectors in spaces of two or more dimensions. In this framework, an element is a representation of the relations between vectors in the state space. The elements involving the trajectory in the model's state space, S_M, are constrained by the elements involving the trajectory in the world's state space, S_W, which contains the actually occurring sequences of vectors (values of variables). As in the Tarskian case, a model is coherent to the extent to which it satisfies constraints directing the co-acceptance of elements from the model and the corresponding elements from the world.

Different kinds of models will require different kinds of elements, but it should always be possible to define the coherence of the model in terms of the extent to which it satisfies constraints between elements of the model and elements of the world. Hence the notion of fit between a model and the world can go beyond Giere's map analogy and be specified more generally as a coherence problem. While metaphysically useful, this view of correspondence between a model and the world is of limited practical use. Many aspects of the world that models are intended to capture are not directly observable: we can not directly measure the properties and relations of hypothetical entities such as subatomic particles. Hence practically, we can at most assess the degree of the fit between the elements of the model and world that concern observable objects, and use that to guess the overall fit between all the elements of the model and the corresponding elements of the world. Scientists can proceed more directly, by addressing the question of whether one theory provides a better explanation of the evidence than its competitors, in accord with the theory of explanatory coherence. If one theory coheres with the evidence better than other available theories, then we have reason to believe that it models the world more coherently than the alternatives.

3 MIND AND BODY

Aside from a few wild-eyed philosophers, everyone agrees that there is a world apart from the minds that contemplate it. But no such universal consensus exists concerning the nature of mind. Most cognitive scientists, including researchers in neuroscience, cognitive psychology, and philosophy of mind, adopt a materialist perspective according to which all aspects of mind are ultimately explicable in terms of the brain and the body and world that it inhabits. In contrast, most ordinary people are dualists, taking it for granted that a person is not just a body, but also consists of a nonmaterial soul or spirit. Religions such as Christianity that assume survival beyond death are the source of the everyday metaphysical beliefs that portray a person as a combination of body and soul. What is the evidence for dualism and materialism, and which metaphysical theory is more coherent?

Support for materialism has increased dramatically in recent decades, as neurological data has made possible detailed explanations of more and more mental phenomena in terms of the operation of the brain. Scientists can measure the firing of single cells in brains of cats and monkeys, and correlate these occurrences with the animals' mental activities. Such invasive measurements are not permissible in humans, but other techniques such as brain scans using positron-emission tomography and functional magnetic-resonance imagery have begun to provide detailed information about what the mind is doing during diverse mental operations, including visual perception, word recognition, and memory. In addition, much has been learned about the operation of neural networks in the brain, including how neurons transmit electrical signals to each other and adjust their connections with each other on the basis of experience. Such progress supports the claim that mind can be understood on the basis of the principles of physics, chemistry, and biology that we use to explain the material world in general.

The metaphysical hypothesis of materialism coheres with scientific findings by providing a higher-level explanation of why the operations of the mind and the brain are so strongly correlated. Figure 4.1 shows in simplified form the explanatory structure of materialism. The top-level metaphysical hypothesis says that everything is matter, i.e., that whatever exists consists of physical entities such as quarks, electrons, atoms, molecules, cells, and organisms. Materialism about mind follows deductively from this universal materialism, which of course must be rejected if the mind is not scientifically explicable. But figure 4.1 also displays the explanatory coherence of materialism about the

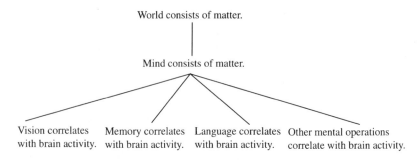

Figure 4.1
The coherence of materialism. The lines indicate positive constraints based on explanation. (See the appendix to this chapter for a much fuller exposition.)

mind, which explains why neuroscience has found such striking correlations between a broad range of mental operations and increasingly well-identified operations in the brain.

Materialism, however, is not the only general way of explaining mental operations. According to idealism, minds operate because everything is mind, but I argued in the last section that idealism is implausible. More plausible is the dualist view that allows that *some* aspects of mind are indeed explicable in material terms, because a person is indeed a body as well as a soul. But the dualist claims that there are other aspects of mind that require explanations based on the existence of a nonmaterial soul. Materialism allegedly is unable to explain such apparent phenomena as the survival of life after death, extrasensory perception, free will, the moral sense, and consciousness.

Let us construct the most powerful case we can for dualism's having greater explanatory coherence than materialism. It would seem that dualism can explain everything that materialism does by virtue of a person having a body, but in addition there is a lot that dualism can explain but that materialism cannot. Dualism is capable of explaining the existence of life beyond death, although survival is itself a hypothesis whose explanatory coherence must be evaluated. The ability of the soul to survive the body would explain various alleged occurrences, such as near-death experiences when people report going through a tunnel toward a bright light and seances when people report communicating with the dead.

Another phenomenon that would seem to require a dualist explanation is extrasensory perception. Suppose, as some advocates of ESP claim, that people are capable of remote viewing, seeing scenes thousands of miles away without any mechanical devices. And suppose that people can perform telepathy, transmitting information from mind to mind without any physical means of transmission. And suppose that people are capable of telekinesis, affecting matter without any physical contact or connection. These kinds of ESP would provide strong support for dualism, because their existence and operation violate current scientific theories and therefore cannot be explained by them.

Other phenomena that have been given a non-materialist explanation include the widespread beliefs in free will and the moral sense, or conscience. We certainly feel that we are acting freely and that we have a sense of right and wrong, and it is not easy to imagine how these feelings can emanate from material processes involving neurons and brain chemicals. The existence of a nonmaterial soul would explain why we appear to have free will and why we can make intuitive moral judgments.

Our experiences of acting freely and making judgments of right and wrong are part of a more general aspect of mind, consciousness. We not only think; we are aware of our thinking, especially of visual and other sensory experiences, as well as emotions and moods.

Consciousness does not seem to be a process like the physical, chemical, and biological ones found in materialist explanations. The dualist contends that consciousness needs a different kind of explanation: only nonmaterial souls are capable of the awareness and qualitative experiences that constitute consciousness. Like survival after death, ESP, free will, and moral intuition, consciousness requires explanation by a nonmaterial component of mind. Figure 4.2 sketches the explanatory coherence of dualism.

The materialist, however, has a good shot at explaining all these phenomena. Materialism cannot explain how minds could survive without brains, but it can explain why people report communication with the dead and near-death experiences. Seances are easily staged, so the materialist can explain them as fraudulent performances. Near-death experiences can be explained neurologically and socially. It is possible that the process of expiring produces a flood of brain chemicals such as endorphins that generate the unusual experiences reported by people who have come close to death. The similarity of the reports may be explained by people having similar brain chemistry, but also by people near death having previously heard of the experiences of other people.

Reports of extrasensory perception can also be explained in materialist terms. Many attempts to demonstrate the occurrence of anomalous phenomena such as remote viewing, telepathy, and telekinesis have been exposed as fraudulent or inadequately designed to rule out chance or bias as alternative explanations of the alleged results. A few attempts have been made to determine the existence of ESP with full scientific rigor, but at best the effects found have been very small and explicable by the alternative hypotheses of fraud or poor experimental design. Because materialism provides explanations of ESP

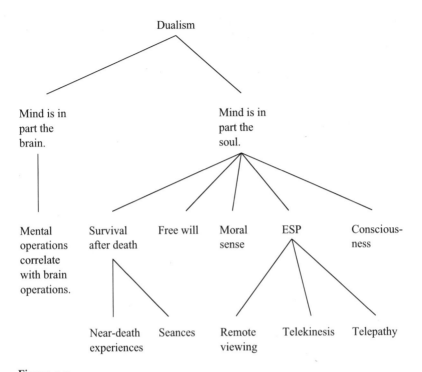

Figure 4.2
The explanatory coherence of dualism. Lines indicate explanatory relations.

that are at least as plausible as the existence of a soul, dualism gains little support from ESP.

Similarly, the semblance of free will and the moral sense can be explained in material terms. We think we have free will because we are not aware of the operations of our brains, just as prescientific people explain the operation of animals and the weather in terms of spirits because of their ignorance of the underlying physical processes. The illusion of free will derives partly from the religious and dualistic culture that most of us are raised in, and partly from the reality of conscious experience that I will discuss shortly. Although we do not have free will in any absolute, dualist sense, we certainly are capable of acting freely in a social sense when our choices are not directly controlled by others or by the defective neurochemistry that produces schizophrenia and other mental disorders. Such freedom suffices for moral and social responsibility: we hold people responsible not because they are free in the sense required for religious doctrines of sin and divine punishment, but because doing so helps to produce desirable outcomes for them and for other members of society.

From a materialist perspective, the existence of moral intuition can be explained in the same way that other kinds of intuitive judgments are explained. When we compile various kinds of information into an overall judgment of the rightness or wrongness of some act such as murder, we are unconsciously producing a coherence judgment that can have a strong emotional content. Chapter 5 describes how ethical judgments can arise from a combination of coherence-based inferences, and chapter 6 shows how these can be combined with emotional evaluation.

Materialism has a fairly easy time offering explanations of near-death experiences, ESP, free will, and moral judgment, but the general phenomenon of consciousness is much more difficult. Even if we find all sorts of neural correlates of sensory experience and awareness, the dualist can still maintain that neurology has not shown how consciousness is produced by the brain. Recently, however, brain scientists have began to develop detailed hypotheses about the neural origins of some aspects of consciousness. For example, Crick (1994) uses what is known about the brain's visual, attentional, and memory systems to conjecture how consciousness might emerge from circuits of interacting neurons. Thus the materialist explanation of consciousness, that it emerges from neural processes, is sketchy but promising.

Some philosophers, e.g., Chalmers (1996), think that consciousness can be used to support dualism on purely conceptual grounds. For example, we can conceive of the existence of zombies, which are physically identical to humans but lack consciousness, so that consciousness is logically independent of bodies. But conceivability is a poor guide to reality, and dualism must be evaluated with respect to its explanatory coherence, not on conceptual grounds tainted by prior beliefs.

To fully assess the competing explanatory coherence of materialism and dualism, we need to combine all the dualist and materialist explanations shown in figures 4.1 and 4.2. The outcome is a much closer call than the debate between idealism and materialism, for there are aspects of mind such as consciousness that are not obviously within the scope of scientific explanation. But even if the materialist explanation of consciousness is currently weak, so is the dualist explanation, for no one has offered any account of how the soul produces consciousness that is any more successful than one for the brain. In the appendix to this chapter I present a fuller analysis of the explanatory coherence of dualism and materialism, which needs to be connected with the question of the existence of God. Dualism is much more plausible if God created souls, and theism loses plausibility if materialist explanations of the existence of the universe are available. Hence the mind-body problem involves theological issues, which are addressed below. First I want to address another traditional philosophical question: whether there are other minds.

4   OTHER MINDS

Here is the traditional philosophical problem of other minds: you know from your conscious experience that you have a mind, but how are you justified in believing that other people, whose consciousness you have no access to, have minds? Like the problem of whether there is a mind-independent world, this problem is rather silly, since no one doubts that there are other minds. We can dispose of the philosophical problem quickly, then move on to the more interesting and pressing psychological question: given that there are other minds, what can we know about them?

One common solution to the philosophical problem is analogical inference: other people's actions are similar to yours, so perhaps they are also similar to you in having minds. Another common solution to the problem of other minds is inference to the best explanation: the hypothesis that other people have minds is a better explanation of their behavior than any other available hypothesis, for example, that they are radio-controlled robots. From the perspective of coherence as constraint satisfaction, analogical inference and best-explanation inference are complementary, not alternative justifications, because analogical- and explanatory-coherence considerations can simultaneously work to justify as acceptable the conclusion that other people have minds. Figure 4.3 shows how analogy-based positive constraints mesh with

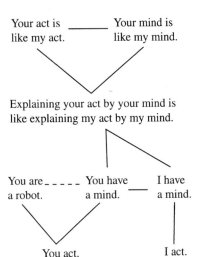

Figure 4.3
Support for the existence of other minds incorporating both explanatory and analogical coherence. Solid lines indicate positive constraints and the dashed line indicates a negative constraint. My hypothesis that you have a mind is evaluated both by comparing its explanatory power with other hypotheses that explain your behavior and by analogy with my explanations of my own behavior.

explanation-based positive constraints to establish the acceptability of the hypothesis that other people have minds. The hypothesis that another person has a mind is supported both by its greater explanatory coherence over competing explanations of your actions and by its analogical coherence based on the similarities between your acts and my acts.

So other minds exist, but how do we know them? First, we understand other people by means of causal attributions in which we form and evaluate hypotheses that explain their behavior. To explain why someone is abrupt on one occasion, you may hypothesize that this person is impatient or that he or she is under pressure from a work deadline. You believe the hypothesis that provides the best available explanation of the person's behavior. A second means of making sense of people is analogy: you can understand people through their similarity to other people or to yourself. For example, you may understand the stresses that your friend is experiencing by remembering an occasion when you yourself experienced similar stresses. This will allow you to predict your friend's likely feelings and behavior.

Causal attribution of mental states is naturally understood in terms of explanatory coherence. The elements are propositions, including the evidence to be explained (observed behavior) and hypotheses about them that would explain the behavior. Suppose, for example, that a normally mild-mannered friend screams at you. Various hypotheses would explain that behavior: perhaps the friend had a stressful day at work, or stopped taking some needed medication, or learned some secret ugly fact about you. What inference you make to explain your friend's behavior will depend on what best fits with your other beliefs: maximizing coherence will lead you to accept the most plausible hypothesis that explains your friend's behavior and to reject the alternative hypotheses. You may hypothesize that your friend screamed at you because of a stressful day at work and further hypothesize that the stressful day was caused by impending layoffs. The result can be a network of propositions of the sort shown in figure 4.4, which shows different hypotheses competing to explain the evidence. Positive constraints can be affected by considerations of simplicity: if a number of hypotheses are required to make an explanation, then the positive constraints between hypotheses and evidence are weakened. For example, if you explain Mary's behavior by supposing that she was

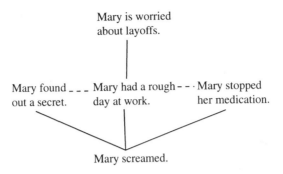

Figure 4.4
An explanatory-coherence network for Mary's screaming. Positive associations are shown with solid lines and negative associations are shown with dashed lines. The evidence that Mary screamed can be explained by three competing hypotheses.

abducted by aliens who mistreated her, you are making a number of hypotheses whose coherence may suffer as a result of a lack of simplicity as well as incompatibility with other things that you believe.

In explanatory coherence, the sources of negative constraints are contradiction and competition. If two propositions logically contradict each other ("Mary is in Florida" versus "Mary is in Toronto"), then there is a strong negative constraint between them. Moreover, in explanatory situations, people tend to treat hypotheses as negatively constraining each other even if they are not strictly contradictory. It is possible that Mary's behavior should be explained because she had a stressful day *and* she stopped taking her medication *and* she found out something about you, but in the absence of evidence linking them, we treat these as independent competing explanations. Explanatory coherence can also be used to assess hypotheses about oneself, as when Mary herself figures out that she screamed because of some previously suppressed hostility.

Another valuable cognitive mechanism for making sense of people is analogy, in which we see one person as similar to another with respect to a complex of properties and relations. I may, for example, increase my understanding of Princess Diana by comparing her to Anna Karenina in Tolstoy's novel. This comparison would be much deeper than just noticing that both are women who came to tragic ends, in that it also involves a set of interlocking relations. Diana was like Anna Karenina in being married to a man, not caring for that man, and being (for a while) passionately involved with another man. The analogy involves noticing not only that Diana corresponds to Anna, but also that Prince Charles corresponds to Anna's husband, and that Diana's lover James Hewitt corresponds to Anna's lover Vronsky.

As we saw in chapter 3, such analogical mapping can be viewed as a coherence process that maximizes the satisfaction of multiple constraints. The elements are hypotheses about what corresponds to what, for example, that Diana corresponds to Anna and that *loves* in Diana's case corresponds to *loves* in Anna's case. One constraint is perceptual and semantic similarity: two elements will tend to correspond to each other if they look the same or have similar meaning. Other constraints are structural: to map *Anna loves Vronsky* to *Diana loves James*, we must consistently map Ann to Diana, loves to loves, and Vronsky to James. Mappings should tend to be one-to-one; without strong reason, we should not map Diana to both Anna and Vronsky. Finally, purpose provides a practical constraint on the mapping, because we should try to come up with mappings that will contribute to the cognitive goals that the analogy is supposed to serve, such as providing an explanation or contributing to a decision.

Analogically making sense of people always involves comparing two individuals, a target to be understood and a source that provides understanding. In the Princess Diana example, the source and target are both other people, but sometimes the source is oneself and the target is another (e.g., empathy), sometimes the target is oneself and the source is another (e.g., some kinds of social comparison), and sometimes both the source and target are oneself (as when a past situation of one's life is used to make sense of a current situation). I can get a better understanding of my own mind by comparing my current situation with a previous one where I knew what I was thinking and feeling.

Empathy is analogical mapping from another to oneself, establishing a correspondence not only between someone else's situation and one's own but also between the other's emotional state and one's own emotional experience. Deep understanding of people's work stress requires not just seeing how their situation corresponds to one that I have been in (unpleasant boss, risk of layoff, etc.) but also appreciating their emotional state (anger, fear). In a purely verbal analogy, I may infer that just as I was angry in my own situation, so the other is likely to be angry in a similar situation. But empathy goes beyond verbal elements by providing a correspondence between some emotional experience of my own and what I can analogically infer to be the emotional experience of the other. By setting up an analogy between another person and myself, I can feel an approximation to what the other feels. Such an analogy should be facilitated if I myself have been in a similar situation. Indeed, Batson et al. (1996) found that women felt greater empathy for someone undergoing a difficult experience if they themselves had had a similar experience (though the same was not true for men). Like other kinds of analogy, empathy can be understood as a coherence mechanism that evaluates a set of correspondences between two people and their situations; empathy differs from other analogies in that the correspondences link representations that are not verbal or visual, but emotional. Additional discussion of empathy must await the account of emotional coherence presented in chapter 6.

We take for granted our ability to understand, at least to a large extent, the minds of others. But people with autism have a greatly diminished ability to comprehend other minds. This deficit has led some autism researchers to postulate that there is an innate mental module for a "theory of mind" that enables people to understand each other. But Uta Frith (1989) cites many studies that show that autistics' problems are much more general than the inability to understand other minds. Their other defects in visual and linguistic reasoning suggest that autistic people suffer from the more general deficit that Frith calls "weak central coherence." O'Laughlin and Thagard (forthcoming) have used coherence models to simulate how autistics make defective inferences in both theory-of-mind and language-understanding tasks. Five-year-old children, unlike three-year-old children and older autistics, can make powerful inferences about the mind of another child who does not see a marble moved from one place to another. Older children infer that the other child will look for the marble in the place that the other thinks it is, rather than in the place where it really is. This sophisticated kind of explanatory-coherence-based inference breaks down when the coherence model is distorted by making inhibition very strong in comparison with excitation, resulting in preference for the most immediately appealing conclusion rather than in the conclusion that maximizes coherence. Similarly, autistics have difficulty processing sentences such as "The girls were climbing over the hedge. Mary's dress remained spotless, but in Lucy's dress there was a big *tear*" (Frith and Snowling 1986). Here "tear" needs to be interpreted as a hole in the dress, not as water in the eye, but autistics are not able to use the context of the sentence to make the interpretation that best fits overall. O'Laughlin and Thagard (forthcoming) show that the same coherence defect (an excess of inhibition over excitation) that produces incorrect inferences in the connectionist coherence model of children's false beliefs also reproduces the autistics' incorrect inferences in the dress example. Thus the theory of coherence as constraint satisfaction has the potential to explain some failures to understand other minds as well as numerous successes.

5   GOD

We can also use the theory of coherence to address another major metaphysical question: does God exist? I shall produce what I think is the best possible argument for the existence of God, based on explanatory and analogical coherence. It will turn out, however, that a full assessment of the coherence of theism, which asserts the existence of an all-powerful nonmaterial being and thus contradicts materialism, supports the conclusion that there is no reason to believe in the existence of a divine being.

For many religious people, belief in the existence of God is not a matter of evidence or reason, but of faith and tradition. But some theists have defended the explanatory coherence of the existence of God. Swinburne writes,

The basic structure of my argument is this. Scientists, historians, and detectives observe data and proceed thence to some theory about what best explains the occurrence of these data. We can analyse the criteria which they use in reaching a conclusion that a certain theory is better supported by the data than a different theory—that is, is more likely, on the basis of those data, to be true. Using those same criteria, we find that the view that there is a God explains everything we observe, not just some narrow range of data. It explains the fact that there is a universe at all, that scientific laws operate within it, that it contains conscious animals and humans with very complex intricately organized bodies, that we have abundant opportunities for developing ourselves and the world, as well as the more particular data that humans report miracles and have religious experiences. In so far as scientific causes and laws explain some of these things (and in part they do), these very causes and laws need explaining, and God's action explains them. The very same criteria which scientists use to reach their own theories lead us to move beyond those theories to a creator God who sustains *everything* in existence. (1996, 2)

Thus according to Swinburne, belief in the existence of God does not require a leap of faith, but can arise from the same explanatory reasoning found in science.

At first glance, the hypothesis that there is a God does seem to have a great deal of explanatory coherence. First, it explains why the universe exists, i.e., because God created it. One traditional argument for the existence of God contends that everything has a cause, so the universe must have a cause, namely God. This is not a deductive argument, for it does not show that the cause of the universe is the omnipotent being that theists usually take God to be. Rather the cosmological argument, as it is called, is best construed as an inference to the best explanation: we should accept the hypothesis that there is a God because it provides the best explanation of the existence of the universe.

But the existence of God can explain more than the universe's existence: it can explain why the universe is as it is, with the specific scientific laws that govern it. Physical laws such as Newton's laws of motion and biological laws such as genetic transmission hold because God designed them that way. Design is especially important for explaining the complexity of biological organisms such as humans. The traditional argument from design says that God is responsible for the wonderful abilities of organisms to function in the world. The argument is partly a matter of explanatory coherence: God's plan explains the complexity and adaptations of organisms. But it also involves an analogy between God's design and human design. William Paley (1963) compared the complexity of the world to that of a watch and argued analogically that just as a watch has a designer, so does the physical and biological world. Intricately adapted organs such as the eye are taken as signs of God's existence.

If, contrary to the argument made earlier in this chapter, humans consist of souls as well as bodies, then God's existence can be used to explain the existence of souls. Because souls are nonmaterial, their existence is not explicable scientifically, so a different metaphysical explanation is required. Souls exist because an all-powerful nonmaterial being created them.

The existence of God would also provide an explanation for miracles and religious experience. Miracles occur because God occasionally intervenes in the world, and he sometimes interacts with people, providing them with religious experiences. In addition, many people believe that God is the source of morality, providing an explanation of why there is right and wrong and why most people believe there is right and wrong. In sum, we get an impressive picture of the coherence of theism, shown in figure 4.5. The figure is incomplete in that it does not show the analogical connections between the explanation of biological complexity in terms of God's design and the explanation of complexity in artifacts in terms of human design.

The explanatory coherence of theism appears overwhelmingly impressive until one begins to examine alternative explanations of the phenomena taken to support it. The metaphysical hypothesis of materialism contradicts

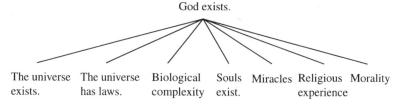

Figure 4.5
The explanatory coherence of theism.

theism and provides alternative explanations of the apparent support for the hypothesis of God's existence. There are various nontheistic explanations of the existence of the universe: perhaps the universe has always existed, or perhaps it came into being spontaneously as the result of random energy fluctuations in quantum fields. Obviously, we lack good evidence for either of these two hypotheses, but then there is no direct evidence of divine creation either. It might seem that they complicate the materialist hypothesis by requiring extra assumptions in the explanation of the existence of the universe, but the theistic hypothesis also requires additional assumptions, for example, that God decided to create the universe and had the power to do so. With respect to explanation of the existence of the universe, the theistic explanation has no clear advantages over the materialist ones.

Why is the universe governed by its physical laws? The materialist explanation here is partly reductive and partly historical. The reductive part comes from the assumptions that biological laws derive from chemical laws and chemical laws from physical laws, and that physical laws derive from the fundamental forces and particles that operate universally. Although science is not currently able to fill out these derivations completely, there is abundant knowledge of some of the crucial dependencies. For example, biological laws of genetic inheritance have their basis in chemical laws involving molecules such as DNA, and chemical molecular interactions are based on the operations of atoms and subatomic particles. Why do these fundamental entities behave the way they do? Here we can at most hazard a historical explanation, based on the early development of matter after the big bang around twenty billion years ago. Science cannot explain exactly why the present laws of nature came to be, but then theism cannot explain why God chose to construct a world that falls under Newton's laws of motion.

Much more can be said concerning the materialist explanation of biological complexity. The argument from design lost its cogency in 1859, when Charles Darwin published *On the Origin of Species,* describing how evolution by natural selection could produce new species with complex organs. Darwin explicitly considered divine creation as the alternative to evolution in explaining biological facts, but mounted a long and impressive argument that organisms including humans could evolve by natural means (Thagard 1992b, chap. 6). In the 140 years since the *Origin* appeared, an astonishing amount of evidence has accumulated that is best explained by the theory of evolution by natural selection, supplemented by the more recent theory of genetics, which explains how traits are transmitted from one generation to another and how variation can occur. The analogy between human design of artifacts and biological design of organisms has been progressively undercut by the substantial amount of evidence that biological complexity can arise from nonintentional means such as genetic variation and natural selection.

A modern version of the argument from design is based on the *anthropic principle,* according to which "all the seemingly arbitrary and unrelated constants in physics have one strange thing in common—these are precisely the values you need if you want to have a universe capable of producing life" (Glynn 1997, 22). Physicists have argued that if the physical constants such as the values for gravitational force or electromagnetic force had varied much from the actual values, then the universe would be very different and life would not have evolved. Glynn takes the anthropic principle as pointing to a religious explanation of why the fundamental constants have the values that they do. God must have picked those values of the constants in order to ensure that life would evolve. This explanation requires many assumptions: that God exists, that God wanted life like that found on Earth to evolve, and that the only way God could produce such life was by choosing the currently observed values for the physical constants. At best, this is a weak explanation: according to explanatory coherence principle E2c, the more hypotheses it takes to explain something, the lower the degree of coherence. Science does not do any better in explaining the values of the physical constants: there are strange speculations about our universe being one of many evolving from black holes in previous universes. In general, however, the hypothesis that the values of the physical constants are happy accidents is as plausible as the hypothesis that they are the result of divine design, unless one already believes that God designed the world.

The other alleged evidence for God's existence fares even worse in the explanatory battle with materialism. I argued earlier in this chapter that explanatory coherence supports materialism over dualism. Because there is no good reason to believe that souls exist, we cannot use their existence as evidence for the existence of God. Here materialism does not offer an alternative explanation, only a rejection of the alleged fact to be explained. Similarly, miracles are not a fact to be explained: the materialist denies that they occur. What does need to be explained is that some people report that miracles have occurred, but it is easy to account for these reports on the basis of individual and social delusions. Similarly, psychological explanations are available for why people have religious experiences, which derive from social experiences and individual needs to believe in contact with God. I have already argued, in discussing dualism, that materialist explanations of the moral sense are possible and plausible, so no theistic explanation is needed.

From a psychological perspective, it is misleading to discuss arguments about dualism and arguments about the existence of God separately from each other. Theism and dualism go hand in hand, and evidence for one supports the other. It is difficult to diagram the full complexity of such coherence-based inferences, but in the appendix I provide an encoding of the propositions and coherence relations involved in assessing dualism and theism together as challenges to materialism, and I describe a computer simulation that supports my claim that materialism is more coherent.

So far my analysis of the coherence of theism has concentrated on what the existence of God might be able to explain and has ignored a great deal of evidence that traditional theism has difficulty explaining. The billions of people who have existed during the past one hundred thousand years or so have undeniably undergone a great deal of suffering, arising from famine, war, disease, death, and other afflictions. These occurrences would not be a problem for a theist who believed that a malevolent god created humans in order to observe their pain, but Christians and most other theists believe that God is inherently good and wants the best for people. Thus theism seems to be incoherent with the huge amount of evil in the world. The standard theistic explanation of evil in the world is free will: it maintains that God wanted people to be free to make their own choices. But, as the discussion of dualism showed, there is reason to believe that free will in the absolute sense is an illusion. And even the assumption of free will does not explain the existence of so much suffering not derived from human actions, such as the occurrence of diseases that cause physical and emotional suffering.

In contrast, there is an obvious materialist explanation of human suffering. People are biological organisms subject to disease, famine, and death just like all other species of animals. We differ from other animals in having greater intellectual capacity, which unfortunately is sometimes used to inflict suffering on other people through wars and other actions. Human suffering thus has natural biological, psychological, and sociological explanations that do not require invoking any extra ill-supported hypotheses such as free will.

As the appendix shows in more detail, the conflict between materialism and theism requires that the latter be rejected as part of the maximally coherent explanation. Why, then, is belief in God so widespread? The reasons are partly sociological, in that people are brought up by parents and other teachers who pass on their religious beliefs. The reasons are also party psychological, in that belief in God provides solace and hope to many people, who otherwise would experience despair at the difficulties that life carries with it. Chapter 6 describes how our coherence judgments are intermixed with emotions.

In his fullest argument for the existence of God, Swinburne (1990) concludes that the hypothesis of God's existence is *probable*, given evidence such as the existence and nature of the world. He neglects to consider that the meaning of probability as applied to explanatory hypotheses is problematic, and that the assessment of hypotheses requires consideration of alternative explanations. Chapter 8 provides a systematic comparison of the relation of probabilistic reasoning and explanatory coherence.

In the middle of the twentieth century, metaphysics fell into disrepute when the logical positivists contended that metaphysical questions are unanswerable and meaningless because they are not subject to empirical confirmation and refutation. As it turned out, the positivists' view of scientific inference was much too narrow and would have condemned most of science as unscientific. But inference to scientific theories is naturally construed in terms of explanatory coherence (Thagard 1992b), and exactly the same kind of inference can be used to address metaphysical questions such as the existence of God. Analogical and deductive coherence are also relevant. There is, therefore, nothing inherently disreputable about metaphysics, although many who have claimed to pronounce upon the fundamental nature of reality have produced implausible theories. There is no conflict between science and metaphysics, only between science and bad metaphysics. At the edges of science, metaphysical questions about the fundamental nature of reality inevitably arise, and they can be answered by the same kinds of coherence-based inferences found within science.

6 SUMMARY

A coherence theory of knowledge and inference can be used to justify a realist theory of truth, the world, and other minds. Simultaneously, coherence considerations lead one to reject as implausible such nonmaterial entities as spirits, souls, and gods. Just like scientific theories, metaphysical hypotheses about the fundamental nature of reality can be evaluated with respect to their explanatory and other kinds of coherence.

7 APPENDIX: THE COMPARATIVE COHERENCE OF MATERIALISM, DUALISM, AND THEISM

A full comparative analysis of the coherence of materialism needs to integrate all the hypotheses and evidence involved in assessing it with respect to nonmaterialist explanations offered by dualists and theists. Dualism and theism are usually discussed in isolation from each other, but both psychologically and logically they go together. I have not conducted a survey, but I suspect that virtually all theists are dualists and almost all dualists are theists, whereas materialists are typically atheists. Theism explains dualism, through God's creation of human souls, so allegedly nonmaterialist aspects of mind such as consciousness and the moral sense provide some evidence for theism. It is natural, therefore, to evaluate the coherence of materialism, theism, and dualism simultaneously. Fortunately, the computational model of coherence developed in chapters 2 and 3 makes this easy to do. What follows is input to the explanatory coherence program ECHO that builds a constraint network and uses the algorithms described in chapter 2 to maximize coherence. This input produces the network shown in figure 4.6. The result of running the program ECHO on this network is that the materialist hypotheses are strongly accepted and the dualist and theistic ones are rejected (figure 4.7). Materialism is more coherent than the combination of dualism and theism.

In the input I have constructed, materialist hypotheses leave unexplained evidence proposition E16, the exis-

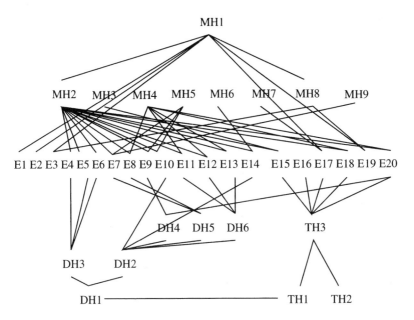

Figure 4.6
The comparative coherence of materialism, dualism, and theism. Lines indicate relations of explanation or implication. Incoherence relations between competing hypotheses are not shown.

tence of universal laws. And theistic hypotheses leave unexplained evidence proposition E19, the suffering of people from diseases and natural disasters. Most important, I have not included a theistic or dualistic explanation of E1 to E3, which are shorthand for the great many physical, chemical, and biological phenomena that science has provided detailed materialistic explanations for over the past several centuries. Overall, the greater explanatory coherence of materialism over the theistic/dualistic alternative is primarily the result of the many theoretical and experimental successes of the sciences.

Many people would disagree with the particular analysis provided in this appendix. My coherence calculation

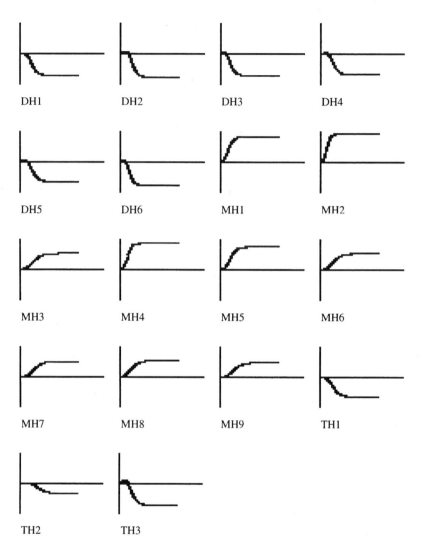

Figure 4.7
Graphs of activation levels of units representing explanatory hypotheses in a connectionist run of ECHO using the input in this appendix. Note that the materialist hypotheses MH1 to MH9 become activated (accepted), while the dualist and theistic hypotheses are rejected.

shows only that *if* you accept the input that follows, *then* materialism has greater coherence than its competitors. To dissenters, I recommend the exercise of producing alternative coherence analyses. The main point of this section has not been to provide a definitive refutation of the existence of God, but rather to illustrate how coherence assessments can be applied to metaphysical questions.

Input to ECHO

Materialist hypotheses

(proposition MH1 "Everything consists of matter and energy.")

(proposition MH2 "Minds consist of matter and energy.")

(proposition MH3 "The universe has always existed, or came to be randomly.")

(proposition MH4 "People are prone to fraud, illusion, and other psychological failings.")

(proposition MH5 "People acquire beliefs and attitudes through education and socialization.")

(proposition MH6 "Consciousness emerges from brain activity.")

(proposition MH7 "Biological complexity emerges from natural selection.")

(proposition MH8 "People are biological organisms.")

(proposition MH9 "Brains near death undergo physical changes.")

Dualist hypotheses

(proposition DH1 "Minds consist of matter and soul.")

(proposition DH2 "Minds consist partly of soul.")

(proposition DH3 "Minds consist partly of matter.")

(proposition DH4 "People have free will.")

(proposition DH5 "People survive after death.")

(proposition DH6 "People have extrasensory perception.")

Theistic hypotheses

(proposition TH1 "God exists.")

(proposition TH2 "God is all powerful.")

(proposition TH3 "God created and designed the universe.")

Evidence

(proposition E1 "Many physical phenomena")

(proposition E2 "Many chemical phenomena")

(proposition E3 "Many biological phenomena")

(proposition E4 "Vision correlates with brain activity.")

(proposition E5 "Memory correlates with brain activity.")

(proposition E6 "Memory correlates with brain activity.")

(proposition E7 "People report near-death experiences.")

(proposition E8 "People report contact with the dead in seances.")

(proposition E9 "People feel they have free will.")

(proposition E10 "People have a moral sense.")

(proposition E11 "Remote-viewing experiments")

(proposition E12 "Telekinesis experiments")

(proposition E13 "Telepathy experiments")

(proposition E14 "People have consciousness.")

(proposition E15 "The universe exists.")

(proposition E16 "The universe has laws.")

(proposition E17 "Biological complexity")

(proposition E18 "People report miracles.")

(proposition E19 "People suffer from disease and natural disasters.")

(proposition E20 "People suffer from the evil actions of others.")

Contradictions

(contradict MH1 DH1)

(contradict MH1 TH1)

Materialist explanations

(imply (MH1) MH2)

(imply (MH1) MH8)

(explain (MH1) E1)

(explain (MH1) E2)

(explain (MH1) E3)

(explain (MH2) E4)

(explain (MH2) E5)

(explain (MH2) E6)

(explain (MH2 MH5 MH9) E7)

(explain (MH2 MH4) E8)

(explain (MH2 MH5) E9)

(explain (MH2 MH5) E10)

(explain (MH2 MH4) E11)

(explain (MH2 MH4) E12)

(explain (MH2 MH4) E13)

(explain (MH2 MH6) E14)

(explain (MH2 MH3) E15)

(explain (MH1 MH7) E17)

(explain (MH2 MH4) E18)

(explain (MH1 MH8) E19)

(explain (MH2 MH4) E20)

Dualist explanations

(imply (DH1) DH2)

(imply (DH1) DH3)

(explain (DH2) DH4)

(explain (DH2) DH5)

(explain (DH2) DH6)

(explain (DH3) E4)

(explain (DH3) E5)

(explain (DH3) E6)

(explain (DH5) E7)

(explain (DH5) E8)

(explain (DH4) E9)

(explain (DH2) E10)

(explain (DH6) E11)

(explain (DH6) E12)

(explain (DH6) E13)

(explain (DH2) E14)

Theist explanations

(explain (TH1) DH1)

(explain (TH1 TH2) TH3)

(explain (TH3) E15)

(explain (TH3) E16)

(explain (TH3) E17)

(explain (TH3) E18)

(explain (TH3 DH4) E20)

Ethics and Politics

In Toronto in 1995, Paul Bernardo was convicted of the prolonged sexual torture and murder of two young women. Since Canadian law does not admit capital punishment, he was sentenced to life in prison. Some people who had long argued the immorality of capital punishment felt strongly inclined to judge that execution would nevertheless be appropriate for Bernardo's extraordinarily heinous crimes. How should such people overcome the incoherence in their ethical views? This chapter shows how justification of ethical principles and particular judgments can be accomplished by taking into account deductive, explanatory, analogical, and deliberative coherence. Like epistemic justification, discussed in chapter 3, ethical justification involves the interaction of several kinds of coherence, with the major addition being the role of deliberative coherence in decision making.

Many ethical theorists have taken coherence to be central to the justification of judgments of right and wrong (Brink 1989, Daniels 1996, De George 1990, DeMarco 1994, Ellis 1992, Hurley 1989, Richardson 1994, Sayre-McCord 1996, Swanton 1992). For example, Rawls writes, "A conception of justice cannot be deduced from self-evident premises or conditions on principles; instead, its justification is a matter of the mutual support of many considerations, of everything fitting together into one coherent view" (Rawls 1971, 21; see also Rawls 1996, 26, 53, etc.). Unfortunately, ethical theory has remained vague about the nature of coherence and about how ethical principles and judgments can be evaluated with respect to coherence. The term "wide reflective equilibrium" is used to describe a state in which a thinker has achieved a mutually coherent set of ethical principles, particular moral judgments, and background beliefs. But how people do and should reach reflective equilibrium has remained poorly specified. This chapter shows how we can justify ethical principles (such as that capital punishment is wrong) and particular judgments (such as that Paul Bernardo should be executed) by taking into account a wide range of coherence considerations.

To show that ethical decision is a coherence problem, it is necessary to define the elements, the positive constraints, and the negative constraints that operate in ethical thinking. Ethical conclusions require a complex interplay of four different kinds of coherence: deductive, explanatory, deliberative, and analogical. Each of these kinds of coherence involves different kinds of elements and constraints that contribute to an overall conclusion of what ethical principles and judgments to accept. Reflective equilibrium requires integrated assessment of deductive coherence (fit between principles and judgments), explanatory coherence (fit of principles and judgments with empirical hypotheses), deliberative coherence (fit of judgments with goals), and analogical coherence (fit of judgments with other judgments in similar cases).

As I presented it in chapter 1, cognitive naturalism holds that many philosophical issues are intimately connected with the cognitive sciences, including psychology, linguistics, neuroscience, and artificial intelligence. By applying a psychological/computational theory of coherence to ethics, this chapter demonstrates the relevance of cognitive naturalism to ethics.

1 DELIBERATIVE COHERENCE

Standard decision theory says that rationality consists in maximizing the satisfaction of preferences or utilities, but it says nothing about why people have their preferences and utilities. In contrast, Thagard and Millgram (1995; Millgram and Thagard 1996) developed a coherence theory of decision making that involves the evaluation of personal goals as well as actions that potentially accomplish those goals. According to this theory, the elements in deliberative coherence are actions and goals, and the primary positive constraint is facilitation: if an action facilitates a goal, then there is a positive constraint between them. For example, the action of executing Paul Bernardo (or the action of life imprisonment) will facilitate the goal that Paul Bernardo not murder again. Negative constraints arise because some actions are incompatible, since, for example, we cannot both execute Bernardo and imprison him for 50 years. Just as explanatory coherence gives some priority to propositions that state empirical evidence, so deliberative coherence gives some priority to intrinsic goals, ones that an agent has for basic biological or social reasons rather than because they facilitate other higher goals. But just as empirical evidence can be overridden for reasons of explanatory coherence, intrinsic goals can also be revised and overridden for reasons of deliberative coherence, which evaluates intrinsic goals (final ends) as well as instrumental goals and actions. More exactly, deliberative coherence can be specified by the following principles, analogous to those given for explanatory, deductive, analogical, conceptual, and perceptual coherence in chapter 3:

Principle L1: Symmetry   Coherence and incoherence are symmetrical relations: if factor (action or goal) F_1 coheres with factor F_2, then F_2 coheres with F_1.

Principle L2: Facilitation   Consider actions $A_1, \ldots, A_n$ that together facilitate the accomplishment of goal G. Then (a) each A_i coheres with G, (b) each A_i coheres with each other A_j, and (c) the greater the number of actions required, the less the coherence among the actions and goals.

Principle L3: Incompatibility   (a) If two factors cannot both be performed or achieved, then they are strongly incoherent. (b) If two factors are difficult to perform or achieve together, then they are weakly incoherent.

Principle L4: Goal priority   Some goals are desirable for intrinsic or other noncoherence reasons.

Principle L5: Judgment   Facilitation and competition relations can depend on coherence with judgments about the acceptability of factual beliefs.

Principle L6: Decision   Decisions are made on the basis of an assessment of the overall coherence of a set of actions and goals.

These principles show that deliberative coherence and explanatory coherence have essentially the same structure. Actions are like hypotheses in that they are evaluated with respect to their coherence with each other and with goals that can have a degree of priority on their own, just as evidence can. Both the facilitation relation in deliberative coherence and the explanation relation in explanatory coherence are based on causal connections: actions can cause goals to be satisfied, and hypotheses can state the causes of observations. Despite their isomorphism, however, deliberative and explanatory coherence need to be kept distinct, since the former concerns what to do and the latter concerns what to believe. We could translate a potential action into a kind of hypothesis, e.g., translate "Execute Bernardo" into the proposition "Executing Bernardo is the best thing to do." But there is no natural translation of goals into evidence, and the facilitation relation that links actions and goals is not the same as explanation, even though both rely on causation: actions do not explain goals. Once networks of elements and constraints are constructed, deliberative and explanatory coherence are computed in the same way, by the algorithms described in chapter 2. But the elements and constraints for deliberative coherence are sufficiently different from those for explanatory coherence that the two kinds of coherence should not be assimilated.

The most novel feature of this account of deliberative coherence is that it allows goals to be evaluated for their coherence with other goals and actions in much the same way as actions are evaluated. Principle L4 assumes that some goals are favored for intrinsic biological or social reasons, but even these goals are evaluated for their overall coherence with other goals. To anticipate an example from chapter 6, hunger may generate the goal of eating from a plate of doughnuts, but other goals such as staying healthy or not looking gluttonous may suppress the goal of eating the doughnuts.

Deliberative coherence is relevant to ethical decisions that take into account the consequences of actions. Someone might argue that executing Bernardo will be cheaper than imprisoning him under special security for life; thus execution facilitates the goal of saving Canadian taxpayers money, unless (as in the United States) the high cost of appeal procedures makes capital punishment more expensive than life imprisonment. The deterrence-based argument for capital punishment also can be reframed as a matter of deliberative coherence: the action of executing murderers facilitates (it is claimed) the goal of preventing murders. Putting it in this way makes it clear how deliberative coherence depends in part on explanatory coherence. The judgment that an action facilitates a goal depends on a causal judgment about the relation between the action and the goal, and the plausibility of the causal judgment is a matter of explanatory coherence.

In individual decision making, an agent may maximize coherence of actions and goals for the agent alone. Ethical decisions, however, require us to consider what is objectively good, not just for the agent, but also for other people involved. Something is nonmorally good for an agent if and only if it would satisfy an objective interest of the agent (Railton 1986). Normatively, actions should be chosen on the basis of the extent to which they facilitate the objective interests (goals) of all concerned. Thus in deciding whether to execute Paul Bernardo, we take into account the interests of the victims' families, Bernardo himself, and anyone else affected. I am assuming that ethical egoism is false, on the grounds that egoism, or any view that tries to derive ethics only from individual preferences, is incoherent with empirical knowledge about human psychology and sociology and with plausible ethical principles.

Whereas deductive coherence (discussed below) involves a quasi-Kantian concern with general moral principles, deliberative coherence involves a consequentialist concern with goals of those affected by ethical decisions. From the point of view of a coherence theory of ethics, the Kantian and consequentialist positions need not be seen as radically conflicting. Rather, each identifies one kind of coherence that goes into an overall judgment of right and wrong. In everyday debates on ethical issues, people often swing between questions of principle and questions of practical effects. Seeing ethical coherence as involving both deductive and deliberative coherence shows why this can be so. Deliberative coherence is, however, different from a straightforward consequentialist calculation of the costs and benefits of different actions, because it also assesses the extent to which different goals are important and hence contribute to the assessment of costs and benefits.

Questions of objective interests are closely tied with empirical hypotheses about the wants/interests mechanism of human beings. Evidence from biology, psychology, sociology, and anthropology will be needed to evaluate hypotheses concerning what kinds of actions contribute to the interests of human beings. Thus deliberative coherence is intimately tied with explanatory-coherence evaluation of hypotheses about the nature of humans and their societies. Deliberative coherence does not reduce to explanatory coherence, but depends on it in very useful ways that allow for the possibility of revising views about what is good for people and thereby revising decisions about what to do. For example, the families of Paul Bernardo's victims may naturally want to see him killed, but whether execution would bring some relief from their grief is an empirical question. Without psychological evidence about the effects of executions in similar cases, we do not have grounds for saying whether execution is really in the objective interests of the victims' families.

For utilitarians and other ethical consequentialists, something like deliberative coherence is all there is to ethical decisions. But strict consequentialism generates some implausible judgments, justifying, for example, the horrible mistreatment of a few individuals if it produces the greatest good for the greatest number. Kantian ethics postulates universal principles that establish rights and duties to overrule consideration of consequences of actions. Adoption and application of such ethical principles can be understood in terms of deductive coherence.

For deductive coherence as applied to ethics, the elements are propositions, including both general principles and particular moral judgments. As chapter 3 specified, the main positive constraint is established by the relation of deduction: if one proposition is deducible from another, then there is a positive constraint between them that will tend to make them either accepted together or rejected together. I assume here a psychologically realistic notion of deduction that avoids such trivialities as having a logically contradictory proposition entail every proposition or a logically necessary proposition being entailed by every proposition. In the context of coherence theory, deductive constraints operate quite differently from logical inference, where from $p \rightarrow q$ and p we can infer q by modus ponens, and from $p \rightarrow q$ and not q we can infer not p by modus tollens. As I argued at the end of chapter 3, coherence judgments do not have the kind of step-by-step linear reasoning found in formal logic, but instead require fitting everything together using constraints that are typically soft rather than hard. A soft constraint produces a tendency to accept two positively constrained elements together, but this constraint can be overruled if overall coherence maximization suggests that one of the elements be accepted and the other rejected.

In ethics, positive constraints arise when principles deductively entail judgments, as when the principle that capital punishment is wrong entails that Paul Bernardo should not be executed. Alternatively, the principle that capital punishment is justified for heinous murders implies that Bernardo should be executed. Negative constraints arise because of contradictions between propositions, for example, between the two principles just stated and

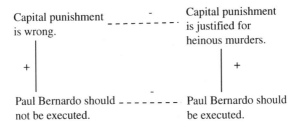

Figure 5.1
Constraint network for the Bernardo case. Solid lines indicate positive constraints, while dashed lines indicate negative constraints.

between the two judgments just stated. Figure 5.1 shows a simple constraint network that shows the relations among these four propositions.

Obviously, the constraint network shown in figure 5.1 does not offer a solution to the coherence problem, since there are two equally coherent solutions: accepting that capital punishment is wrong and that Paul Bernardo should not be executed while rejecting that capital punishment is justified and that he should be executed, or vice versa. Figure 5.1 should be expanded to include higher-level principles such as that killing people is wrong, which entails that capital punishment is wrong, as well as additional judgments about particular cases of capital punishment. Evaluation of ethical coherence based solely on fit of principles and judgments will generally be open to the standard objection to coherence theories that incompatible sets of propositions can be equally coherent. We will see, however, that broadening ethical coherence to incorporate judgments of explanatory and deliberative coherence can help to overcome this problem by introducing empirical information.

As chapter 3 discussed, deductive coherence is important outside ethics too, for example, in axiom selection in mathematics. Rarely are axioms selected because they are self-evident. Rather, axioms are selected because they entail the desired theorems, which are in turn accepted because they follow from the axioms. Mathematicians do not proceed from axioms to theorems, nor backwards from desired theorems to axioms; rather they attempt to come up with deductively coherent packages of axioms and theorems. Similarly, ethical principles are not self-evident, but must be selected on the basis of deductive coherence with particular judgments, taking into account additional kinds of coherence.

Particular ethical judgments are also not to be taken as self-evident. Much current ethical theorizing places great weight on intuitions that are established by thought experiments involving hypothetical cases. For example, Thomson (1971) defended the permissibility of abortion by asking you to imagine yourself being kidnapped and having your circulatory system connected to that of a famous violinist in order to save his life. The intuition that you are not obliged to support the violinist for nine months in order to allow his kidneys to recover is then used to support the intuition that abortion is permissible. Cummins (1998) argues convincingly that ethical intuitions as well as other philosophical intuitions derived from thought experiments have little justificatory force, because they are generated from beliefs and tacit theories. Ethical intuitions are thus different from the observations that get a degree of priority in explanatory coherence and from the mathematical intuitions that get a degree of priority in deductive coherence applied to mathematics. Deductive coherence in ethics requires us to find a fit between our general principles and our particular judgments, but I see no reason to give our particular ethical judgements any degree of intuitive priority. Clearly, then, my theory of ethical coherence is not a form of intuitionism. Intuitions should be viewed not as special inputs to the process of ethical judgments, but as outputs that reflect an overall assessment of what makes sense. Often such outputs have a salient emotional dimension, as chapter 7 discusses.

3   EXPLANATORY COHERENCE

Ethics requires attention to explanatory coherence whenever (as frequently occurs) ethical decisions depend in part on evaluation of empirical hypotheses. Particular judgments such as that Paul Bernardo should be punished depend on factual claims such as that he actually committed the crimes of which he was accused. General principles such as adoption of capital punishment can also be closely tied to factual claims: one common argument for capital punishment is that it is desirable as a deterrent to future crimes, which depends on the empirical hypothesis that having capital punishment as a possible punishment reduces crimes of certain sorts. Evaluation of this hypothesis depends on a very complex evaluation of evidence, such as comparison of countries or states with and without the death penalty. The hypothesis that capital punishment is a deterrent must mesh with a variety of sociological and psychological evidence if it is to be put to ethical use.

How can deductive and explanatory coherence interconnect? The principle that preventing serious crimes is good and the empirical hypothesis that capital punishment helps to prevent crimes together entail that capital punishment is good. These three propositions form a mutually constraining package, as shown in figure 5.2. Unlike a pure deductive principle or moral judgment, however, the empirical hypothesis is subject to a kind of coherence in which empirical evidence is given priority. Priority does not mean that the results of observations *must* be accepted,

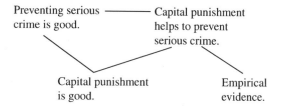

Figure 5.2
Deductive coherence depending on an empirical hypothesis. All lines indicate positive constraints based on deductive or explanatory coherence.

only that there is a soft constraint that tends to make them accepted. Now we begin to see how coherence judgments might discriminate objectively between competing sets of principles and judgments: whenever the entailment relation between principles and judgments depends on empirical hypotheses, the coherence of the ethical judgments can be affected by the explanatory coherence of the empirical hypotheses. An opponent of capital punishment might argue that killing innocent people is wrong, and that capital punishment sometimes kills innocent people, so that capital punishment is wrong. This entailment depends on the empirical hypothesis that sometimes innocent people are executed in countries and states that have capital punishment. People who are convinced on the basis of explanatory coherence that the empirical hypothesis that capital punishment sometimes leads to execution of innocent people, and convinced on the basis of explanatory coherence that the hypothesis that capital punishment serves as a deterrent is false, will tend to find more coherent the conclusion that capital punishment is wrong.

From a logical perspective, it might seem odd that if p and q together entail r, then there are pairwise constraints between p and q, between p and r, and between q

and r. However, as in explanatory coherence, these constraints capture the tendency for p, q, and r to fit together as a package of propositions to be accepted or rejected together. Of course, other coherence considerations can lead to some of them being accepted while others are rejected. For a given individual, entailment and explanation relations establish constraints between two elements if the individual believes, on the basis of other coherence judgments, that the relations hold. Logical omniscience and deductive closure have no place in a naturalistic account of inference.

Thus evaluation of ethical principles requires considerations of explanatory coherence as well as deductive coherence and striving for wide rather than narrow reflective equilibrium. But deductive and explanatory coherence are quite similar, in that both involve propositional elements with positive and negative constraints that can be maximized. The interpenetration of deductive and explanatory coherence gives us some hope that ethical deliberation can be affected substantially by empirical evidence. Adding analogical coherence shows another way of broadening ethical coherence.

4 ANALOGICAL COHERENCE

Not all ethical argument considers general principles (deductive coherence) or consequences (deliberative coherence). People often argue for moral principles and judgments analogically, supporting a conclusion in one case by comparing it to a similar case whose moral status is more obvious. The morality of capital punishment is similarly subject to analogical dispute: is execution of a murderer comparable to killing a defenseless victim, or is it somehow similar to acts of self-defense? Applying an analogy to an

Table 5.1
Correspondences between source and target analogs in arguing that capital punishment is wrong

Source	Target
holds(abductor, victim)	holds(state, prisoner)
kills(abductor, victim)	executes(state, prisoner)
wrong(kills(abductor, victim))	wrong?(executes(state, prisoner))

ethical issue requires transferring a moral judgment from an accepted case to a contested case: if capital punishment is relevantly similar to killing a defenseless victim, an act that is obviously wrong, then capital punishment can also be judged to be wrong. Assessing relevant similarity requires establishing correspondences between the source analog, about which an ethical judgment has already been made, and the target analog, to which the ethical judgment is to be applied.

As chapter 3 described, establishing correspondences between source and target analogs can be viewed as a coherence problem involving several different kinds of constraints. The elements are hypotheses about what features of the analogs correspond to each other. Table 5.1 is a simple representation of two analogs. To perform an analogical mapping between these analogs, we need to create mapping hypotheses, such as that *kills* in the source analog corresponds to *executes* in the target analog and that *victim* in the source corresponds to *prisoner* in the target. Once these correspondences are established, analogical inference can support the conclusion that it is wrong to execute a prisoner by mapping *wrong?* to *wrong*.

In the multiconstraint theory of analogy of Holyoak and Thagard (1995), positive constraints are based on semantic and visual similarity, with people tending to map semantically similar predicates such as *kill* and *execute*. Additional positive constraints are based on syntactic structure: if *holds* in the source is mapped to *holds* in the target, then the corresponding arguments will also be mapped: *abductor* to *state* and *victim* to *prisoner*. Structure also provides negative constraints based on a preference for one-to-one mappings; accepting the mapping hypothesis that *abductor* corresponds to *state* will tend to lead to rejection of the mapping hypothesis that *abductor* corresponds to *prisoner*. Finally, an additional set of positive constraints arises from the purpose of the analogy, what it is designed to accomplish. In ethical deliberations, the purpose of the analogy is to transfer the ethical judgment about the source over to an ethical judgment about the target.

Analogical arguments are rarely convincing on their own, but they can contribute to the overall coherence of a view. Darwin, for example, used an analogy between artificial and natural selection as one of the ingredients in his case for the explanatory coherence of his theory of evolution. Similarly, analogy can help to establish the deductive and deliberative coherence of an ethical conclusion. A defender of capital punishment might argue that just as it may be legitimate to kill an attacker such as Bernardo in self-defense, so it may be legitimate for society to defend itself against murderous psychopaths like Bernardo by executing them. The argument involves both deductive coherence and fit between principles and judgments (killing in self-defense is right; a victim's killing Bernardo would have been justified) and analogical coherence (the comparison between killing for self-defense and execution). Of course, a critic of capital punishment will attempt to undermine this analogy and employ different ones to suggest the applicability of different principles.

From the perspective of the *multicoherence* theory of ethics proposed here, reaching ethical conclusions turns out to be a complex psychological process. Normatively, people can proceed as follows in establishing ethical principles and judgments:

1. Identify deductive elements (principles, judgments) and positive and negative constraints among them.

2. Identify deliberative elements (actions, goals) and positive and negative constraints among them.

3. Identify explanatory elements (hypotheses, evidence) and positive and negative constraints among them.

4. Identify constraints linking the explanatory elements with the deductive and deliberative elements.

5. Identify analogical elements (mapping hypotheses) and positive and negative constraints among them.

6. Identify constraints linking the analogical elements with the deductive, deliberative, and explanatory elements.

7. Finally, use algorithms to maximize coherence by accepting some elements and rejecting others in the way that approximately maximizes satisfaction of the positive and negative constraints.

While this procedure is normatively appealing, it is probably too much to expect of people, given their psychological resources. At the level of consciousness, working memory is far too limited to simultaneously entertain all the different elements that go into such a complex coherence judgment. Perhaps simultaneous maximization of all the constraints goes on automatically at the unconscious level, just as the brain makes sense of complex visual inputs to produce a coherent interpretation of a scene. More likely, though, the mind must proceed more sporadically, alternating between focusing on one kind of coherence and focusing on another, or concentrating on some elements and then on others (see Hoadley, Ranney, and Schank 1994). Instead of systematically identifying different kinds of constraints, people focus for a while on a particular kind of coherence, such as the deductive fit between principles and judgments, then shift to other kinds of coherence, such as deliberative. Within each focus the mind reaches a tentative coherence conclusion based on the elements and constraints currently active, producing evaluations of elements that can then feed into coherence calculations involving different elements and constraints. This sporadic, unsystematic way of reaching ethical conclusions is obviously subject to the main weakness in any imperfect maximization procedure: instead of reaching a global maximum that achieves the highest possible extent of constraint satisfaction, people may get stuck in a local maximum that, although better than immediately available alternatives, is still inferior to other ways of maximizing constraint satisfaction. One charitable way of explaining the incessant controversies in ethics is by noting the complexity of ethical coherence and conjecturing that disputants have simply fallen into different local maxima.

Those who find inconsistencies in their ethical views, such as the people mentioned at the beginning of this chapter who believe both that capital punishment is wrong and that Paul Bernardo should be executed, can at least attempt to implement the seven-step procedure stated at the beginning of this section. The result should be to bring to bear a wide complex of principles, judgments, actions, goals, hypotheses, evidence, and mapping hypotheses in a way that may suggest how either to abandon the principle that capital punishment is wrong or to reject the judgment that Paul Bernardo should be executed. In either case, coherence with a large number of other considerations will be what determines ethical belief change.

It is important to note that the process by which people reach ethical conclusions is often social: "We press each other toward coherence, and these pressures help nudge us toward consensus" (Gibbard 1990, 204). From the perspective of the individual, it may seem rather arbitrary what elements (concepts, propositions, analogs, etc.) make up the coherence network, but the arbitrariness is much diminished in a social context in which people with different ethical judgments introduce competing elements to be integrated into each other's coherence networks. We do not have to worry about there being an unlimited number of trivial elements that are minor variants of each other, as in Goodman's (1965) "grue" predicates in confirmation theory, so long as ethical coherence is viewed as taking place in human minds in real social contexts. Attention to the content of ongoing controversies should enable us to identify for each ethical issue the relevant elements and constraints. Chapter 7 discusses how consensus can arise through coherence and communication.

6   PUTTING IT ALL TOGETHER

But how do minds amalgamate the various concerns—deductive, explanatory, analogical, and deliberative—that go into an overall coherence judgment? On the traditional view of inference, ethical conclusions would have to somehow integrate the conclusions of a variety of arguments presented one at a time. From the constraint-satisfaction view of coherence, in contrast, inference is not a matter of step-by-step argument, but rather of assembling a set of constraints whose satisfaction is to be maximized in parallel. Figure 5.3 shows how constraints

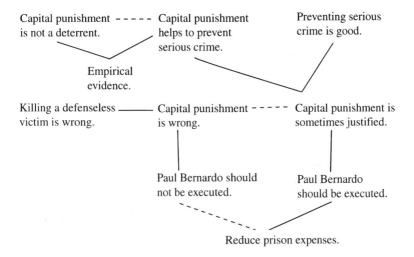

Figure 5.3
Constraint network showing interconnections of explanatory, deductive, analogical, and deliberative coherence. Solid lines are positive constraints, and dashed lines are negative constraints.

derived from deductive, explanatory, analogical, and deliberative coherence can all be incorporated into a single constraint network. The figure shows only a fraction of the considerations that would go into a full assessment of the morality of capital punishment, but it serves to show how a wide variety of constraints can be incorporated into a single network. I have run a computer simulation using the following programs together to produce a common network:

· ECHO (Thagard 1992b) creates constraints based on whether the hypothesis that capital punishment is a deterrent explains the evidence. ECHO is also used to approximate the deductive relation that justifies capital punishment as following from the principle that preventing serious crime is good, as well as other deductive relations such as the one between "Capital punishment is wrong" and "Bernardo should not be executed."

• ACME (Holyoak and Thagard 1989) creates constraints based on the analogical mapping between capital punishment and killing defenseless victims.

• DECO (Thagard and Millgram 1995) creates constraints based on consequences such as that capital punishment reduces prison expenses.

Because ECHO, ACME, and DECO all use the same connectionist algorithm for maximizing coherence (chapter 2), the computer simulation succeeds in reaching a conclusion based simultaneously on all the considerations shown in figure 5.3.

Of course, this simulation does not settle the enormously difficult ethical issue of whether capital punishment is justified. It does serve, however, to show how various kinds of coherence considerations can combine to produce an overall judgment. To fully capture individual judgments about capital punishment, it would be necessary to combine assessment of the ethical issue with metaphysical views of the sort discussed in chapter 4. People who believe that God ordains that murderers be put to death will obviously reach a different conclusion than others whose coherence calculations are restricted to secular matters.

7   THE COHERENCE OF ABORTION

The complexity of ethical coherence is further illustrated by debates concerning the morality of abortion, which contain a variety of deductive, explanatory, deliberative, and analogical considerations. Baird and Rosenbaum (1993) contains the U.S. Supreme court judgment on *Roe v. Wade*, which is clearly based on a mixture of coherence considerations, along with various essays for and against abortion that also illustrate the multifariousness of coherence. Deductive arguments are used by both sides of the issue. Defenders of abortion argue that the illegitimacy of the state's banning abortion follows from a right to privacy, whereas critics of abortion claim that its immorality follows deductively from the principle that murder is wrong. Of course, neither of these deductive arguments is convincing to the other side, since they depend on the legitimacy of the principle stated and on the acceptability of additional premises required to make the argument sound, for example, that abortion is murder.

Other arguments invoked in the abortion case point to issues of deliberative coherence, for example, on the pro side that prohibiting abortion will lead to injuries of numerous women undergoing illegal abortions, and on the con side that abortion causes distress both to fetuses and to women who have abortions. As in the issue of capital punishment, deliberative coherence often interacts with explanatory coherence: factual claims such as that making abortion illegal would cause suffering both from illegal abortions and unwanted children need to be empirically evaluated on the basis of how well they fit with theories and observations in psychology and sociology. Explanatory coherence can also interact with deductive coherence, for example, when theists infer that abortion is wrong because God forbids it. This deductive argument presupposes that there is a God, a hypothesis that can be evaluated on the basis of its explanatory coherence.

Analogical coherence also enters into judgments about the morality of abortion, since arguments often rely on comparison to practices such as infanticide or hypothetical cases such as described earlier of the one being involuntarily connected with a violinist. Analogy also plays a major role in legal judgments, when abortion is treated as a case that should be settled in ways similar to precedents such as the judgment that prevented states from banning contraception. Whether abortion is deemed as analogous to legally acceptable practices such as contraception or as analogous to proscribed practices such as infanticide depends on a variety of deductive, explanatory, and deliberative considerations. Analogies contribute to the assessment of explanations and actions, just as the assessment of explanations and actions contributes to the evaluation of analogies. There is no circularity here, because all kinds of coherence can be simultaneously computed by global maximization of satisfaction of different kinds of constraints.

Thus, like capital punishment, the ethical assessment of abortion depends on a combination of deliberative, explanatory, deductive, and analogical coherence. I have attempted not to provide such an assessment here but only to indicate how the different kinds of coherence combine to influence judgments about the morality of abortion.

8   NORMATIVE ISSUES

My theory of ethical coherence is intended to be both descriptive and prescriptive, characterizing how people think ethically when they are thinking at their best. Epistemology can be "biscriptive," i.e., simultaneously descriptive and prescriptive (Thagard 1992b, 97). But linking the descriptive and the normative is more problematic in ethics than it is in epistemology. In philosophy of science, we can take as exemplars of scientific inference those scientists who have made the most important contributions to the growth of knowledge: Newton, Darwin, Einstein, and so on. In ethics we do not have recognized inferential experts whom we can view as exemplars. The most influential ethical theorists have tended to be dogmatic in defending monolithic approaches to ethics, for example, exclusively in terms of Kantian rights and duties or exclusively in terms of utilitarian consequences. My more eclectic coherence approach makes possible incorporation of a wide variety of ethical considerations but must face the question of whether putting them all into a coherent soup will produce judgments that are objectively right. My response is that when dealing with difficult ethical issues such as capital punishment and abortion, we should feel obliged to take into account all the different kinds of issues that have been taken to be relevant to the morality of such practices. One of the advantages of the coherence theory is that it can incorporate the full range of arguments that ethicists have used in a more piecemeal fashion to support their own conclusions. The requirement of taking into account a broad range of considerations is analogous to the requirement in epistemology that anyone evaluating an hypothesis on the basis of its explanatory power should take into account the full range of empirical evidence and alternative hypotheses.

Still, difficult normative issues arise in the application of ethical coherence. We saw in the discussion of empirical issues in ethics that explanatory coherence can affect deliberative coherence when judgments of likely consequences of actions are based on causal theories and evidence. In a coherence system, however, there is a danger that deliberative coherence will have an undesirable effect on explanatory coherence, as when people adopt hypotheses for personal gain rather than on the basis of evidence. There is substantial psychological evidence that people's goals do affect their evaluation of evidence (see Kunda 1990).

Normatively, however, we want explanatory coherence to affect deliberative coherence and not vice versa. This issue is addressed further at the end of chapter 6.

Another difficult normative issue concerns the construction of constraint networks, such as the one shown in figure 5.3. Different people may put different weights on the positive and negative constraints connecting the various elements in the network. At the extremes, a devout Kantian might put zero weight on any empirical considerations, and a utilitarian might put zero weight on anything else. My first response is to point out that the extreme versions of both these approaches have familiar incompatibilities with most people's ethical judgments: Kantian rules such as never to tell lies are too rigid to apply universally, and utilitarian calculations that count the pleasure and pain of strangers equally with the pleasure and pain of loved ones are impossible for most people. My second response is to point to the multifarious nature of actual ethical arguments that embrace different kinds of ethical concerns, including both Kantian and utilitarian ones. I do not have an algorithm for establishing the weights on people's constraints, only the hope that once discussion establishes a common set of constraints, coherence algorithms can yield consensus. I return to the topic of consensus in chapter 7. Now I turn to the discussion of important normative issues in politics.

9 POLITICS: JUSTIFYING THE STATE

The term *politics* is usually defined as the art or science of government, so the first normative political issue is whether there should be any government at all. Do organized nation states have legitimate authority over their members, or is government an illicit infringement on the freedom of people forced to submit to the decrees of a state? Anarchists, who advocate the abolition of government, claim both that there is no justification for the state and that its elimination will produce a society in which people's lives are improved. Traditional anarchists like Mikhail Bakunin and Peter Kropotkin advocated elimination of the state in favor of a cooperative socialism in which people would provide mutual aid. In contrast to this sort of left-wing anarchism, there is a more recent and currently more popular brand of right-wing anarchism, which advocates full-fledged free-market capitalism as the alternative to current government (Sanders and Narveson 1996). At the extremes, left- and right-wing thinkers converge on rejection of the state, although the utopian forms of government-free life that they envision are very different.

What response can one give to the rejection of the state by various anarchists? Foundationalists, who think that politics, like epistemology and ethics, requires indubitable truths, must find incontrovertible axioms and implications that lead to the conclusion that the state is justified. But such a foundation is no more likely to be found in politics than in epistemology or ethics. Instead, we need to look for a coherentist justification of the state that combines deliberative, analogical, explanatory, and deductive considerations.

In particular, the question of whether people should live in a state or in socialist or capitalist anarchy is largely a matter of deliberative coherence. At a crude level, here are the actions to choose from:

• Establish a nation state that has authority over its citizens.

• Abolish the state in favor of socialist cooperation.

• Abolish the state in favor of capitalist free markets.

Both left- and right-wing anarchists assume that people will be better off without the state, but in what respects? What are the goals with respect to which the deliberation concerning the existence of the state should take place? It is impossible to establish deductively the goals that political deliberation should accomplish, but three stand out prominently in political arguments. I shall call them the *F-constraints*: freedom, flourishing, and fairness. Deliberation both about whether there should be a state and about what form the state should take can be framed in terms of how different ways of organizing people contribute to satisfaction of these three constraints. Other kinds of coherence, particularly analogical and explanatory, will interact with deliberative coherence to produce a coherentist justification of particular forms of the state.

Without intending to give it any kind of priority, I listed freedom as the first F-constraint. Freedom (autonomy, liberty) is the ability of individuals to make personal and economic decisions without interference by the state or other people. Initially it might seem that anarchism is clearly the way to maximize freedom, but eliminating the state may in fact increase interference by other people, who are also unconstrained by the state. We need to weight carefully the relative extent to which the options of (1) having a state, (2) right-wing anarchism, and (3) left-wing anarchism promote freedom.

Similarly, we need to weight the contributions that different forms of government and nongovernment make to human flourishing, which encompasses both happiness and excellence. People flourish not only when they enjoy pleasure and lack pain, but also when they accomplish the things that humans do best, including intellectual accomplishments (such as science, philosophy, and art) and physical accomplishments (such as athletics). Anarchists from both the right and left assume that people will not only have more freedom without the state, they will also flourish more without state interference. Evaluating these assumptions requires explanatory and analogical considerations, described below.

The final F-constraint is fairness, which concerns the extent to which there is equality in the distribution of freedom and flourishing. Consider a society in which most people enjoy great degrees of flourishing and freedom at the expense of some people who are totally deprived of these benefits, perhaps because they are slaves to the well-off. Such a society is so unfair that most people would consider that it is not justified by the freedom and flourishing it provides for those who are well-off. I see no way in which the F-constraints can be subordinated to each other, even though they have interactions. Freedom, for example, seems historically to contribute to flourishing, but that does not mean that is valuable only for its role in promoting flourishing. In different historical contexts, there may be varying ways in which the different F-constraints enhance or weaken each other's satisfaction.

Different traditions in political and social philosophy have emphasized different constraints. For libertarians, the primary constraint is freedom from interference by others, with little concern for flourishing or fairness. For utilitarians, the only constraint on ethical and political justification is maximizing the greatest happiness for the greatest number, which falls under my constraint of flourishing. Various theorists, from socialists and anarchists to liberals such as John Rawls, have stressed fairness as a key constraint on any admissible political system. My view is that we should take all three of these constraints seriously in trying to justify the state and particular versions of it. It is an open and difficult question what the relative weights of these constraints should be; I conjecture that differences in political philosophy arise primarily from different weightings of the importance of freedom, flourishing, and fairness.

How can we use freedom, flourishing, and fairness to compare having a state versus left- and right-wing anarchism? The answer involves both analogical and explanatory coherence. Explanatory coherence is relevant to assessing the causal claims that underlie facilitation relations that produce judgments of deliberative coherence. We need to assess the claim that eliminating the state would facilitate freedom, flourishing, and fairness. Unfortunately, there is no evidence that we can use to assess the explanatory coherence of this claim, because complex human societies have lived under some form of government at least since around 2800 B.C., when Sumerian city states were in operation. There simply is no evidence that life without the state has facilitated or would facilitate freedom, flourishing, and fairness.

Anarchism also fares poorly when analogical coherence is taken into account. Even though there have been no state-free episodes to establish facilitation relations directly, one might argue analogically that a future stateless society might have the good features of some past situation that was less state-dominated than current societies. But what are the analogs one can use? For right-wing anarchists, perhaps the best choice would be capitalist governments before the twentieth-century rise of the welfare state increased state involvement. But it would be very hard to make the case that nineteenth-century residents of Britain or the United States had lives superior to people in those countries today. Perhaps there was more abstract economic freedom than now exists, but health and education—crucial ingredients in flourishing—were far inferior to current standards. Moreover, fairness was intensely violated by the great discrepancies in political participation (the right to vote was limited) and wealth. The claims of right-wing anarchists to satisfaction of the F-constraints are thus bereft of explanatory and analogical coherence. Of course, they may well claim that the only constraint that matters to them is freedom, so that failures of right-wing anarchism to afford gains in flourishing and fairness are irrelevant. But the restriction to only one constraint is arbitrary and insupportable. Anarchism may follow deductively from some principle that says that freedom is all that matters, but that principle does not cohere with what we know about human needs and desires. Myopic concentration on freedom is no more appealing than the opposite view that freedom may be largely ignored in order to increase general flourishing and fairness.

Left-wing anarchists are even shorter on plausible analogs than right-wing anarchists. For examples of stateless societies run on principles of cooperation and social aid, one can look only to relatively small groups, such as communes and Israeli kibbutzim. However, there are two reasons why these analogs do little to support the claim that socialist anarchism would support freedom, flourishing, and fairness. First, the analogy between anarchist experiments in small groups and running a complex society without a state is very weak: there are huge differences between running a society with millions of people and running a group of twenty or one hundred people. Second, even on a small scale, anarchistic, socialistic experiments have not been very successful in the long run. The Israeli kibbutz movement was strong in the 1950s, but today there are only weak remnants trying to survive as quasi-capitalist enterprises. Other anarchist experiments have degenerated into chaos or despotism. So analogies do little to support left-wing anarchism.

Therefore, in order to facilitate freedom, flourishing, and fairness, having some form of government is preferable to having no state at all. Of course, states have varied enormously in the degree to which they satisfy these constraints, which raises the question of what kind of government is best. Given the evidence that the best of modern states contribute substantially to freedom, flourishing, and fairness and the lack of evidence that anarchism in any form would even come close to performing so well, we can dispense with the skeptical question of whether the state is justified at all and move on to the much more interesting and important question of what kind of state is best.

10 WHAT KIND OF STATE?

The question of whether the state is justified is of purely philosophical interest, since hardly anyone seriously considers the complete abolition of the state. But the question of what kind of state to have is very much alive in many contexts. For example, in the wake of the collapse of communism, people in Eastern European countries are faced with deciding what kind of government should replace it. Should they move towards a kind of laissez-faire capitalism at the opposite extreme from socialism, or should they look for a middle road closer to social democracies such as Sweden, or should they revert to a version of socialism without the extreme restrictions on freedom found under communism? Choices in most Western states are less extreme, ranging between social democracy and welfare capitalism in Western European states and Canada, and between welfare capitalism and laissez-faire capitalism in the United States. We can now explore how freedom, flourishing, and fairness fare in various societies to help answer the question of what kind of state is best.

Deciding what kind of state to adopt is primarily a matter of deliberative coherence subject to the three F-constraints. But what are the options? Derbyshire and

Derbyshire (1997) provide a systematic comparison of 192 current states, which they classify into the following political systems:

• Liberal democracy, with representative government and individual freedom, e.g., the United States
• Emergent democracy, like liberal democracy, but with limited political stability, e.g., Poland
• Communism, with state ownership and one-party control, e.g., China
• Nationalistic socialism, with charismatic leaders, e.g., Libya
• Authoritarian nationalism, with one-party dominance, but not socialist, e.g., Indonesia
• Military authoritarianism, e.g., Nigeria
• Islamic nationalism, e.g., Iran
• Absolutism, with no constitutional government, e.g., Saudi Arabia

If these are the eight options for choosing a kind of state, then choice is relatively easy. The 73 liberal democracies not only surpass the other states in freedom, they also by and large have much greater degrees of flourishing, as measured by such variables as wealth, health, and education. As for fairness, the liberal democracies make voting generally available, and their distribution of wealth is generally no worse than that of other kinds of state. Hence liberal democracy is clearly superior to all other current forms of government with respect to the F-constraints.

Choice gets more difficult if we try to select among different variants of liberal democracy. We can distinguish at least the following variants, distinguished by the increasing extent to which the state is involved in the economy:

- Laissez-faire capitalism, e.g., nineteenth-century Britain
- Welfare capitalism, e.g., Britain since the Second World War and the United States since Roosevelt's New Deal
- Social democracy, e.g., Sweden

To decide which of these to prefer, we need to make a much more fine-grained assessment of freedom, flourishing, and fairness. Ideally, we would need to conduct a full survey with informative measures of the degree to which current countries and ones in the recent past have satisfied the F-constraints. No such surveys currently exist, but there have been other surveys that address some of the relevant issues.

For a start, the Fraser Institute, a Canadian economic think tank, publishes an index of economic freedom, which attempts to measure one aspect of freedom. This index aims to measure the extent to which individuals are free to choose for themselves and engage in voluntary transactions with others, and have their rightly acquired property protected from invasions by others (Gwartney and Lawson 1997, 2). The index contains seventeen components, divided into four major areas:

- Money and inflation: protection of money as a store of value and medium of exchange
- Government operations and regulations: freedom to decide what is produced and consumed
- Takings and discriminatory taxation: freedom to keep what you earn
- Restraints on international exchange: freedom of exchange with foreigners

The political bias of this way of measuring freedom is evident: it is part of the Fraser Institute's mission to reduce taxation and other forms of government involvement in

Table 5.2
Summary rankings of the economic-freedom ratings by the Fraser Institute, 1997, showing the top twenty countries

Rank	Country	Freedom rating
1	Hong Kong	9.6
2	Singapore	9.4
3	New Zealand	9.2
4	United States	9.1
5	United Kingdom	9.0
6	Canada	8.8
7	Argentina	8.7
8	Netherlands	8.6
8	Panama	8.6
8	Australia	8.6
8	Luxembourg	8.6
8	Ireland	8.6
13	Switzerland	8.5
14	Japan	8.3
14	Denmark	8.3
14	Norway	8.3
17	Belgium	8.2
17	El Salvador	8.2
17	Finland	8.2
17	Germany	8.2

Source: Gwartney and Lawson 1998, p. 22.

the economy. Although this measurement of economic freedom is not an adequate substitute for the freedom constraint, it is a methodologically interesting way of beginning to quantify ideas about freedom. Table 5.2 reproduces part of the Fraser Institute's 1998 ratings of economic freedom.

Aspects of flourishing can also be measured with some degree of approximation. Although it is in many ways limited as an indicator of human flourishing, the United

Nations Human Development Index (HDI) provides an interesting first approximation. The HDI is a composite of three basic components of human development:

• Longevity, measured by life expectancy
• Knowledge, measure by a combination of adult literacy and mean years of schooling
• Standard of living, measured by purchasing power, based on real GDP per capita adjusted for the local cost of living

Table 5.3 lists the top finishers in the most recent assessment. There does not appear to be any strong correlation with the economic-freedom-index results shown in table 5.2. Nor can we demonstrate that the three components of the HDI correlate strongly with human happiness and achievement of excellence, although it is not implausible that they do. But the methodology of the HDI shows that it is in principle possible to assess the extent to which different countries have enabled their citizens to flourish. By extension, once the countries are classified according to what kind of government they have, we can begin to assess the contributions of different kinds of states to human flourishing. In contrast to the economic-freedom tally, which was dominated by states inclined toward laissez-faire policies, states with relatively more state intervention in the economy and social planning tended to do well according to the human development index.

One major weakness in both the HDI and the economic-freedom index is that they look only at aggregates and neglect questions concerning the distribution of freedom and flourishing. The United Nations does, however, offer measures of poverty and gender inequality that address these issues to some extent. A fairness index needs to be developed to measure the extent to which there is an equitable distribution of economic and social goods not limited by gender, race, and ethnicity. If the aim of this

Table 5.3
Top twenty countries in the 1997 United Nations Human Development Index

HDI rank	Country	Life expectancy at birth (yrs.) 1994	Adult literacy rate (%) 1994	Combined 1st, 2nd, 3rd level gross enrollment ratio (%) 1994	Real GDP per capita (PPP$) 1994	Human Development Index (HDI) 1994
1	Canada	79.0	99.0	100	21,459	0.960
2	France	78.7	99.0	89	20,510	0.946
3	Norway	77.5	99.0	92	21,346	0.943
4	USA	76.2	99.0	96	26,397	0.942
5	Iceland	79.1	99.0	83	20,556	0.942
6	Netherlands	77.3	99.0	91	19,238	0.940
7	Japan	79.8	99.0	78	21,581	0.940
8	Finland	76.3	99.0	97	17,417	0.940
9	New Zealand	76.4	99.0	94	16,851	0.937
10	Sweden	78.3	99.0	82	18,540	0.936
11	Spain	77.6	97.1	90	14,324	0.934
12	Austria	76.6	99.0	87	20,667	0.932
13	Belgium	76.8	99.0	86	20,985	0.932
14	Australia	78.1	99.0	79	19,285	0.931
15	U.K.	76.7	99.0	86	18,620	0.931
16	Switzerland	78.1	99.0	76	24,967	0.930
17	Ireland	76.3	99.0	88	16,061	0.929
18	Denmark	75.2	99.0	89	21,341	0.927
19	Germany	76.3	99.0	81	19,675	0.924
20	Greece	77.8	96.7	82	11,265	0.923

Source: http://www.undp.org/hdro/. "PPP" stands for "purchasing power parity."

section were to argue for a particular form of state, I would need to attempt to quantify the extent to which different countries satisfy the fairness constraint. My aim, however, is more methodological: to show that in principle we can assess different kinds of states with respect to the extent to which they satisfy the F-constraints. Although the assessment is obviously a very challenging project in social science, and although the tough issue of how to weight the constraints of freedom, flourishing, and fairness remains unsolved, we can at least begin to see how the problem of justifying particular forms of states can be seen as a coherence problem.

It is unusual for people to undergo major changes in their political views during their lifetimes, but it sometimes happens. Consider, for example, the student radicals of the 1960s who abandoned the traditional liberal democratic views that they grew up with in favor of more revolutionary ones. Or consider the neoconservative intellectuals of the 1970s and 1980s, some of whom had been much more radical in their youth. What is involved in the shift from being a liberal to a left-wing radical, or from a leftist to a neoconservative espousing the virtues of laissez-faire capitalism? Evidence to answer this question is limited, but the coherence perspective suggests that we should look at changes such as the following:

• Changes in beliefs about human nature, based on explanatory and analogical coherence

• Changes in beliefs about the efficacy of different political strategies, again based on explanatory and analogical coherence

• Changes in the weights attached to the F-constraints, altering the relative priority given to freedom, flourishing, and fairness

It is difficult to say to what extent the latter process is a rational one. Emotional changes of the sort discussed in chapter 6 will also be relevant.

Choosing what kind of state to adopt is largely a matter of deliberative coherence with the F-constraints, but analogical reasoning can also contribute. Negative analogies are particular states that we do *not* want future states to be like, for example, Nazi Germany and the Soviet

Union under Stalin. Positive analogies are particular states that have aspects that we might want to emulate, for example, the freedom of the United States and the fairness of the Scandinavian social democracies. Analogies may myopically limit deliberative coherence, since they focus on past examples rather than novel future state organizations that surpass previously available ones, but they can provide positive and negative suggestions about what to keep and what to avoid in designing the state. As in the assessment of the ethical coherence of capital punishment, explanatory coherence becomes relevant to assessing the plausibility of relevant empirical claims concerning the efficacy of different kinds of political organization. For example, the claim that a particular kind of state promotes prosperity must be evaluated against the historical evidence. Hence, justifying the state and the more specific task of choosing what kind of state to adopt are both coherence problems.

11   CONCLUSION

This chapter has proposed a multicoherence theory of ethical thinking according to which people reach ethical and political conclusions by approximately maximizing the satisfaction of deductive, explanatory, deliberative, and analogical constraints. There are at least four reasons why this theory should be adopted as a normative account of how people should reason about right and wrong.

First, the multicoherence theory of ethics can handle the complexity of moral reasoning. This chapter has shown the relevance of all four kinds of coherence to the evaluation of whether capital punishment and abortion are right or wrong. It would not be hard to show that other major ethical issues similarly involve a mixture of deductive, explanatory, deliberative, and analogical considerations.

Second, the multicoherence theory is naturalistic in that it is consistent with substantial amounts of evidence showing that the processes of parallel constraint satisfaction are important in human cognition (Holyoak and Spellman 1993; Thagard 1996, chap. 7). If vision, language understanding, hypothesis evaluation, concept application, and analogy are all coherence processes, it should not be surprising that ethical thinking is also a coherence process. The ethical theory developed in this chapter is not naturalistic, however, in the sense of claiming that moral judgments are reducible to scientific facts about the natural world. Judgments about right and wrong are often closely tied with scientific judgments, as we saw with the interconnections among deductive, deliberative, and explanatory coherence. But these connections do not *reduce* deductive and deliberative coherence to explanatory coherence. Ethical questions are not simply factual questions, but they are sufficiently linked with empirical issues that we can hope that agreement on psychological, biological, and economic issues can contribute to agreement on ethical issues. My multicoherence account of coherence provides a much fuller account of ethical inference than is found in recent naturalistic accounts that emphasize either perceptionlike neural networks (Churchland 1995, Flanagan 1996) or metaphor (Johnson 1993, 1996; Lakoff 1996). These accounts capture aspects of conceptual and analogical coherence, but neglect the contributions of deductive and deliberative coherence to ethical judgments.

Third, the coherence view of ethics and politics proposed here avoids the two major problems of foundationalist approaches to ethics and epistemology. The first problem is that, for epistemology as for ethics, no one has ever been able to find a set of foundations that even comes close to receiving general assent. The coherentist approach has no need for a priori intuition or contractarian artifice. The second problem is that proposed foundations are rarely substantial enough to support an attractive epistemic or ethical edifice, so that foundationalism degenerates into skepticism. In contrast, the multicoherence theory of ethics, like coherence theories of knowledge, recommends that we jump into issues in midstream, revising ethical beliefs as necessary to increase overall coherence, without attempting the impossible task of rederiving all ethical principles and judgments from first principles.

Finally, the multicoherence theory proposed here has the advantage over previous coherentist approaches to ethics that it employs a clearly stated and computationally implemented account of what it is to maximize coherence. Explanatory, deliberative, and analogical coherence all have computational models that have been applied to numerous complex real-world cases. Amalgating these kinds of coherence with the deductive coherence of ethical principles and judgments is nontrivial, but the sporadic, incremental way in which people generally shift focus among different kinds of coherence can be seen as a rough approximation to a more ideal process of global maximization of constraint satisfaction. We do not always maximize coherence, but sometimes we manage nevertheless to make quite good sense of right and wrong.

I have so far neglected an important psychological aspect of ethical thinking. When people make ethical and political judgments, there is usually a strong emotional component. People feel very positively about what they view as right, and they feel strong negative emotions about what they view as wrong. Chapter 6 develops a theory of emotional coherence that shows how to integrate the coherence considerations discussed in this chapter with emotional matters.

In contrast to the vague notions of coherence used by many ethical theorists, the theory of coherence as constraint satisfaction can provide a detailed and computable model of how different kinds of coherence can contribute to ethical judgments. Deliberative coherence involves choosing actions and goals on the basis of their coherence and incoherence with other actions and goals. Deliberative coherence is essential to ethical judgments, but deductive, explanatory, and analogical coherence can also contribute. This theory of ethical coherence is intended to be both descriptive of how people make ethical judgments and prescriptive of how they should. Political judgments involving the justification of the state and the choice of a kind of state are based on ethical coherence, particularly on deliberative coherence with respect to the goals of freedom, flourishing, and fairness.

Like most philosophical and psychological writings about inference, my discussion of coherence has so far ignored the important role of emotion in human cognition. This chapter presents a theory of emotional coherence and describes its implementation in a computational model that has been applied to interpersonal trust and other important psychological phenomena that involve both inference and emotion, including empathy and nationalism. The theory and model are then extended to encompass "metacoherence" and the emotional impact of overall assessments of coherence relevant to understanding beauty, humor, and cognitive therapy.

1   THE IMPORTANCE OF TRUST

When Jimmy Carter ran for President in 1976 in the wake of Watergate, he told the voters, "You can trust me." After Tony Blair was elected Prime Minister of England in 1997, he responded by telling the voters, "You have put your trust in me. I will not let you down." In elections, politicians often try to convince the voters that they are more trustworthy than their opponents, and incumbents work to maintain the trust of their constituents (Bianco 1994, Fenno 1978). The political importance of trust is also seen in international relations, where opportunities for agreement and cooperation can be missed because of distrust between nations (Larson 1997). When U.S. Secretary of State Albright visited Israel in Se7ptember 1997, she told the Israelis and the Palestinians that in order to overcome their conflicts, they need to establish a climate of trust.

Fukuyama (1995) has recently emphasized the economic importance of trust, particularly in the organization of the workplace. Manufacturers such as Toyota have been successful in increasing quality and productivity in part because they have established factories in which there is trust between workers and managers. Business partnerships and deals are much easier to arrange when there is trust rather than distrust among the participants. The sociological importance of trust has been noticed by such writers as Gambetta (1988), Kramer and Tyler (1996), Lewis and Weigert (1985), and Misztal (1996).

Everyday life would be impossible without trust. Dealing with spouses, partners, friends, and myriad other people with whom we interact is immensely facilitated when we can trust them; suspicion and distrust make interactions unpleasant and often unsuccessful. Social psychologists such as Deutsch (1973) and Holmes (1991) have described the central role played by trust in interactions and relationships. Many mundane decisions, such as hiring a baby-sitter to look after one's children, are largely decisions whether the person hired can be trusted.

The concept of trust is also philosophically important. In political philosophy, a focus on trust as both a passion and a policy provides an alternative to the contractarian emphasis on rational egoism (Dunn 1993). In real life prisoner's dilemma situations, for example, the decision to cooperate or defect is typically based not on the abstract logical considerations of game theory, but on informed and emotional decisions about whom to trust (Deutsch 1973). Trust is also important for epistemology, because knowledge is not just a matter of an individual working out everything alone. Rather, especially in modern science, the development of knowledge depends crucially on collaboration and communication, both of which require epistemic trust (Hardwig 1991, Thagard 1999).

Trust is a matter of both inference and emotion. The inference of whether to trust people depends on combining many kinds of information about them into a coherent system that generates a positive or negative emotional reaction to them. Leaving emotion aside for the moment, I will review the coherence theory of inference developed in chapters 2 and 3.

2 COHERENCE-BASED INFERENCE

The conception of inference familiar since Aristotle and the Stoics is based on formal logic, according to which we infer a conclusion from a set of premises in accord with rules of inference. Probably the most frequently applied rule is modus ponens: if p then q; p; therefore q. But this view of inference is problematic, because, as Harman (1986) and Minsky (1997) pointed out, we should not always infer q from *If p then q* and p, since sometimes it is more appropriate to abandon p or *If p then q*. To take a trust-related example based on the 1997 influx of Czech Gypsies to Canada and England, suppose you have the common stereotype that Gypsies are dishonest. You might be prone to make the following inference:

If Karl is a Gypsy, then Karl is dishonest.

Karl is a Gypsy.

Therefore, Karl is dishonest.

But what if Karl has just returned intact the wallet that you dropped on the street? Then you have reason to believe that Karl is not dishonest, so you might consider revising one or both of the premises that led to the conclusion that Karl is dishonest. Alternatively, you might hypothesize that Karl really is dishonest and that he returned your wallet only to ingratiate himself with you. The inference you make about Karl's dishonesty will depend on how the conclusion and the premises generating it fit with everything you know. Inference is a matter of coherence.

Explanatory coherence is highly relevant to trust, because it is the mechanism by which we infer the motives and plans of another. In the Gypsy example, the evidence that Karl returned your wallet led you to consider different hypotheses that would explain why he returned it. In general, you will tend to trust people when you can infer from what you know about them that they have motives and plans that contribute to your own goals. Hypotheses about motives and plans need to be evaluated with respect to how well they explain the evidence about someone in comparison with hypotheses about other motives and goals.

A more automatic kind of inference is performed as the result of conceptual coherence, in which the elements are concepts representing, in the interpersonal case, attributes of people such as stereotypes, traits, and behaviors. The positive constraints arise from observations and positive associations, for example, the prejudiced association that Gypsies are dishonest. Negative constraints arise from negative associations, for example, between returning money and being dishonest. Kunda and Thagard (1996) showed that many psychological phenomena involving impression formation and the application of social stereotypes can be understood in terms of conceptual coherence. Conceptual coherence is relevant to trust when it produces inferences about stereotypes, traits, and behaviors based on positive and negative associations. We tend to trust people who have characteristics, such as honesty, that are associated with trustworthiness, while we distrust people who have contrary traits, such as mendacity.

Analogical coherence differs from the explanatory and conceptual kinds in that it is primarily based not on general hypotheses or concepts, but on particular cases. In analogical inference, we infer something about a person or situation on the basis of its similarity with other persons or situations. The relevance to trust is that we tend to come to trust people who are similar to other people that we trust, while distrusting people who remind us of people whom we have learned to distrust.

Deliberative coherence involves deciding what to do on the basis of interrelations of competing actions and goals (chapter 5). The actions and goals are elements that are positively constrained by facilitation relations (e.g., an action facilitates a goal) and are negatively constrained by incompatibility relations (e.g., when two actions cannot both be performed). The decision to trust someone involves considering the implications of all that you know about the person that is relevant to the accomplishment of your goals. Deductive and perceptual coherence seem only tangentially related to trust judgments.

A major problem for the theory of coherence-based inference concerns how the different kinds of coherence can be integrated with each other (Thagard and Kunda 1998). How do explanatory, conceptual, and analogical coherence interrelate? How do we integrate possibly incompatible conclusions based on different kinds of coherence? From a coherentist perspective, there is only one rule of inference: accept a representation if and only if it coheres maximally with the rest of your representations. A partial answer to the question of integration, as well as an insight into the role of affect in judgments of trust, can be gained by means of a theory of emotional coherence. Emotional coherence is not a seventh kind of coherence, but rather an expanded way of considering the elements and constraints already described.

3 EMOTIONAL COHERENCE: THEORY

In the theory of coherence described in chapter 2, elements have the epistemic status of being accepted or rejected. We can also speak of degree of acceptability, which in connectionist models of coherence is the interpretation of the degree of activation of the unit that represents the element. I propose that elements in coherence systems have, in addition to acceptability, an emotional *valence*, which can be positive or negative. Depending on the nature of what the element represents, the valence of an element can indicate likability, desirability, or other positive or negative attitude. For example, the valence of Mother Theresa for most people is highly positive, while the valence of Adolf Hitler is highly negative. Many other researchers have previously proposed introducing emotion into cognitive models by adding valences or affective tags (Bower 1981, 1991; Fiske and Pavelchak 1986; Lodge and Stroh 1993; Ortony, Clore, and Collins 1988; Sears, Huddy, and Schaffer 1986).

Just as elements are related to each other by the positive and negative nonemotional constraints described in the last section, they also can be related by positive and negative valence constraints. Some elements have intrinsic positive and negative valences, for example *samaritan* and *serial killer*. Other elements can acquire valences by virtue of their connections with elements that have intrinsic valences. These connections can be special valence constraints, or they can be any of the epistemic constraints. For example, if someone has a positive association between the concepts of *Gypsy* and *dishonest*, where *dishonest* has an intrinsic negative valence, then *Gypsy* can acquire a negative valence. However, just as the acceptability of an element depends on the acceptability of all the elements that constrain it, so the valence of an element depends on the valences of all the elements that constrain it.

Crucially, the valence of an element depends not just on the valences of the elements that constrain it, but also on their acceptability. Attaching a negative valence to the concept *Gypsy*, if it does not already have a negative valence from previous experience, depends both on the negative valence for *dishonest* and the acceptability (confidence) of *dishonest* in the current context. The inferential situation here is analogous to expected-utility theory, in which the expected utility of an action is calculated by summing, for various outcomes, the result of multiplying the probability of the outcome times the utility of the outcome. The calculated valence of an element is like the expected utility of an action, with degrees of acceptability analogous to probabilities and valences analogous to utilities. There is no reason, however, to expect degrees of acceptability and valences to have the mathematical properties that define probabilities and utilities.

Because the valence calculation depends on the acceptability of all the relevant elements, it can be affected by all the kinds of coherence described above. In particular, explanatory, conceptual, and analogical coherence can all contribute to the acceptability of elements and hence affect the valence of an element linked to those elements. To foreshadow the account proposed below, whether you trust someone depends largely on the valence attached to the person based on all the information you have about him or her. This is obviously not intended to be a general theory of emotions, which involve much more than positive and negative valence.

The basic theory of emotional coherence can be summarized in three principles analogous to the qualitative principles of coherence stated in chapter 2:

- Elements have positive or negative valences.

- Elements can have positive or negative emotional connections to other elements.

- The valence of an element is determined by the valences and acceptability of all the elements to which it is connected.

To make emotional coherence more clearly applicable to psychological phenomena such as trust, I will now describe a computational model that specifies a mechanism for combining epistemic- and emotional-coherence calculations.

4 EMOTIONAL COHERENCE: MODEL

As chapter 2 showed, coherence can be computed by a variety of algorithms, but the most psychologically appealing model, and the model that first inspired the theory of coherence as constraint satisfaction, employs artificial neural networks. In this connectionist model, elements are represented by units, which are roughly analogous to neurons or neuronal groups. Positive constraints between elements are represented by symmetric excitatory links between units, and negative constraints between elements are represented by symmetric inhibitory links between units. The degree of acceptability of an element is represented by the activation of a unit, which is determined by the activation of the all the units linked to it, which takes

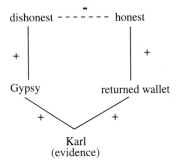

Figure 6.1
Simple connectionist network with excitatory (+) and inhibitory
(−) links. All links are symmetric, with activation originating at
the evidence node and flowing upward.

into account the strength of the various excitatory and
inhibitory links.

For example, in figure 6.1 there are five units representing the Gypsy inference already described. The Karl
unit is activated, and then activation spreads to what is
known about Karl, i.e., that he is a Gypsy and returned
the wallet. Activation then spreads to the units for dishonest and honest, which inhibit each other. Depending on
the strengths of the links to these two concepts, one of
them may become more active and suppress the other.
Activation spreads around the system until all units reach
stable activation levels, which typically takes 50–100
cycles. Activations can range between 1 (fully accepted)
and −1 (fully rejected), and elements whose units have final
activations above 0 are deemed accepted.

It is straightforward to expand this kind of model
into one that incorporates emotional coherence. In the
expanded model, called "HOTCO" for "hot coherence,"
units have valences as well as activations, and units can
have input valences to represent their intrinsic valences.

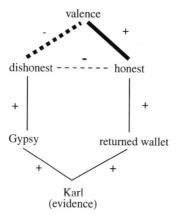

Figure 6.2
The network in figure 6.1 supplemented with valence inputs (thick lines).

Moreover, valences can spread through the system in a way very similar to the spread of activation, except that valence spread depends in part on activation spread. Figure 6.2 shows the network from figure 6.1 expanded to include a valence input to the concepts of *honest* and *dishonest*, the former positive and the latter negative. Just as activation spreads up the network from *Karl* to *honest* or *dishonest*, so valence spreads down the network to *Karl*. If *honest* becomes activated, then its positive valence will spread to *returned wallet* and then to *Karl*. The network of someone who is prejudiced against Gypsies would have a negative valence link directly to the *Gypsy* node.

The valence of a unit u_j is the sum of the results of multiplying, for all units u_i to which it is linked, the activation of u_i times the valence of u_i, times the weight of the link between u_i and u_j. The actual equation used in HOTCO to update the valence v_j of unit j is the following:

$$v_j(t+1) = v_j(t)(1-d) + \text{net}_j(\text{max} - v_j(t)) \text{ if net}_j > 0$$
$$= \text{net}_j(v_j(t) - \text{min}) \text{ otherwise}$$

Here d is a decay parameter (say 0.05) that decrements each unit at every cycle, min is a minimum valence (−1), max is maximum valence (1). From the weights w_{ij} between each unit i and j, we can calculate net$_j$, the net valence input to a unit, thus:

$$\text{net}_j = \Sigma_i w_{ij} v_i(t) a_i(t)$$

Updating valences is just like updating activations (see McClelland and Rumelhart 1989) plus the inclusion of a multiplicative factor for valences. The equation for net valence input, combining both activation (like probability) and valence (like utility), is similar to ones proposed by Anderson (1974), Deutsch (1973), Fishbein and Ajzen (1975), and Lodge and Stroh (1993). The difference in the parallel model HOTCO is that the valence calculation is done locally and interactively, with an overall judgment emerging from the simultaneous application of the valence equation to numerous interconnected units.

To see how this works, we can step through how HOTCO processes the simple example in figure 6.2. Initially, the *Karl* evidence node has activation 1 and the valence input node has valence 1; the other four nodes have low default activation and valence values: 0.01. At the first round of network updating, activation flows from *Karl* to the *Gypsy* and *returned wallet* nodes, and valence flows from the valence node to *dishonest* and *honest* nodes, decreasing the valence of the former and increasing the valence of the latter. At the second round of updating, activation flows from *Gypsy* to *dishonest*, and from *returned wallet* to *honest*, but valence does not flow in the reverse direction because on the previous step *dishonest* and *honest* had not yet been activated. But at the third round of updating these two units do have both valences and activations, so they can now spread positive valence to *Gypsy* and negative valence to *returned wallet*. Moreover, because of the inhibitory link between *dishonest* and *honest*, they tend to suppress each other's activations and valences. By the fourth round of updating, valence has begun to spread to the *Karl* node, representing an overall emotional attitude toward Karl. What this attitude will be in the end will depend on the strengths of the various links between the nodes in the network. For example, if there is a strong activation link between *returned wallet* and *honest* and there is a strong valence link between *valence* and *honest*, then *Karl* will end up with a positive valence. Typically it takes around 50 to 60 cycles of updating before the network has achieved stable activations and valences.

The term "valence" is borrowed from Gordon Bower's (1981, 1991) model of cognition and affect, but my model differs from his in that the kinds of inference that HOTCO employs are more complex than the simple associationistic ones that Bower discusses and that figures 6.1 and 6.2 display. A full account of emotional coherence has to include not only the sort of conceptual coherence involved in the Gypsy example, but also the contributions of explanatory, analogical, and deliberative coherence. The model is shown more fully in figure 6.3, which indicates more generally how evidence input can meld with emotion input to yield an emotional appraisal of the observed person or situation. HOTCO incorporates the previous computational models ECHO (explanatory coherence), DECO (deliberative coherence), IMP (conceptual coherence), and ACME (analogical mapping). All of these can contribute to the coherence inferences in the middle of figure 6.3 that determine how activation spreads from the evidence input node to various nodes representing hypotheses and other elements. Simultaneous with the spreading of

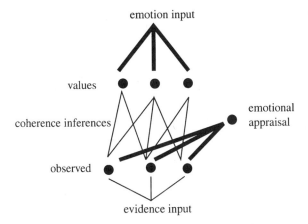

Figure 6.3
A general model of emotional coherence, not showing the many interconnected units that may be involved in coherence inferences. Thick lines are valence links. All links are symmetric, but activation flows up from the evidence input, and valences flow down from the emotion input.

activation determined by links established by explanatory, deliberative, conceptual, and analogical coherence, there is spreading of valences from the emotion input at the top of the diagram. As intermediate nodes acquire both activations and valences, valences spread down to the *observed* nodes that describe a person or situation, and then converge to produce an overall emotional appraisal of that person or situation. The next section shows how this works using a detailed example involving trust.

5 EMOTIONAL COHERENCE AND TRUST

One possible application of emotional coherence to trust would be that the extent to which people trust each other is determined directly by emotional coherence. That is, you trust a person P to the extent that P has a positive valence. This conjecture is too simple, however, because trust is not always a universal attribute of a person, for it may be relative to a particular goal or situation: I may trust someone to wash my car but not to mind my children or invest my money. In these cases, the elements of emotional appraisal are very specific, not just *Karl* but *Karl as car washer*. Moreover, although positive valence may give a good overall indication of whether you *like* someone, likability and trustworthiness can be independent of each other. You can like affable and charming people without trusting them (if they are unreliable), and trust gruff or awkward people without liking them (if they are reliable with respect to the task to which trust is relevant). Hence there is more to trust than simply attaching a positive valence to a person, although such a valence may well be a large part of what produces the positive valence for the more specific node representing *trusting a person P to do X.*

A more concrete example will help to make these distinctions clear. In 1997 my wife and I needed to find someone to drive our six-year-old son, Adam, from morning kindergarten to afternoon day care. One solution recommended to us was to send him by taxi every day, but our mental associations for taxi drivers, largely shaped by some bizarre experiences in New York City, put a very negative emotional appraisal on this option. We did not feel that we could trust an unknown taxi driver, even though I have several times trusted perfectly nice Waterloo taxi drivers to drive *me* around town.

So I asked around my department to see if there were any graduate students who might be interested in a part-time job. The department secretary suggested a student, Christine, who was looking for work, and I arranged an interview with her. Very quickly, I felt that Christine was someone whom I could trust with Adam. She was intelli-

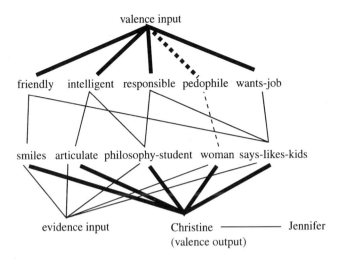

Figure 6.4
Emotional appraisal of a potential baby-sitter. Thin lines indicate
activation links, while thick lines indicate valence links. All links
are positive except for the two dashed lines, which are negative.
Activation spreads only along activation links, but valences
spread along both valence links and activation links.

gent, enthusiastic, interested in children, and motivated to
be reliable, and she reminded me of a good baby-sitter,
Jennifer, who had worked for us some years before. My
wife also met her and had a similar reaction. Explanatory,
conceptual, and analogical coherence all supported a positive emotional appraisal, as shown in figure 6.4.

Conceptual coherence encouraged such inferences
as from *smiles* to *friendly*, from *articulate* to *intelligent*,
and from *philosophy graduate student* to *responsible*.
Explanatory coherence evaluated competing explanations
of why she says she likes children, comparing the hypothesis that she is a friendly person who really does like
kids with the hypothesis that she has sinister motives
for wanting the job. Finally, analogical coherence enters

the picture because of her similarity with our former baby-sitter Jennifer with respect to enthusiasm and similar dimensions. A fuller version of figure 6.4 would show the features of Jennifer that were transferred analogically to Christine, along with the positive valence associated with Jennifer.

In the HOTCO simulation of this case, evidence input spreads activation to the units representing what is known about Christine (smiles, etc.), at the same time as valence input spreads valences to the units that have intrinsic valences (friendly, etc.). Then, as these units become active as the result of the coherence-based inferences, they spread valences down to the units that activated them. For example, just as *smiles* spreads activation to *friendly*, *friendly* spreads positive valence to *smiles*, which then spreads positive valence to *Christine*, whose valence is also being affected by other units, including ones representing Christine's analog, Jennifer. The result is an overall positive emotional appraisal of Christine as someone to be trusted. Thus coherence-based inferences, combined with emotional inputs, can yield a kind of emotional Gestalt impression of someone to be trusted. In figure 6.4, the valence output node for *Christine* represents not simply the fact that I like Christine, but also a positive emotional attitude attached to the decision to trust her with Adam. The emotional valence attached to Christine serves to integrate all the information relevant to assessing her as a baby-sitter, blending many coherence and valence considerations into a single emotional reaction accessible to consciousness. A judgment to trust people is more than just a judgment about the probability that they will do what is expected. For most people, trust and distrust are associated with positive and negative emotions, respectively.

Fenno (1978) describes how members of the U.S. House of Representatives present themselves to their constituents in order to gain their trust, attempting especially to convey three impressions: qualification, identification, and empathy. Representatives want their constituents to infer that they are qualified for the job, and accordingly provide brochures listing their background, experience, and accomplishments. With this information representatives provide evidence of competence, and they also try to convey to voters that they are sufficiently honest to qualify for the job. These inferences involve both conceptual and explanatory coherence. The voters can infer that the candidate is competent because that competence is associated with previous accomplishments, and they can infer that the candidate is honest because this attribute is associated with previous behaviors and provides the best explanation of some of those behaviors.

The second trust-generating impression, according to Fenno (1978, 59), is identification, where the message that voters get from the candidate is, "You can trust me because we are like one another." This is a kind of analogical inference, in which voters decide that candidates who are like them on various cultural dimensions are also like them in being trustworthy.

Third, every House member conveys a sense of empathy with his constituents, giving the impression of understanding and caring about their situations. This is a matter of explanatory coherence: the constituents infer that the best explanation of member's expressions of care and understanding is that he or she really does care or understand. Empathy can sometimes fail, as when Canadian Prime Minister Kim Campbell gave a speech at a shelter in Vancouver's Skid Row during the 1992

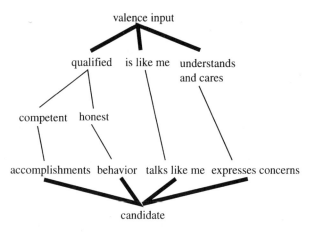

Figure 6.5
Emotional appraisal of a political candidate. Thin lines indicate activation links, while thick lines indicate valence links. Alternative interpretations are not shown in the figure, which does not distinguish the different activation links that derive from conceptual, explanatory, and analogical constraints.

Canadian election. She told the residents of the shelter that she too had known loss and disappointment, for she had once wanted to be a concert cellist. The weakness of the analogy between her history and the condition of the Vancouver derelicts undermined her attempt to convince them of her empathy.

Figure 6.5 illustrates how emotional coherence can generate an inference and feeling that a candidate is to be trusted. It does not show the details of the conceptual, explanatory, and analogical connections that can generate an emotional Gestalt towards a candidate, but serves to display how information converges to generate a positive or negative impression. Empathy is a particularly interesting kind of emotional inference, and I will now show how it can be understood in terms of emotional coherence.

According to Barnes and Thagard (1997), empathy is a kind of emotional analogy, in which person *A* constructs an emotional image of person *B* by mapping *B*'s situation onto a similar situation previously experienced emotionally by *A*. In contrast to the current cognitive models of analogical mapping (e.g., Holyoak and Thagard 1989; Falkenhainer, Forbus, and Gentner 1989), what is mapped is not propositional information, but a feeling or an image of a feeling (Barnes 1998 discusses emotional images). When I have empathy for you, I do not just recognize abstractly that you are similar to me: I actually feel something like what you feel. This account of empathic analogy can be enhanced by viewing it in the context of the theory of emotional coherence.

Here is another example of empathy. When new graduate students arrive from overseas, they are often overwhelmed by arriving in a very different country and university and by having to work in English, if that is not their native language. My best shot at understanding their mental state comes from remembering my own disorientation when I went to study in Cambridge, England, in 1971. Everything seemed different and odd: the colleges, the town, the people, the food, the money, etc. Despite having only minor language difficulties, it was months before I felt I knew what I was doing. Because foreign students' situations are relevantly similar to mine many years ago, I can project my remembered emotional state of bewilderment and anxiety onto them, using my imagination to amplify its intensity because of the greater cultural and linguistic differences that they may face.

From the perspective of emotional coherence theory, empathy is more than just retrieving an emotion-laden

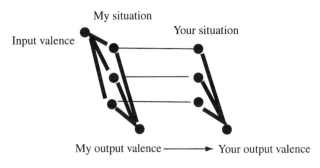

Figure 6.6
Empathy and emotional coherence. My situation serves as a source analog to generate an emotional valence that I transfer to you in your situation. Thick lines indicate valence links, thin lines indicate analogical links, and the arrowhead indicates transfer of valence.

source to map onto a given target. Empathy-producing source analogs can be generated, not just remembered, as when I generate an England-only-worse analog for my foreign student or when I generate a loss-of-English-Canadian-language-and-culture analog to help understand Quebec nationalism (see next section). In both those constructed analogs, I am generating a situation that produces an emotional image based on the emotional coherence of the situation, which has different aspects whose valences contribute to its overall valence. Once I establish a correspondence between my imagined situation and yours, I can ascribe to you an emotional valence for your situation that is similar to the emotional valence that I ascribe to my situation.

Figure 6.6 portrays schematically how I do an analogical mapping that enables me to transfer the valence of my situation to your situation. The elements in my situation have input valences that produce an overall output valence for the whole situation. Once the elements in my situation have been mapped to the elements in your situation, then the valences of these elements can spread over to the elements in your situation and then produce an output valence for your situation similar to the output valence for my situation. In this way I can feel some approximation to how you feel.

Figure 6.6 is oversimplified in that it portrays empathy as merely a matter of analogical mapping. In fact, a full range of coherence inferences may be involved in (1) understanding your situation, e.g., making inferences about your beliefs and goals, (2) figuring out what elements to add into my constructed analog of your situation, and (3) computing the valence of my constructed situation that serves as a source analog situation. Moreover, empathy is not just a matter of positive and negative valence, but also requires transfer of the full range of emotional responses. Depending on his or her situation, I need to imagine someone's being angry, fearful, disdainful, ecstatic, enraptured, and so on. As currently implemented, HOTCO transfers only positive or negative valences associated with a proposition or object, but it can easily be expanded so that transfer involves an *emotional vector* that represents a pattern of activation of numerous units, each of whose activation represents different components of emotion. This expanded representation would also make possible the transfer of "mixed" emotions.

Empathy is relevant to trust in different ways. The last section described how politicians use empathy to generate trust: people are inclined to trust people who have empathy for them. U.S. President Bill Clinton is noted for his empathic ability, or at least for his ability to appear empathic. If you have empathy for me, leading you to understand me positively by transferring your emotional states, then I will be more likely to trust you. Empathy is often cited as a crucial ingredient in psychotherapy, and one of its contributions is to enhance trust as well as understanding. Of course, empathy does not always lead to positive valuations: mapping what I know about you onto what I know about me in a similar situation may lead me to project a negative valence onto you if I realize that I would likely act badly in the situation in which you are in.

Trusting people often involves inferring their motives and intentions, but it can also involve inferring their emotional states. I am unlikely to trust someone who I have reason to believe is seething with concealed anger against me. On the other hand, I am likely to trust and like someone who trusts and likes me. Thus if empathy (analogical mapping of the emotion that I would experience if I were in a similar situation) suggests that if someone attaches a positive valence to me, then I can attach a positive valence to him or her. Alternatively, putting yourself in someone else's shoes may strongly suggest that the person's valences are negative, and thus reduce your inclination to like and trust him or her.

To sum up, emotional coherence suggests the following recipe for how to achieve empathic understanding of a person P:

1. Take what you know of P's personality and situation, and use explanatory and other kinds of coherence to make inferences about it that supplement the given information.

2. Use analogical coherence to retrieve a similar situation from your own experience. (See Thagard, Holyoak, Nelson, and Gochfeld 1990 for a model of analog retrieval.)

3. Use imagination to enhance the retrieved situation so as to bring it closer to P's.

4. Use coherence-based inferences and emotional coherence to generate a valence for your constructed situation.

5. Project this valence onto P as representing P's likely emotional state in that situation.

I now turn to another political application of empathy, arguing that Canada's dealings with Quebec nationalists requires empathic understanding of their goals and of the emotional coherence of their belief system.

7 NATIONALISM

In 1996 the province of Quebec voted in a referendum concerning whether Quebec should separate from Canada and become a sovereign nation. The referendum was defeated, but only by less than 1 percent of the vote, and a substantial majority of those whose first language is French voted in favor of separation. To much of the world, which views Canada as one of the world's best countries to live in, Quebec separatism seems very puzzling; indeed, it seems bizarre to most Canadians outside Quebec. A typical reaction is, "What do these people want? Leaving Canada doesn't make any sense. They're just being emotional."

Nationalism is clearly an emotional issue: many people feel very strongly about the nations and ethnic groups to which they belong, and they often have strong negative emotions towards other nations and ethnic groups (Caputi 1996, Group for the Advancement of Psychiatry 1987, Ignatieff 1991, Kecmanovic 1996, Stern 1995). According to the theory of emotional coherence, however, emotions are not inherently irrational, since they may be tied to coherence judgments that are rooted in evidence, for example via explanatory coherence (see the section on normative issues at the end of this chapter). Without trying to assess whether nationalism is rational or not, I want to try to understand it as a phenomenon involving emotional coherence. In particular, we can get a better understanding of Quebec separatism by constructing a profile that integrates considerations of emotions and coherence.

A good place to start is the writings of René Lévesque, the first leader of the Parti Québécois, which was formed in 1967 with a platform of achieving Quebec independence. The reasons for establishing the new party were eloquently stated in the book *Option Québec*:

We are Québécois.

What that means first and foremost—and if need be, all that it means—is that we are attached to this one corner of the earth where we can be completely ourselves: this Quebec, the only place where we have the unmistakable feeling that "here we can be really at home."

Being ourselves is essentially a matter of keeping and developing a personality that has survived for three and a half centuries.

At the core of this personality is the fact that we speak French. Everything else depends on this one essential element and follows from it or leads us infallibly back to it. [Historical background given.]

All these things lie at the core of this personality of ours. Anyone who does not feel it, at least occasionally, is not—is no longer—one of us.

But *we* know and feel that these are the things that make us what we are. They enable us to recognize each other wherever we may be. . . .

This is how we differ from other men and especially from other North Americans. (Lévesque 1968, 1–15)

Lévesque describes how French in Quebec is threatened by the dramatically dropping birth rate among francophones and the strong preference shown by immigrants to the province to learn and work in English rather than French.

The appeal of Quebec separatism can be understood in terms of strong emotional inputs and outputs that are part of deliberative coherence. As the above quotation suggests, Québécois have intense desires to feel at home in their own province, to speak French, and to avoid assimilation into the dominant English-speaking environment of the rest of Canada and North America. Lévesque and his colleagues who started the Parti Québécois strongly believed that sovereignty was the only means to avoid assimilation. Figure 6.7 provides a rough sketch of this attitude. A computational model of this view provides a strong positive valence to feeling at home and speaking French, and a strong negative valence to assimilation. These valences then spread to the options of separation versus staying in Canada, with the former receiving a strong positive valence and the latter reaching an emotional state akin to repugnance.

Of course, the issue is a lot more complicated than figure 6.7 indicates. The valence links presume a number of empirical projections that depend on empirical evidence: critics of Quebec sovereignty deny that staying in Canada will lead to the elimination of French, pointing to such phe-

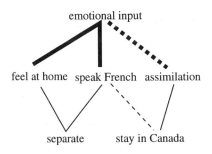

Figure 6.7
A sketch of the emotional coherence of Quebec separatism. Thick lines indicate valence links. Thin lines indicate facilitation relations that are part of deliberative coherence. Dashed lines indicate negative links.

nomena as the bilingualism of the federal government and the growth of French immersion programs in English Canada. In response, sovereigntists point out that the trend outside Quebec among native French speakers is, in fact, strongly towards assimilation. Probably the most effective argument used by antiseparatist forces has been economic: Quebec can prosper within Canada, but risks economic disaster by going on its own. Lévesque and other sovereigntists pointed to a number of models for an economically viable Quebec, particularly the European Economic Community, in which numerous countries are economically drawing closer and closer together for mutual benefit. Analogously, Quebec could be part of a North American common market with the United States and what's left of Canada.

My goal in this section is not to assess the costs and benefits of Quebec separatism, but rather to understand its emotional appeal. For sovereigntists, the economic problem of separation is only a short-term one that can be taken care of by negotiating a new economic arrangement. Hence separatism has only a small negative impact on the goal of economic well-being. In the battle of emotional analogies, separatists look to the European Community, the Scandinavian union (following the peaceful separation of Norway from Sweden in 1905), and the recent peaceful separation of Slovakia from the Czech Republic. They resist analogies with much uglier situations, such as the American Civil war, Northern Ireland, and Bosnia. Blanchette and Dunbar (1997) collected 234 analogies used in the 1996 Quebec referendum. Separatists have a strong emotional attachment to feeling at home and preserving their national personality, both of which are tied in with preserving French as the dominant language of Quebec. They also have a belief that negotiations within Canadian federalism have failed, as in such incidents as the forced repatriation of the constitution from Great Britain to Canada in 1982 and the failure of the Meech Lake accord in 1990. The result is that separatists arrive at an intense emotional conviction in favor of forming their own country.

Daniel Latouche (1990, 89) wrote, "When will you English Canadians get it through your thick collective skull that we want to live in a French society, inside and outside, at work and at play, in church and in school. Is this so difficult to understand?" English Canadians generally fail to understand why this goal is so strong for Québécois, and why many francophones believe that the goal cannot be achieved within Canada. English Canadians do not feel the anger that arises from the perception of a long history of humiliation, stretching from the conquest of Quebec by England's troops in 1760 through the more recent constitutional wrangles and referendum defeats. Because English Canadians do not have the kind of passionate nationalism found in Quebec or even in the United States, it is difficult for them to have an empathic understanding, based on mapping their own emotions, of why Québécois feel so strongly about their cultural identity. Moreover, although some Canadian cultural institutions are undoubtedly threatened by the American entertainment juggernaut, at least there is no fear that English will be wiped out. In contrast, the Québécois can infer from past behavior and current utterances of many English Canadians that the English do not care about preserving Quebec culture. This inference is based on the high explanatory coherence of the hypotheses that the English have little comprehension and appreciation of the French demands.

Nationalism has often been an evil force in human history, as witnessed in atrocities of the Nazis and in recent Balkan conflicts. But it can have a positive side when it is directed, as a kind of self-preservation, toward maintaining cultural practices that are important to the people who perceive themselves as a nation. Personally, I have virtually no ethnic identification and, like most anglophone Canadians, only a weak emotional attachment to my native country. Understanding political movements like Quebec separatism requires me to imagine how badly I would feel if I had the prospect, for myself or my children, of being unable live and work in my native language. This empathic understanding involves a kind of analogical coherence in which I transfer my emotional attitude to another in a similar situation. It is probably easier for an Israeli, a German, an Italian, or even an American to understand Quebec nationalism than for an English Canadian, but empathy can be generated if one works at it. It is an interesting question why some French Canadian leaders, such as Pierre Trudeau and the current Prime Minister Jean Chrétien, have little appreciation of the separatist position. Perhaps they do have an empathic understanding that is overruled by other considerations, such as valuing universal rights and freedoms more highly than nationalist aspirations.

Let me emphasize that I am not trying to give a kind of romantic glorification of the sort of aggressive nationalism that urges a people to see themselves as superior to all foreigners and that can be used to justify conquest. The fact is, however, that nationalism is clearly in part a matter of emotion, and it can also be a matter of deliberative, explanatory, and analogical coherence. Defensive nationalism, based on the goal of preserving a culture, is not obviously either irrational or immoral. Convincing Quebec to stay *happily* in Canada will require much more than dire threats about the negative economic and political consequences of separation. Such threats leave untouched the strong feelings about home, personality, and language that drive separatism. Rather, Canadian unity will require convincing francophones in Quebec that their language and culture are safe within Canada. If this task is accomplished, emotional coherence may point toward accommodating Quebec nationalism without destroying Canada.

8 METACOHERENCE

The applications of the HOTCO model so far described have attached value to particular objects or situations. But emotions also involve more general kinds of evaluations. When a situation "makes sense" to us, we feel a general well-being, whereas a situation that we are unable to comprehend can cause anxiety. The usually pleasant feeling that something makes sense involves an overall assessment of coherence, in contrast to the confusion and anxiety that often accompany incoherence. I call these *metacoherence* emotions, because they require an overall assessment of how much coherence is being achieved.

On the theory of coherence sketched earlier, the coherence of a partition of elements into accepted and rejected is determined by the extent to which positive and negative constraints are satisfied. If the elements are related by highly incompatible constraints, it is possible that the best partition will not be very good, so that the overall coherence of the system is low even though the partition maximized it. Scientists faced with highly conflicting evidence supporting different theories may choose the theory that is best, given the overall evidence, but remain uncomfortable with their conclusion because of low overall coherence. For example, Newtonian mechanics dominated physics throughout the nineteenth century, but some scientists found it to be imperfectly coherent because it gave incorrect predictions about the orbit of Mercury. Similarly, in everyday life we sometimes make optimal decisions that we are not generally happy with, as when we are forced to make the best of a bad situation. A student, for example, may decide to go to a community college rather than a university because of financial constraints, but be unhappy about not having the chance to pursue more advanced studies. I interpret this as a case where the valence attached to an action is positive, but the emotional reaction to the overall judgment is negative because the best action leaves important goals unsatisfied.

Another metacoherence emotion is surprise, which reflects a judgment that a situation has occurred differently from what was expected. Such failed expectations are noticed when the most coherent interpretation of a situation is replaced by another coherent interpretation that differs from it substantially. For example, if I am watching a hockey game in which one team is leading 5 to 0 at the end of the first period, I will be surprised to find that the game turned out to be a victory for the team that was behind. Surprise is a function of the extent to which elements switch status from accepted to rejected or vice versa, with the greatest surprise contributed by elements that go from being strongly accepted or strongly rejected to the opposite.

A theory of emotional coherence should therefore incorporate overall judgments of coherence and incoherence, happiness and sadness, surprise, and other general emotions. It is easy to expand the HOTCO program by writing functions that calculate the overall coherence and valence satisfaction of the system (chap. 2, section 4), but such global calculations are at odds with the model's connectionist assumptions. Rather, judgments of coherence, happiness, and surprise should emerge from local assessments made by particular units. Figure 6.8 provides a rough picture of how this should work. The various

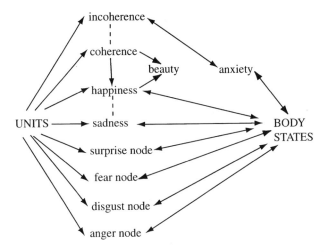

Figure 6.8
Metacoherence nodes (lowercase) in relation to cognitive units and body states. Dashed lines are negative constraints.

cognitive units that represent elements involved in explanatory, conceptual, and other kinds of coherence collectively activate nodes representing coherence, incoherence, happiness, and so on, which also have connections with other emotion nodes and bodily states. It is natural to think of the cognitive units, emotion nodes, and body states as together constituting a dynamic system with a very large state space representing all the different combinations of activations, valences, and values of other variables. Particular emotions, of which there are hundreds if one can judge from the number of emotion words in English and other languages, correspond to regions in this state space.

In the computational model HOTCO, the coherence and incoherence nodes receive activation from each of the cognitive units according to the local coherence of each active unit. An individual unit can assess its own coherence status by determining the extent to which its own

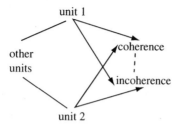

Figure 6.9
Two units affecting the coherence and incoherence nodes, which
inhibit each other. The dashed line is a negative constraint.

constraints are satisfied, taking account of its positive and
negative links to other units. If a unit is active and it has
a positive link to another unit, then the constraint is satisfied only if the other unit is also active. Alternatively, if an
active unit has a negative link to another active unit, then
that unit must not be active if the constraint is to be
satisfied. In HOTCO, each unit has a unidirectional link
to the coherence node, to which it passes on its degree of
constraint satisfaction, and a unidirectional link to the
incoherence node, to which it passes on its degree of constraint *non*satisfaction. Hence the activation of the coherence and incoherence nodes depends on the coherence of
the individual cognitive units. Figure 6.9 gives a more
detailed picture of the linkages. The coherence and incoherence nodes mutually inhibit each other, so that one or
the other will tend to become active, representing an
overall judgment of how much the whole situation makes
sense. As figure 6.8 suggested, general coherence influences
emotions such as happiness, while incoherence influences
emotions such as anxiety. There may be individual differences in the strengths of the links between the nodes: in
people with a high tolerance for incoherence, the link
between the incoherence and anxiety nodes will be particu-

larly weak, and in people with a great appreciation for coherence, the link between the coherence and happiness nodes will be particularly strong.

In social psychology, the cognitive dissonance theory of Festinger (1957) has been used to account for a wide variety of phenomena. Shultz and Lepper (1996) presented a computational model of cognitive dissonance in terms of parallel constraint satisfaction, using ideas very similar to those found in coherence models such as ECHO. However, dissonance is not simply cold incoherence, but also has an affective dimension involving negative emotions such as anxiety and discomfort (Cooper and Fazio 1984). Such emotional reactions are more fully modeled using HOTCO's metacoherence nodes than by traditional connectionist systems based solely on parallel constraint satisfaction.

HOTCO also uses a local mechanism to activate the general happiness and sadness nodes, which are affected by both the activation and the valence of each node. If an active unit has positive valence, it affects the activation of the happiness node to an extent that is a function of the unit's activation as well as its valence. On the other hand, if an active unit has negative valence, it affects the activation of the sadness node to an extent that is a function of the unit's activation and magnitude of negative valence. The happiness and sadness nodes inhibit each other, so the system will tend to settle into a state in which happiness is dominant, sadness is dominant, or both are neutral. Figure 6.10 shows the structure, similar to that in figure 6.9. But whereas in figure 6.9 the activation of the coherence nodes depends on the units' calculation of their degree of constraint satisfaction, in figure 6.10 the activation of the happiness and sadness nodes depends on the units' activations and valences.

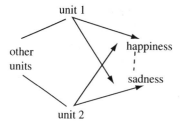

Figure 6.10
Two units affecting the happiness and sadness nodes.

Finally, let us consider how HOTCO produces judgments of surprise. After the network of cognitive units settles, each unit records its final activation. When new information is added to the network and it settles again, each unit compares its new activation with its previous activation, and the difference represents the extent to which the new information has produced a surprising result for that unit (I owe this way of implementing surprise to Cameron Shelley). Each unit conveys to the surprise node the extent to which it is locally surprised, so that many nodes affect the general surprise node shown in figure 6.8, which interacts with body states such as accelerated heart rate. There are both pleasant and unpleasant surprises, so the overall emotional state of the system depends on the activation of other nodes, such as the ones for happiness and sadness.

These extensions to HOTCO show how emotion nodes that represent metacoherence judgments can be implemented in ways that allow local calculations at the level of individual cognitive units to produce general emotional reactions. These metacoherence-based reactions make possible an understanding of the very complex emotional states involved in beauty and humor.

From symphonies to sunsets, beautiful objects produce pleasure and happiness, so beauty obviously has a large emotional component. But it also has a large coherence component, as many philosophers of art have noticed. R. G. Collingwood confidently asserted, "Beauty is the unity or coherence of the imaginary object; ugliness its lack of unity, its incoherence. This is no new doctrine; it is generally recognized that beauty is harmony, unity in diversity, symmetry, congruity, or the like" (1925, 21). The doctrine that beauty is unity in diversity originated with the eighteenth-century thinker Frances Hutcheson, who said, "The figures which excite in us the ideas of beauty seem to be those in where there is *uniformity amidst variety*. . . . The variety increases the beauty in equal uniformity. . . . The greater uniformity increases the beauty amidst equal variety" (Hutcheson 1973, 40–41). The eminent mathematician G. H. Hardy also saw beauty as connected with coherence: "A mathematician, like a painter or poet, is a maker of patterns. . . . The mathematician's patterns, like the painter's or the poet's, must be *beautiful*; the ideas, like the colours of the words, must fit together in a harmonious way" (1967, 84–85). In a beautiful object, diverse elements come together coherently to produce positive emotions, whereas in an ugly object the elements do not fit together and tend to produce negative emotions.

The metacoherence architecture depicted in figure 6.8 above provides a model of how the human mind might generate beautiful experiences. The cognitive units represent different aspects of an object, for example, the features of a human face. Particular features may have input valences attached to them, for example, eyes that are large and colorful, but the beauty of a face depends not just on the individual features but on how well these fit with each other. Faces have numerous built-in constraints, for example, that the eyes should be the same size and above the nose. If the constraints are well satisfied, then the face generates a high degree of perceptual coherence, which in turn generates positive emotions. A misshapen face, on the other hand, violates conventional constraints on facial structure, producing perceptual incoherence and a negative emotional reaction.

Beauty and ugliness can be intellectual as well as perceptual, as in Hardy's remark about mathematics and in T. H. Huxley's famous complaint about a beautiful theory being killed by an ugly fact. In the poem "Ode on a Grecian Urn," John Keats even goes so far as to identify beauty and truth:

When old age shall this generation waste,
Thou shalt remain, in midst of other woe
Than ours, a friend to man, to whom thou say'st,
"Beauty is truth, truth beauty,"—that is all
Ye know on earth, and all ye need to know.

Without going that far, we can still recognize that scientists, like mathematicians, often use beauty as a guide to truth. According to Zemach, "An account that is rich, powerful, dramatic, elegant, coherent, and simple—that is, beautiful (*unity in variety* is the oldest definition of Beauty)—is probably true" (1997, 64).

McAllister (1996, 40) identifies four classes of aesthetic properties of scientific theories: form of symmetry, invocation of a model, visualizability/abstractness, and metaphysical allegiance. The last three of these are easily interpreted as matters of coherence. On McAllister's account, invocation of a model is a matter of analogy between a source domain, such as the solar system, which provides a model of a target domain, such as the atom. Such modeling is a matter of analogical coherence, and an apt analogy that satisfies the constraints of similarity, structure, and purpose as discussed by Holyoak and Thagard (1995) often inspires positive emotions. Visualizability requires construction of a mental image that guides our understanding of a phenomenon, and thus would seem to combine perceptual and explanatory coherence, as when classical electromagnetic theory portrays the interaction of two electrons as the gradual intensifying of a repulsive electrostatic force. By the metaphysical allegiance of a theory McAllister means its fit with claims about the ultimate constituents of the world and with norms of reasoning about them. For example, a modern physicist might react with anger, disgust, or laughter to anyone who proposed a theory that the planets are carried around the sun by demons.

The remaining aesthetic property of scientific theories is symmetry, which is also related to emotional coherence. Rosen writes, "What makes a theory beautiful? This is, of course, a subjective matter, and in science too, beauty is in the eye of the beholder. But an opinion poll would reveal that simplicity and symmetry play decisive roles in determining whether a theory appears beautiful or not to most scientists" (1975, 121). Simplicity is part of explanatory coherence, which favors hypotheses that accomplish their explanations using fewer auxiliary hypotheses (Thagard 1992b), so its contribution to beauty can be handled in terms of coherence. But what can we make of symmetry?

Some kinds of symmetry can be understood in terms of analogical and perceptual coherence. For example, the bilateral symmetry of human faces consists of an isomorphic mapping between the two sides: the left side of the face is usually analogous to the right side. Symmetry as a kind of analogy is also apparent in McAllister's description of Einstein: "The symmetry that Einstein valued, and which he judged classical physical theory to possess to an insufficient degree, is one in virtue of which a theory offers explanations of the same form for events deemed physically equivalent" (1996, 43). The principle underlying this value is something like the idea that analogous phenomena should have similar explanations. Such symmetry is easily accommodated within analogical and explanatory coherence. When a theory gives analogous explanations to similar phenomena, it achieves two kinds of coherence simultaneously and can therefore be perceived as beautiful.

But symmetry is broader than bilateral perceptual symmetry or internal explanatory analogy. In general, a structure is said to be symmetric under a transformation if and only if the transformation leaves the structure unchanged. Many kinds of transformations establish symmetries, including spatial ones like flipping and rotation, but also conceptual ones like substitution of terms in parallel verbal constructions.

Can symmetry in general be brought within the scope of coherence theory so that its contribution to beauty can be explained in terms of emotional coherence? Following Rosen (1995), we can quantify the degree of symmetry of an object or system as the number of transformations that operate on it and preserve structure. A square, for example, is more symmetric than a triangle, because there more ways of transforming it that preserve its basic structure. Each transformation can be thought of as a kind of analogical mapping of the system to itself, with the transformed system required to be at least approximately equivalent to itself. But symmetry is not a matter of just one transformation, so it cannot be understood in terms of a single internal analogy. Rather,

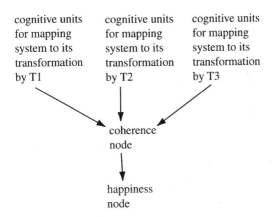

Figure 6.11
Symmetry as coherence of multiple self-analogies.

symmetry is a matter of a system having *multiple* internal analogies: many transformations of a system are analogous to it. The more such internal analogies, the greater the degree of symmetry. Symmetry, then, turns out to be a kind of metacoherence, in that it involves a summary of various judgments of analogical coherence. A fractal picture, for example, is highly symmetric, in that there are many ways of transforming it that do not change its appearance. Figure 6.11 schematizes the general relation of symmetry to analogical coherence. The more transformations that generate coherent analogies, the more activation is passed to the coherence node and the more positive is the emotional response. On the other hand, if transformations fail to produce good analogies, many constraints will be unsatisfied and the incoherence node will be activated, which produces a negative emotional reaction. Thus symmetry, like uniformity and simplicity, is an aspect of beauty that can be understood in terms of emotional coherence.

The last section gave an emotional-coherence account of the cognitive processes involved in finding something to be beautiful, and related processes can be involved in finding something to be funny. The relevance of emotional-coherence theory to humor is summarized in the following theses:

• Humor involves a shift from one coherent interpretation of an utterance or situation to a different coherent interpretation.

• This coherence shift generates the emotional state of surprise, using metacoherence mechanisms that attend to shifts in activation levels of units in a neural network representing components of the interpretations.

• Aspects of the utterance or situation generate other emotions, such as happiness, that interact with surprise to produce the overall emotional state of mirth.

Consider, for example, the following definition: "A drug is a substance that, when injected into a laboratory rat, produces a scientific paper." Until the reader or listener gets to the last two words, this sentence generates a coherent interpretation involving the expectation of a biochemical account of what a drug is. But the last two words shift to another, unexpected and surprising interpretation that defines "drug" in terms of the activities and motivations of scientists; we have production by a scientist rather than production in a rat. But surprise is not the only emotion involved: it would be even more surprising but not particularly funny if the sentence ended "produces a shower curtain." For the joke to be funny, the new interpretation must be coherent on its own terms and must generate other emotions, in this case glee at the thought that the whole purpose of drugs is to generate scientific research, which makes fun of scientific researchers. Puns are another form of humor that combine coherence and incoherence. If someone remarks "That's very punny," there is both a fit and an incompatibility between the usual interpretations of "pun" and "funny."

Emotional coherence is also evident in the following example of a humorous analogy:

The juvenile sea squirt wanders through the sea searching for a suitable rock or hunk of coral to cling to and make its home for life. For this task, it has a rudimentary nervous system. When it finds its spot and takes root, it doesn't need its brain anymore, so it eats it! (It's rather like getting tenure.) (Dennett 1991, 177)

This story initially generates a coherent biological interpretation, with some surprise and amusement generated by learning the unusual fact that there is an organism that eats its own brain, which is incoherent with what we know about animals' eating behavior. But the real surprise comes with the parenthetical comparison with getting tenure. If the comparison were surprising but unconnected, it would not be funny: there is no point in saying "It's rather like getting a sun tan." Rather, humor arises because of coherence and emotion. First, there is a coherent analogical mapping that we can generate between the sea squirts eating their brains and tenured professors ceasing to use theirs (Shelley, Donaldson, and Parsons 1996). Second, in addition to surprise, this analogy generates emotions such as glee directed at brainless professors. Humor is thus emotional coherence, with surprise and other emotions, arising from two coherent interpretations. (Many other examples of humorous analogies are discussed in Thagard and Shelley, forthcoming.)

This account of humor subsumes other theories of humor that have been historically influential (for reviews, see Keith-Spiegel 1972 and Lefcourt and Martin 1986). According to the incongruity theory, humor arises because an utterance or situation brings together disparate ideas in a surprising manner. On my account, incongruity is the incoherence between the initial coherent expectations in an utterance or situation and the final coherent interpretation after something surprising occurs. Another theory of humor is the superiority account, according to which humor functions to disparage someone or something. Not all humor aims at superiority, but my drug and sea squirt examples show how superiority-related emotions such as glee and gloating can be part of a humorous reaction based on emotional coherence. Such emotions tied to feelings of superiority increase the emotional intensity of the coherence-surprise reaction, and humor is the interactive sum of the cognitive/emotional response.

Finally, emotional coherence theory can accommodate the emotional-release theory of humor. Humor sometimes arises in tense and anxious situations and provides a welcome release. For example, in a difficult social situation, breaking the ice with an amusing comment can shift from one interpretation of the situation attended with negative emotions such as fear of failure and to another coherent interpretation with more positive emotional content. Nervous novice public speakers are sometimes advised to imagine they are talking to a naked audience— a surprising shift that reduces the anxiety of the situation. Many jokes start with taboo subjects such as sex and other bodily functions, then shift them to a less threatening interpretation. (Did you hear about the man with five penises? His pants fit like a glove.) Emotional release comes through a shift that is emotional as well as cognitive, producing a particularly emotionally intense kind of surprise, since it involves shifts in activation not only of cognitive nodes but also in nodes that carry the overall emotional interpretation of the situation. Hence from the perspective of the theory of emotional coherence we can see why emotional release is an important part of humor.

My account of humor is somewhat similar to the catastrophe theory of jokes proposed by Paulos (1980), but it is less metaphorical. Humor involves a sudden shift from one state of the cognitive/emotional network to another and is therefore like a catastrophe in the mathematical sense. It is more concrete, however, to think of humor in terms of the mathematics of dynamic systems such as HOTCO networks. The initial coherent interpretation establishes a particular state of the dynamic system defined by the activation and valence values of the various cognitive and emotional nodes of the integrated cognitive/emotional network. But the punch line of the joke or the humorous event of the situation shifts the system into another stable state distant from the original one. Humor, like other emotional changes, involves a shift from one region in the state space of the system to another. Implicit in this account is the conception of an emotional state as a region in the state space of a dynamic system constituted by the activation and valence values of the nodes. The relevant dynamic system should be construed even more broadly to include a wide range of physiological states of the organism in which the neural network resides. Thus an emotion is a region of state space of a system that includes not only the cognitive/emotional neural network, but also the somatic states that influence and are influenced by the neural network. Emotional changes are then shifts from one region of the state space to another region with different cognitive, metacoherence, and somatic states. Cognitive therapy, which can be used for producing positive emotional shifts, can similarly be understood in terms of emotional coherence.

Cognitive therapy is an effective method for treating a variety of emotional disorders, including depression. Unlike psychoanalysis, it does not require detailed delving into a patient's past, but instead concentrates on helping the patient to replace unrealistic beliefs and goals with more reasonable ones (Ellis 1962, 1971; Beck 1976). Beck writes,

In order to understand the cognitive approach to the treatment of depression, it is necessary to formulate the problems of the depressed patient in cognitive terms. These characteristics of depression can be views as expressions of an underlying shift in the depressed patient's cognitive organization. Because of the dominance of certain cognitive schemas, he tends to regard himself, his experiences, and his future in a negative way. These negative concepts are apparent in the way the patient systematically misconstrues his experiences and in the content of his ruminations. Specifically, he regards himself as a "loser." ... The cognitive approach for counteracting depression consists of using techniques that enable the patient to see himself as a "winner" rather than a "loser," as masterful rather than helpless. (1976, 264 ff.)

The cognitive therapist works with patients to revise beliefs and goals in ways that produce more positive appraisals of themselves and their situations.

Cognitive therapy is not merely a matter of pointing out to patients the unreasonableness of some of their beliefs and goals. Beck describes a depressed woman who was convinced that she had been a failure as a mother and concluded that she should kill herself and her children. He says, "This kind of depressive thinking may strike us as highly irrational, but it makes sense within the patient's conceptual framework" (Beck 1976, 16). Her negative views of herself suggested to her that she should commit

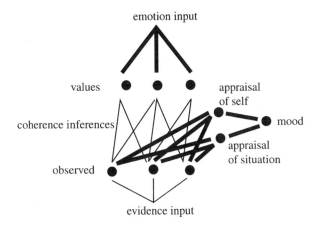

Figure 6.12
Mood changes affected by emotional coherence, expanded from figure 6.3.

suicide, and she felt she had to kill her children too to prevent them from experiencing comparable misery.

The theory of emotional coherence explains both why cognitive therapy can be difficult and why it can be successful. Figure 6.12 is an expanded version of figure 6.3, which showed how numerous coherence inferences can generate an emotional appraisal. For depressives, a coherent set of inferences imply a negative evaluation of the self as well as of his or her situation. Activations spread up from evidence input and valences spread down from emotion input, interacting to produce negative appraisals of self and situation. These negative appraisals produce a negative mood node, which then tends to keep the appraisal nodes negative. Cognitive therapy requires introducing new evidence and reforming coherence relations in ways that produce a change in the emotional appraisal of the self and the situation. For example, the therapist could help the depressed woman considering suicide to recall times when she had been a good mother to her children and thereby help her to revise her belief that she is a failure. Revision of this belief along with others could then change her overall emotional appraisal of herself and her situation, which could lead to a dramatic improvement in her mood. (Moods are ongoing affective states that are both modes of appraisal and states of action readiness; see Frijda 1993.) Mood changes are a kind of emotional Gestalt shift produced by a change in emotional coherence, driven in part by a shift in the inferences made in the belief network but crucially accompanied by shifts in valences attached to various nodes that affect the overall valence of the nodes representing the patient and her situation. Cognitive therapy assumes that inferential changes can affect emotional reactions, but it lacks a theory of how inference works and how it interconnects with emotional changes. These gaps are filled by my account of coherence-based inference as constraint satisfaction linked with valence adjustments.

In contrast to cognitive therapy, psychodynamic therapy based on Freudian ideas places more emphasis on unconscious motivational processes. Westen (2000) argues that optimal treatment of patients may require integration of cognitive and psychodynamic methods, along with delving into problematic and conflicting motives and irrational beliefs. From the perspective of HOTCO, cognitive therapy is aimed at altering the cognitive constraints based on explanatory and other kinds of coherence, whereas psychodynamic therapy pays more attention to the fundamental emotional constraints implemented as valence links. Whereas cognitive therapy often achieves short-term success in alleviating depression by helping patients to readjust their belief systems, long-term therapy may be required to overcome fundamental emotional conflicts.

What reason is there to believe the account of emotional coherence presented above? First, the theory of emotional coherence provides a unified explanation of numerous diverse psychological phenomena of great theoretical and practical importance. This chapter has provided a qualitative account of emotional coherence and has also shown how the theory can be implemented in a computational model with well-defined structures and processes that illuminate phenomena ranging from trust to cognitive therapy. Second, introspections and anecdotes support the view that trust, distrust, and nationalism have an emotional component, and empathy is by definition emotional. It would be desirable to go beyond introspection to show that the theory of emotional coherence can explain more quantitatively the results of psychological experiments, but the relevant experiments concerning the emotional impact of coherence have not been done. Independent of issues of emotion, the theories of explanatory, conceptual, and analogical coherence have had substantial empirical applications, serving to explain a wide variety of results of psychological experiments. Hence there is psychological evidence that inference is coherence-based, but the theory of emotional coherence awaits experimental test. The third support for the theory of emotional coherence comes from recent results in neuroscience, which were in part its inspiration.

In his provocative book *Descartes' Error* (1994), Damasio describes a group of patients with damage to the ventromedial region of the brain's frontal lobe. Such patients are typically physically capable and have most of their mental capacities intact, but their behavior, the result of severely flawed decision making, can be very odd. Elliott, for example, had been a good husband and father and successful in business. Then surgery to remove a tumor in the ventromedial area had left him apparently intellectually intact, but prone to decisions that proved disastrous for both his career and his marriage. Damasio argues that the importance of the ventromedial prefrontal cortices derives from their role in linking cognitive information about particular situations with signals that he calls "somatic markers," which are body states mediated by the emotional centers of the brain: the hypothalamus and amygdala. To put it briefly, the problem with ventromedial-damaged patients is that their decisions are cut off from their emotions, with the result that they have lost touch with what really matters to them.

Damasio's views map nicely onto my theory of emotional coherence. Valence inputs can be interpreted as based on somatic markers that the amygdala associates positively or negatively with particular things or situations. Interactions between the amygdala and the frontal cortex, where coherence-based inferences are presumably made, generate somatic markers that correspond to positive or negative valence outputs. In the case of trusting a babysitter, these somatic markers correspond to my "gut feeling" that a taxi driver was not to be trusted with my son Adam but that Christine was. In terms of HOTCO, the problem with Damasio's patients with ventromedial damage is that their coherence calculations have become severed from valence inputs and outputs.

According to LeDoux (1996), the amygdala has projections to many cortical areas, and the amygdala has a greater influence on the cortex than the cortex has on the amygdala. These influences support the assumption of the HOTCO model that coherence-based activations and emotion-generating valences are intertwined. Inference and appraisal go hand in hand, with emotional appraisal of a situation evolving in parallel with inferences about it. The HOTCO model is also consistent with the thorough review of affective neuroscience by Panksepp (1998), who observes, "The emotional systems are centrally placed to coordinate many higher and lower brain activities" (1998, 27), and notes, "Affective and cognitive processes are inextricably intertwined in higher brain areas, such as the frontal and temporal cortices" (1998, 315). LeDoux also reports, however, that not all emotional reactions require cortical processing, for there is a direct connection from the sensory thalamus to the amygdala. Hence for some visual stimuli, preferences need no inferences (Zajonc 1980). My account of emotional coherence applies only when appraisal is based on complex inferences, not to more direct emotional reactions to salient perceptual stimuli.

Psychological experiments are required to evaluate the plausibility of the following theoretical claims concerning judgments involving representational elements:

• The valence of an element depends on both the valences and the acceptability of the elements connected to it by coherence relations.

• Explanatory, conceptual, and analogical coherence all contribute to the resulting valence of an element.

• Judgments of trust are inherently emotional and are affected by input valences.

• Judgments of trust are also affected by explanatory, conceptual, and analogical coherence considerations that contribute to output valences.

My colleagues and I are currently planning experiments that manipulate valences and coherence to determine their effect on emotional judgments about people.

Since Plato and Aristotle, philosophical and popular thought have generally assumed a contrast between rationality on the one hand and emotion on the other. This divide, however, has been challenged by such writers as de Sousa (1987), Frank (1988), Oatley (1992), and Stocker and Hegeman (1996). My concern in this chapter has largely been to give a descriptive theory of trust and other applications of emotional coherence, but in naturalistic philosophy of the sort I practice, the descriptive and the normative are closely intertwined (Thagard 1988, 1992b).

I see three reasons for considering emotional coherence as being prescriptive as well as descriptive of trust, telling us generally when we *should* trust people as well as when we do. First, the standard models of rationality in decision making have little application to real-life situations. It is usually not possible to perform expected-value calculations based on probabilities and utilities, because we rarely know the relevant probabilities and utilities, which are dubious psychological constructs in comparison with goals and emotions. Second, it is a standard normative principle that ought implies can, so that no one can be held responsible for not doing the impossible. You cannot turn off your amygdala: removing emotions from decisions is psychologically impossible, although there are undoubtedly steps that can be taken to dampen the effects of destructive emotions. So normative principles ought not to require that we eliminate emotions from decisions. Third, if Damasio is right, you may not want to turn off your amygdala, because to do so would cut your analytical decision making off from crucial emotional information about what really matters to you. For human beings, emotion-free decision making is likely to be highly defective decision making, contrary to what you might believe from the Star Trek characters Mr. Spock and Data, who purport to possess cold rationality.

I am not, of course, romantically espousing uncritical guidance by emotional intuitions, which may be of dubious quality. Explanatory, analogical, and conceptual coherence can all be viewed normatively as well as descriptively, and there are better and worse ways of performing inferences based on them. For example, explanatory inference based on neglect of alternative explanatory hypotheses is likely to lead to premature acceptance of weak hypotheses. The normative course I recommend, well within people's capabilities, is the integration of emotional inputs with coherence-based inference to yield emotionally marked and objectively desirable outcomes.

There are important cases where emotional coherence may be in conflict with other kinds of coherence. Consider, for example, the presidential candidate Jack Stanton in the novel *Primary Colors* (1996). Stanton is presented as having two major weaknesses: women and fast food. He knows that it is better for his health and appearance if he avoids doughnuts and other unhealthy foods, but frequently eats them anyway. Similarly, his womanizing is a threat to his marriage and his political ambitions, both of which he presumably values more highly than his illicit affairs, yet he seems incapable of acting in his best interests. It is easy to see from the theory of emotional coherence and the computational model HOTCO how weakness of will can arise. Valences are affected not only by permanent, reasoned valences attached to goals such as being healthy, slim, faithful, and politically successful, but also by the activation of the relevant nodes. Emotion input can be of two kinds, the first arising from reasoned judgments of the value of a goal, such as eating doughnuts, the second arising from physiological reactions to a stimulus, such as a box of doughnuts. When faced with the doughnuts, or perhaps just the thought of the doughnuts, Stanton's doughnut node becomes strongly activated physiologically, so that the node representing the action *eat doughnuts* receives a strong valence. Deliberative coherence is swamped by emotional coherence, and this results in normatively inappropriate weakness of will. Similarly, as in my Gypsy example, social prejudice based on negative stereotypes may lead to irrational actions. Thus emotional coherence may generate normatively inappropriate judgments and behavior, although it may also be an important component in integrative reactions to complex situations.

Religious belief may survive because of the comfort and hope that it provides, despite the lack of evidence for it (chapter 4). Belief in God can be a great consolation, bringing assurance that everything will work out in one's life and that existence continues after death. Hence theism survives because of its emotional appeal, as well as because of the transmission of religious traditions from parents to children. Normatively, however, metaphysical hypotheses such as the existence of God should be evaluated on the basis of their coherence with evidence, not on the basis of desirability or tradition. HOTCO currently allows activations to influence valences, but does not allow valences to influence activations, so that the desirability of a conclusion does not have an effect on its acceptability. It is therefore incapable of modeling wishful thinking or the kind of motivated inference discussed by Kunda (1987, 1990).

Currently, HOTCO allows the activation of units, which represents the acceptance or believability of elements, to influence valences, which represent emotional attitudes toward the elements. Influence in the other direction is obviously dangerous: we should not believe something just because it makes us happy to do so. But recent experiments by Ziva Kunda, Drew Westen, and their colleagues show that emotional attitudes can have a strong influence on factual inferences, and HOTCO can be extended to allow valences to influence activations.

Sinclair and Kunda (1999) have found that the motivation to form a particular impression of an individual can prompt the inhibition of applicable stereotypes that contradict one's desired impression and the activation and application of those that support it. For example, experimental participants who were prejudiced against Blacks inhibited the negative Black stereotype when motivated to esteem a Black individual because he had praised them. In contrast, participants motivated to disparage a Black individual because he had criticized them did apply the Black stereotype, rating the individual as relatively incompetent. Thus inference about a person's competence can be affected by whether it is in one's self-interest to view him as competent or incompetent.

In terms of HOTCO, the experimental results of Sinclair and Kunda can be interpreted as showing that valences measuring the desirability of an inference can influence the activations measuring the plausibility of the inference. The simplest way to allow valences to influence activations would be to rewrite the equation for updating activations to take valences into account. Then the activation of a unit would be a function both of input activations and of the valence of the unit. Belief would then depend directly on positive feeling. However, in Kunda's (1990) work on motivated reasoning, people do not just believe something because it makes them happy: they have to do extra cognitive work to retrieve memories that support their desired beliefs. The results of Sinclair and Kunda (1999) suggest that in addition to a motivated memory search, there is a more direct process whereby valences can sometimes influence activations.

To model this process, I plan to add to HOTCO a special class of units, called "evaluation units," which correspond to representations that have both a cognitive and an affective dimension. For example, the proposition *Frank is good* has a degree of belief, but it also has an intimate connection with the affect attached to the representation *Frank*. The unit representing *Frank is good* should thus have its activation influenced both by other activations (e.g., of the unit *Frank is a criminal*) and by the valence of the associated unit representing *Frank*. I propose that the activations of evaluation units should be a function both of input activations and of input valences from associated units. Conversely, the valences of units such as *Frank* should be influenced by the activations of evaluation units such as *Frank is good*.

Similarly, I conjecture that the participants in the experiments of Sinclair and Kunda have an evaluation unit for *I am good* that has an activation that depends in part on the valence of the correlative *I* unit. The ongoing positive valence of the *I* unit will tend to keep the *I am good* unit active, which in turn will tend to support a unit representing the belief that the Black individual's praise of the participant was accurate. This *Praise is accurate* unit is positively linked to a unit asserting the competence of the individual, which is negatively linked to the participant's negative Black stereotype of incompetence. Thus the positive valence attached to the *I am good* node will tend to inhibit application of the negative aspects of the Black stereotype. On the other hand, if the participant is criticized by the Black professional, then maintaining a positive valence for the *I* unit will encourage judging the professional to be incompetent.

A similar mechanism should be able to account for experimental results of Westen and Feit (forthcoming). They studied people's inferences during the Clinton-

Lewinsky scandal of 1998, and they found that political judgments bore minimal relation to knowledge of relevant data, but were strongly predicted by people's feelings about Democrats and Republicans, Clinton, feminism, and infidelity. Factual hypotheses concerning what Clinton did or did not do should have been evaluated solely on the basis of their fit with the available evidence. But Westen and Feit's data suggest that the evidence had a small influence on people's inferences in comparison with their positive or negative feelings about Clinton and the two political parties involved. I propose to account for these results by giving HOTCO a *Clinton* unit with positive or negative valence that influences the activation of a unit for *Clinton is good*. Then the positive activation of this unit will tend to suppress the activation of a unit representing the hypothesis that Clinton is guilty, and hence to support alternative explanations of why witnesses said what they did about Clinton, for example, that they were encouraged by the Republicans. The explanatory coherence of the hypothesis about Clinton's guilt will thus be directly affected by the emotional coherence of that conclusion, just as people's confidence in the existence of God is determined by its emotional desirability. Similarly, in the O. J. Simpson trial, some jurors may have been influenced in their assessment of the evidence by their motivation to view Simpson as a good person and their emotional attitudes toward the Los Angeles police. I plan to develop a computational model of motivated inference that will apply to biased reasoning in law and science as well as to the experiments of Kunda, Westen, and their colleagues.

Trust, empathy, and the other topics of this chapter are by no means the only psychological phenomena that the theory of emotional coherence might help to explain. As chapter 5 described, judgments of right and wrong are based on interrelated explanatory, analogical, deductive, conceptual, and deliberative considerations. It is evident from both personal introspection and the behavior of others that ethical judgments are also often highly emotional. The emotive and cognitive aspects of ethical judgment are usually treated by philosophers as orthogonal to each other, but the theory of emotional coherence shows how they can be brought back together. In the 1940s, philosophers influenced by logical positivism espoused emotivism, the doctrine that value judgments in ethics and aesthetics merely express emotions. The theory of emotional coherence shows how ethical and other value judgments can be simultaneously emotionally and cognitively coherent. The theory of emotional coherence and the computational model HOTCO are limited in that they do not deal with the full variety of human emotional responses, but they serve to show how inference can at least sometimes be both emotional and rational. Cognitive naturalism can thus take into account the affective side of human thinking as well as the cold, inferential side. The next chapter will show that cognitive naturalism can also take into account some of the social dimensions of knowledge.

14 SUMMARY

Inference often involves not only accepting or rejecting mental representations, but also adjusting positive and negative emotional attitudes towards what is represented. Trust is based on explanatory and other kinds of coherence, but it also involves acquiring an emotional attitude or valence associated with the object to be trusted. Acquiring a valence is a parallel constraint-satisfaction process much like the process of accepting or rejecting representations based on their coherence with other representations. The HOTCO model shows how emotional assessment can be integrated with explanatory and other kinds of coherence to produce judgments of trust and other value-laden decisions, such as those involved in empathy and nationalism. Emotions can also involve more general kinds of evaluations that require an overall assessment of how much coherence is achieved. Such metacoherence assessments are relevant to understanding beauty, symmetry, humor, and the mood changes that occur as the result of cognitive therapy.

7   *Consensus*

Philosophical and psychological discussions of coherence, including the ones in the previous six chapters, are generally concerned with coherence in the mind of a single person. But the achievement of coherent systems of representations is a social process as well as an individual cognitive one. In many reasoning tasks, from evaluating scientific theories to making ethical decisions, people often rely on information received from others. The effective functioning of many kinds of groups, from scientific research teams to corporate divisions, requires that their members reach consensus about what to believe and what to do.

This chapter presents a theory of consensus based on coherence and communication. It presumes that individuals reach their own conclusions by evaluating the relative coherence of competing positions, and that consensus arises in a group when communication ensures that the individuals in the group share approximately the same set of elements that contribute to coherence evaluation. Conferences and other social processes that serve to increase communication thereby help scientists and medical practitioners to reach common conclusions about what to believe and what to do.

This chapter presents a computational model of consensus formation that clarifies how coherence and communication can lead to agreement. The model is unavoidably a great simplification of consensus formation in real groups, but it serves to highlight some of the key factors in the achievement of consensus. After describing the model's application to arguments at recent medical consensus conferences concerning the causes and treatment of peptic ulcers, I discuss a second application to debates concerning the origin of the moon. The desired result of the model is increased appreciation of the epistemic contributions of medical consensus conferences, as well as a deeper understanding of the general process of consensus. At the end of the chapter I discuss why consensus is more difficult to achieve in ethics than in science.

1   CONSENSUS IN SCIENCE AND MEDICINE

Since 1977 the U.S. National Institutes of Health have held more than one hundred consensus-development conferences. The purpose of these conferences is to produce consensus statements on controversial issues in medicine that are important to health-care providers, patients, and the general public. Many countries besides the United States hold similar events to help establish effective medical practices based on the best evidence available. Typically, experts on a medical issue make presentations to a panel or jury, who weigh the evidence and produce a consensus report reflecting their evaluation.

In other areas of science, consensus formation takes place less formally. It is common for controversial issues to be debated at conferences, but without an official panel to report a consensus. Implicitly, the entire scientific community serves as a kind of jury to evaluate competing theories on the basis of available evidence. Consensus does not always arise, but especially in the natural sciences it is not unusual for debate to give way to substantial agreement on issues that were previously controversial. For example, a consensus on the origin of the moon arose from a 1984 conference held in Kona, Hawaii. According to one of its organizers, G. Jeffrey Taylor:

Given the tenacity with which scientists cling to their views, none of us suspected that one of the hypotheses of lunar origin would spring forth as a leading candidate above the others. Certainly none of us thought the postconference favorite would not be one of the three classic hypotheses. Each of these hypotheses had what some considered to be fatal flaws. Each also had ardent supporters. It is a testament to human persistence and imagination that so many scientists tried so hard to adapt their preferences to a growing list of facts. (1994, 41)

Thus in science and medicine, consensus can emerge from controversy.

2   A MODEL OF CONSENSUS

The proposed theory of consensus can be summarized in the following theses:

• People make inferences about what to believe and what to do on the basis of judgments of coherence (chaps. 2–3). In particular, scientists evaluate competing theories by their comparative explanatory coherence, and they evaluate alternative practical actions using deliberative coherence. Coherence can be construed as maximization of constraint satisfaction, and can be computed by connectionist (artificial neural network) and other algorithms.

• Disagreement exists when individuals reach different coherence-based conclusions about what to accept and what to reject. Consensus is achieved by a group when all members of the group accept and reject the same sets of elements, which are representations that can include propositions, such as hypotheses and descriptions of evidence, as well as nonpropositional representations.

• Consensus arises when individuals in a group exchange information to a sufficient extent that they come to make the same coherence judgments about what to accept and what to reject. The information exchange involves both elements to be favored in a coherence evaluation (e.g., evidential propositions that describe the results of observation and experiment) and descriptions of the explanatory and other relations that hold between elements.

These theses are rather general and vague, but they can be made much more precise by describing a computational model that implements them and makes possible experimentation with different ways in which coherence-based consensus can develop.

The new consensus model, called CCC for "consensus = coherence + communication," builds on the computational models of coherence described in chapter 2. In all of these models, conclusions are reached by maximizing satisfaction of constraints among elements that represent aspects of the inferential situation. Hence we can understand the inferences of individual members of a group in terms of each of them reaching conclusions that try to maximize coherence of their own particular sets of elements and constraints. But how can agreement arise between individuals who accept and reject different elements because they assume different elements and different constraints? In scientific disputes, how can agreement arise between scientists who accept different theories based on evidence and explanations?

Communication makes possible mutual coherence by enabling the transfer between individuals of both elements and constraints. Scientists, for example, can communicate to each other information about the available evidence and about the explanatory relations that hold between hypotheses and evidence. This suggests the following straightforward process of consensus formation in science:

1. Start with a group of scientists who accept and reject different propositions because they reach different coherence judgements because of variations in evidence and explanations.

2. Exchange information between members of the group to change the coherence judgments made by the members.

3. Repeat (2) until the members have acquired sufficiently similar evidence and explanations so that all members accept and reject the same propositions; this is consensus.

The model CCC implements the process by representing each member of a group by a data structure:

Person

Name:

Favored elements:

Constraint input:

Accepts:

Rejects:

For simulations of scientific controversies involving explanatory coherence, the favored elements are propositions describing results of observation and experiments. Calling them "favored" does not mean that they cannot be rejected, only that their acceptance is encouraged in comparison with other elements representing hypotheses (see the discussion of discriminating coherentism in chapter 3). Even favored elements can be rejected if they fail to cohere optimally with other accepted elements. The constraint input includes statements of explanatory and contradictory relations. For example, in the ulcer controversy, the competing hypotheses included these:

AH1   Peptic ulcers are caused by excess acidity.

BH1   Peptic ulcers are caused by bacteria.

As well as other pieces of evidence about how people respond to different kinds of treatment, these hypotheses competed to explain the following primary piece of evidence:

E3   Some people get ulcers.

Constraint input can then include such information as the following:

(explain (AH1) E3)

(explain (BH1) E3)

The model CCC is implemented computationally in the programming language LISP, in which data and function calls are equally well written as lists, so these inputs that are part of the structure for a person can automatically be evaluated and produce new constraints (excitatory and inhibitory links). To evaluate coherence for a particular person, CCC uses the information about favored elements and inputs to create a network of units and links that can be used to spread activation to the units, and this results in the acceptance and rejection of units, which is recorded.

After performing a coherence calculation for all members of a given group, CCC checks for the presence of group consensus, which fails as soon as two members are found who differ in the propositions they accept or reject. Unless consensus already exists, communication begins, which enables members to acquire each other's elements and constraints. There are many ways in which communication might take place; here the ones currently implemented:

Communication mode 1: random meetings Randomly pick two persons P_1 and P_2 to communicate with each other. Then transfer from P_1 to P_2 and vice versa is stochastic, in that whether a constraint input or favored element is transferred depends on a communication probability that ranges between 0 and 1. If communication probability in CCC is set high, then an element or input is more likely to be transferred than if it is set low.

Communication mode 2: lectures followed by random meetings A number of persons representing divergent opinions give "lectures," in which they are able to broadcast their elements and constraints to all other members of the group. Transfer of the information is still stochastic, in that the lecturer succeeds in transferring a favored element or input to a listener only with a certain probability. After the lectures, further communication continues by random meetings.

Although simple, this model can generate interesting experiments about the relative effects of variables such as group size and communication probability on the amount of time it takes to achieve consensus. The model differs dramatically from the only other formal model of consensus of which I am aware. Lehrer and Wagner (1981) present a mathematical means of finding a probability assignment that constitutes the best summary of the total information of a group. They do not address the processes, central to CCC, by which an individual reaches a coherence-based judgment about what to accept and reject, and by which individuals exchange information that affect each other's coherence judgments. On the other hand, their model incorporates an aspect not yet implemented in CCC: members of a group have opinions of the reliability of each other member of a group. A minor change to CCC could incorporate this aspect, which would make the transfer of information from one person to another a function not only of exchange probability but also of the degree of reliability that the receiver attributes to the sender. Because little information about such reliability judgments is available for the cases to which CCC has so far been applied, this important aspect of communication has not yet been implemented. Full implementation of reliability assessments would involve judgments of the trustworthiness of other members of the group, and hence require all the coherence-based inferences described in my discussion of trust in chapter 6. The next section describes experiments done with a more limited simulation of consensus formation in the ulcer controversy.

3 CONSENSUS AND THE CAUSES OF ULCERS

When Barry Marshall and Robin Warren proposed in 1984 that most peptic (gastric and duodenal) ulcers are caused by infection by a newly discovered bacterium, the medical community was highly skeptical. But by 1994 the evidence for their hypothesis had accumulated to such an extent that an NIH Medical Consensus Conference recommended that antibiotics be used to treat duodenal ulcers. It is now standard practice among gastroenterologists to test ulcer patients for the presence of *Helicobacter pylori* infection, whose eradication usually brings about a permanent cure. Thagard (1999) analyzed the cognitive and social processes that contributed to the dramatic shift in medical belief and practice.

The generally accepted view in 1983 that peptic ulcers are caused by excess acidity, and the dominant view in 1994 that bacterial infection accounts for most ulcers, can be represented by the following inputs to ECHO.

Dominant View in 1983

Evidence

(proposition E1 "Association between bacteria and ulcers.")

(proposition E2 "Warren observed stomach bacteria.")

(proposition E3 "Some people have stomach ulcers.")

(proposition E4 "Antacids heal ulcers.")

(proposition E5 "Previous researchers found no bacteria.")

Bacteria hypotheses

(proposition BH1 "Bacteria cause ulcers.")

(proposition BH2 "Stomach contains bacteria.")

Acid hypotheses

(proposition AH1 "Excess acidity causes ulcers.")

(proposition AH2 "Stomach is sterile.")

(proposition AH3 "Bacterial samples are contaminated.")

Bacteria explanations

(explain (BH1 BH2) E1)

(explain (BH2) E2)

(explain (BH1 BH2) E3)

Acid explanations

(explain (AH1 AH2 AH3) E1)

(explain (AH1 AH2 AH3) E2)

(explain (AH1) E3)

(explain (AH1) E4)

(explain (AH2) E5)

(data (E1 E2 E3 E4 E5))

There is no need for an explicit statement of which hypotheses contradict or compete with each other (e.g.,

AH1 and BH1), because the program ECHO automatically identifies hypotheses from different theories that compete to explain the same evidence (Thagard 1992b). ECHO then sets up inhibitory links between units representing pairs of competing hypotheses. When ECHO is run on this input, it reaches the same conclusion that most medical researchers did in 1983: the bacterial theory of ulcers should be rejected.

In contrast, the following input yields acceptance of the bacterial theory:

Dominant View in 1994

Evidence

(proposition E1 "Association between bacteria and ulcers.")

(proposition E2 "Many have observed stomach bacteria.")

(proposition E3 "Some people have stomach ulcers.")

(proposition E4 "Antacids heal ulcers.")

(proposition E6 "Marshall's 1988 study that antibiotics cure ulcers.")

(proposition E7 "Graham's 1992 study that antibiotics cure ulcers.")

(proposition E8 "Several other cure studies.")

(proposition E9 "Bacteria/acid study.")

Bacteria hypotheses

(proposition BH1 "Bacteria cause ulcers.")

(proposition BH2 "Stomach contains bacteria.")

(proposition BH3 "Bacteria produce acid.")

(proposition BH4 "Eradicating bacteria cures ulcers.")

Acid hypothesis

(proposition AH1 "Excess acidity causes ulcers.")

Bacteria explanations

(explain (BH1 BH2) E1)

(explain (BH2) E2)

(explain (BH1 BH2) E3)

(explain (BH1 BH2) BH4)

(explain (BH1 BH3) E4)

(explain (BH3) E9)

(explain (BH4) E6)

(explain (BH4) E7)

(explain (BH4) E8)

Acid explanations

(explain (AH1) E3)

(explain (AH1) E4)

(data (E1 E2 E3 E4 E6 E7 E8 E9))

It is evident, and ECHO simulations confirm, that explanatory coherence based on this information supports accepting the bacterial theory in 1994 even though it was widely rejected earlier.

The consensus problem here is, How did the medical community come to achieve consensus that most peptic ulcers are caused by bacteria? CCC can be used to model consensus formation in this case by creating a population of scientists that includes proponents of the 1983 view and proponents of the 1994 view. Communication in which evidence and explanations are transferred between scientists gradually leads to general agreement. We would expect that the time required for consensus to be reached would be affected by a number of factors, including these:

· The number of members of the scientific community

· The probability of exchange of information on a given encounter

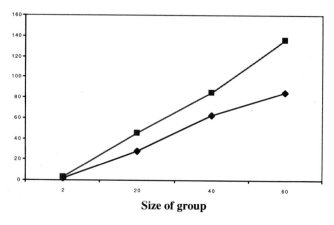

Figure 7.1
Time to consensus in the ulcer simulation, measured by number of meetings before full agreement was reached. The lower line shows the results of simulations that began with lectures. Exchange probability is held constant at 0.5. Results are the mean of five different simulations.

• The occurrence of lectures in which scientists can communicate simultaneously with a large number of other scientists

• The extent to which a superior view is initially distributed in the community

A series of computational experiments with CCC found that each of these factors influence the time to consensus.

Experiment 1 varied the size of the group of scientists seeking consensus, with groups of 2, 20, 40, and 60 members; half of the members started with the dominant view of ulcer causation in 1983, and half started with the dominant view in 1994. Figure 7.1 shows that the time required for consensus to be reached is a function of group size: the larger the group, the greater the number of meetings required to achieve consensus. Figure 7.1 also shows that, regardless of group size, lectures speed up the achievement of consensus. Computational experiment 2 held group size constant and varied exchange probability, which yielded the expected result that higher exchange probabilities produce consensus faster, in both the lecture and no-lecture conditions.

Both experiments 1 and 2 were unrealistic in that they began with half the members of the group of scientists holding each of the two competing theories. Historically, the bacteria theory of ulcers began with Marshall and Warren and then spread only very gradually through the community of gastroenterologists. Accordingly, computational experiment 3, which held group size constant at 40 and exchange probability constant at 0.5, varied proportions of the scientists beginning with the eventually dominant 1994 bacterial theory. In the toughest situation, starting with only 1 proponent of the bacterial theory of ulcers, it takes a long time for opinion to shift, an average of more than 250 meetings. Acceptance of the bacterial theory by the group is initially very slow, but accelerates rapidly as the theory spreads. When the simulation starts with 5 or 10 representatives of the bacterial theory, it reaches consensus much more rapidly, in around 100 meetings. The first simulation, starting with only 1 advocate of the bacterial theory, models much more closely the spread of the theory through the community of gastroenterologists.

The three computational experiments just described show that the CCC model displays some of the consensus behavior that one might expect of a scientific community. Consensus takes longer to achieve when group sizes are larger, when exchange probability is lower, when there are fewer members beginning with the dominant position, and when there are no lectures to jump-start communication. Similar results occur when CCC is applied to a different case, discussed in the next section.

It is rather artificial to have only two positions in the simulations, the 1983 rejection of the bacterial theory of ulcers and the 1994 acceptance. A full simulation of the case would have numerous individuals with many different starting points, arriving at agreement with the eventual consensus at different times. A more detailed account of the developments during the decade would explain more incrementally how beliefs such as AH2, "The stomach is sterile," could drop out of the picture by 1994. Despite the oversimplifications of the computational experiments so far accomplished, CCC provides the start of a model of how scientific consensus can arise through coherence and communication.

Can CCC account for cases where a scientific community fails to reach consensus? The computer simulations of the ulcer case allow exchange of information to be repeated until consensus is reached, but in the real world there are limits on the time and social opportunities for such exchange. Hence a community may not achieve consensus simply because it has not had enough instances of information exchanges with high enough exchange probabilities. If the simulations in figure 7.1 with 60 scientists had been stopped after only 40 interactions, then consensus would not have been achieved. More problematically, there may be communication barriers between scientists that prevent them from receiving each other's evidence and hypotheses, so that the exchange probability for some information drops to 0. Then consensus would never be reached, because the scientists would never end up making the same coherence calculations. I know of no cases in the history of science, however, where such complete communication breakdown has occurred: even the most major scientific revolutions have involved a high degree of comparability of competing theories (Thagard 1992b). Yet when two theories are conceptually very different, scientists may have difficulty understanding the hypotheses proposed by their opponents, and they may have little trust in the evidence adduced by the other side. In such cases, the exchange probability would be very low, so the scientific community and CCC would take a long time to reach consensus.

4 CONSENSUS AND THE ORIGIN OF THE MOON

To run CCC on the dispute concerning the origin of the moon, I encoded the key evidence and hypotheses as input to the explanatory coherence program ECHO largely according to the analysis of the debate by Wood (1986; see also Hartmann, Philips, and Taylor 1986 and Brush 1996). The four main theories were the following:

- Moon-capture hypothesis: a fully formed moon was caught by the earth.
- Coaccretion hypothesis: the moon and earth formed concurrently from a cloud of gas and dust.
- Fission hypothesis: the moon formed by fission from a rapidly spinning earth.
- Giant-impact hypothesis: a Mars-sized body hit the earth.

The relevant evidence concerned comparisons of the composition of the earth and moon, as well as the high angular momentum of the earth-moon system.

CCC has so far been run on the moon example with groups of simulated scientists involving 4, 20, 40, and 60 members. Each simulation begins with one quarter of the scientists holding each of the four theoretical positions. Computational experiments found, as expected, that the amount of time (number of meetings between pairs of scientists) required before consensus is reached increases with the number of scientists, and decreases with higher probability of information exchange. Moreover, starting the simulation with four "lectures" in which proponents of the four theories broadcast to the whole group speeds up consensus formation. The results of these simulations are similar to those described for the ulcer example. They show that CCC is capable of interesting behavior even though it is very simple, compared with the complexities of consensus formation in real scientific communities, and they illustrate the benefits of enhancing the communication process by allowing more rapid lecturelike transmissions of information from one individual to many.

5 BENEFITS OF CONSENSUS CONFERENCES

In an earlier book (Thagard 1999, chap. 12) I assessed medical consensus conferences with respect to seven epistemic standards: reliability, power, fecundity, speed, efficiency, explanatory efficacy, and pragmatic efficacy (the first five of these derive from the work of Alvin Goldman 1992). I will not repeat that analysis here, but I will try to deepen it from the perspective of the CCC model of consensus formation.

The point of medical and scientific consensus conferences should be to help scientific communities reach common conclusions that are reliable (have a good ratio of truths to falsehoods), explanatorily powerful (make sense of the evidence), and practically efficacious (bring about nonepistemic benefits to people). In addition, they should help provide many answers to important questions (power) and make these answers available to many people (fecundity). Speed and efficiency are also relevant epistemic standards, since we want an epistemic practice to produce answers quickly and at low cost. In accord with the CCC simulations of both the moon and ulcer cases, consensus conferences in which scientists begin with lectures and proceed with intense discussions serve to communicate evidence and explanations, and thereby produce speedy, efficient, and explanatorily efficacious decisions. Consensus conferences also increase the speed of interaction of scientists and medical practitioners, by bringing them all together in the same place. This dramatically increases the rate of pairwise and larger interactions between scientists.

Of course, there are many aspects of consensus conferences that are not captured by the CCC model as it currently stands. I have not yet attempted to model the role of the jury panel in meeting together to reach a consensus that is then communicated to a larger group and presumably has a substantial impact on the larger group's consensus. Moreover, the simulations so far have dealt only with issues of explanatory coherence, but there are legitimate and illegitimate ways in which medical decisions are also based on deliberative coherence, which evaluates the extent to which various actions affect goals. The legitimate contribution of deliberative coherence to medical decisions includes calculation of the extent to which different courses of action accomplish medical goals, such as curing as many people as possible, and social goals, such as keeping the cost of medicine down to a level that people and the government can sustain. Such common social goals are favored elements that can be communicated from one decision maker to another in the same way that favored elements representing evidence are communicated between scientists.

On the illegitimate side of theory evaluation, individual judgments about the causes and treatment of disease are sometimes affected by the individual goals of decision makers. Scientists and physicians are not saints, and their inferences may well be affected by their personal goals, such as their finances and their stature in the profession. One of the pioneers of the bacterial theory of ulcers once suggested to me that some gastroenterologists were reluctant to accept the idea of a quick antibiotic cure for ulcers because they would then lose their lucrative gastroscopy businesses and be reduced to conducting colonoscopies, making them no better than proctologists! Because CCC can incorporate any kind of coherence-based inference, it would be easy to incorporate such individual goals and deliberative coherence calculations into its simulations. Like ordinary people, the scientists in a CCC simulation of consensus building would then be liable to what Kunda (1990) calls motivated inference, in which personal goals affect the evaluation of evidence and hence the overall judgment of the reasoner. Moreover, different scientists will have different emotional valences attached to particular hypotheses, which will yield different judgments of emotional coherence.

It is crucial to note, however, that medical consensus conferences, like scientific communications in general, are structured so as to discourage the dissemination of such individual concerns. Medical practitioners cannot stand up and say, "We shouldn't adopt this treatment because it will reduce our income," even if that is what they are thinking. Decisions at consensus conferences are expected to be evidence-based, taking into account all the available data from the most carefully conducted clinical trials. (When I first heard the term "evidence-based medicine," I thought it was redundant, but in fact many medical treatments have yet to be assessed using the randomized and blinded clinical trials necessary to evaluate causal efficacy.) Public talks and comments (although not necessarily informal asides) must conform to the social norm of evaluating disease explanations and potential treatments on the basis of dispassionately presented evidence. Hence what gets transferred between individuals at a consensus conference is not their quirky individual goals, but evidence, explanations, and socially acceptable general goals. Thus consensus conferences can serve to ensure not only that *some* decision be made, but also that the decision made does in fact maximize explanatory and deliberative coherence.

6 CONSENSUS IN VALUE JUDGMENTS

Controversies are common in science and medicine, but so is consensus reached as the result of the collective assessment of evidence. In ethics, politics, and aesthetics, however, it seems that the balance is tipped more toward controversy than consensus. My discussion of coherence and emotion in previous chapters points to several reasons why consensus is more problematic in issues concerning values. Whereas scientific controversies can be settled largely by evaluating the explanatory coherence of hypotheses with respect to the evidence, ethical and other value controversies require integration of the constraints of deliberative coherence. And whereas scientists are required to take seriously the evidence presented by other scientists, decision makers may not share the goals of other decision makers, and there is no immediate normative reason why they should. If your primary goal is world domination and human enslavement, there is no reason why I should give it any priority in my own assessments of deliberative coherence. The emotional valences that you attach to different hypotheses and possible actions need not correspond to my emotional valences.

A collective assessment of deliberative coherence has to be reached on the basis of agreed-upon high-level goals, such as flourishing, freedom, and fairness, as I discussed in chapter 5. But the relative weights of these constraints is an open question, and there is no obvious way that communication can help to overcome weighting differences. How can consensus rationally be reached between proponents of libertarianism, who put top priority on freedom, and proponents of socialism, who put top priority on fairness? The main hope for consensus comes from the possibility of constraint adjustment achieved through explanatory and analogical coherence, as political debaters consider the widest possible range of evidence concerning historical cases, social functioning, and cognitive-emotional processes. Not just cold constraints but also the hot valences that contribute to emotional coherence must be changed.

Broadening consensus formation about what to do so that it includes other kinds of coherence besides deliberative coherence does not always make consensus easier to achieve. For most people, ethical issues are closely tied in with metaphysical ones, because ethical education is commonly part of religion. Consider a person who strongly believes the following propositions:

- God exists.
- God determines what is right and wrong.
- The Bible is God's word.
- The bible says that abortion is wrong.

From these beliefs, it follows deductively that abortion is wrong, so the ethical judgment is strongly constrained by metaphysical beliefs. Achieving a consensus between this person and a proabortion atheist requires dramatic revisions in judgments based on explanatory and other kinds of coherence, as well as deliberative coherence.

Despite these impediments, the prospects for ethical and political consensus are not entirely bleak. By the end of the twentieth century, most educated people have come to agree on many ethical judgments, for example that slavery is wrong. I hope that further increase in understanding of how people think and feel and of how societies work will lead to further consensus.

7 SUMMARY

Consensus in a group can be reached as the result of communication that allows its members to exchange elements and constraints. Thus consensus arises by means of a combination of interpersonal communication and individual coherence assessments. In science and medicine, conferences are one of the means by which communication is increased and convergence on common coherence judgements is encouraged. Consensus in ethics and politics is often more problematic because exchange of goals and constraints in deliberative coherence is much harder to accomplish than exchange of hypotheses and explanations in explanatory coherence.

8

Probability

The model of consensus in the last chapter assumed that scientists evaluate competing hypotheses on the basis of their explanatory coherence. But this is not the only position in current philosophy of science and epistemology, where theory choice and belief revision are often discussed using probability theory. On the probabilistic view, one theory should be preferred to another if it has higher probability given the evidence. This chapter explores the relationship between probabilistic and coherentist approaches to inference.

1   TWO TRADITIONS IN CAUSAL REASONING

When surprising events occur, people naturally try to generate explanations of them. Such explanations usually involve hypothesizing causes that have the events as effects. Reasoning from effects to prior causes is found in many domains, including the following:

• Social reasoning: when friends are acting strange, we conjecture about what might be bothering them.

• Legal reasoning: when a crime has been committed, jurors must decide whether the prosecution's case gives a convincing explanation of the evidence.

• Medical diagnosis: from a set of symptoms, a physician tries to decide what disease or diseases produced them.

• Fault diagnosis in manufacturing: when a piece of equipment breaks down, a troubleshooter must try to determine the cause of the breakdown.

• Scientific theory evaluation: scientists seek an acceptable theory to explain experimental evidence.

What is the nature of such reasoning? The many discussions of causal reasoning over the centuries can be seen as falling under two general traditions, which I will call explanationism and probabilism. Explanationists understand causal reasoning qualitatively, while probabilists exploit the resources of the probability calculus to understand causal reasoning quantitatively. Explanationism goes back at least to Aristotle (1984, vol. 1, p. 128), who considered the inference that the planets are near as providing an explanation of why they do not twinkle. Some Renaissance astronomers such as Copernicus and Rheticus evaluated theories according to their explanatory capabilities (Blake 1960). The leading explanationists in the nineteenth century were the British scientist, philosopher, and historian William Whewell (1967), and the American polymath C. S. Peirce (1958). The most enthusiastic explanationists in this century have been epistemologists such as Gilbert Harman (1973, 1986) and William Lycan (1988). In the field of artificial intelligence, computational models of inference to the best explanation have been developed (Josephson et al. 1994, Shrager and Langley 1990, Thagard 1992b).

The probabilist tradition is less ancient than explanationism, for the mathematical theory of probability arose only in the seventeenth century through the work of Pascal, Bernoulli, and others (Hacking 1975). Laplace and Jevons were the major proponents of probabilistic approaches to induction in the eighteenth and nineteenth century, respectively (Laudan 1981, chap. 12). Many twentieth-century philosophers have advocated probabilistic approaches to epistemology, including Keynes (1921), Carnap (1950), Jeffrey (1983), Levi (1980), Kyburg (1983), and Kaplan (1996).

Probabilistic approaches have recently become influential in artificial intelligence as a way of dealing with the uncertainty encountered in expert systems (D'Ambrosio 1999; Frey 1998; Jordan 1998; Neapolitain 1990; Pearl 1988, 1996; Peng and Reggia 1990). Probabilistic approaches are also being applied to natural-language understanding (Charniak 1993). The explanationist versus probabilist issue surfaces in a variety of subareas. Some legal scholars concerned with evidential reasoning have been probabilist (Lempert 1986, Cohen 1977), while some are explanationist and see probabilist reasoning as neglecting important aspects of how jurors reach decisions (Allen 1994, Pennington and Hastie 1986). In the philosophy of science, there is an unresolved tension between probabilist accounts of scientific inference (Achinstein 1991, Hesse 1974, Horwich 1982, Howson and Urbach 1989, Maher 1993) and explanationist accounts (Eliasmith and Thagard 1997; Lipton 1991; Thagard 1988, 1992b, 1999). Neither the probabilist nor the explanationist tradition is monolithic: there are competing interpretations of probability and inference within the former, and differing views of explanatory inference within the latter.

In recent years it has become possible to examine the differences between explanationist and probabilist approaches at a much finer level, because algorithms have been developed for implementing them computationally. As chapter 3 described, my theory of explanatory coherence incorporates the kinds of reasoning advocated by explanationists and is implemented in a connectionist program called ECHO, which shows how explanatory coherence can be computed in networks of propositions. Pearl (1988) and others have shown how probabilistic reasoning can be computationally implemented using networks. The question naturally arises of the relation between ECHO networks and probabilistic networks. This chapter shows how ECHO's qualitative input can be used to produce a probabilistic network to which Pearl's algorithms are applicable. At one level, this result can be interpreted as showing that ECHO is a special case of a probabilistic network.

The production of a probabilistic version of ECHO highlights several computational problems with probabilistic networks. The probabilistic version of ECHO requires the provision of many conditional probabilities of dubious availability, and the computational techniques needed to translate ECHO into probabilistic networks are potentially combinatorially explosive. ECHO can therefore be viewed as an intuitively appealing and computationally efficient approximation to probabilistic reasoning. We will also see that ECHO puts important constraints on the conditional probabilities used in probabilistic networks.

The comparison between ECHO and probabilistic networks does not in itself settle the relation between the explanationist and probabilist traditions, since there are other ways of being an explanationist besides ECHO, and there are other ways of being a probabilist besides Pearl's networks. But from a computational perspective, ECHO and Pearl networks are much more fully specified than previous explanationist and probabilist proposals, so a head-to-head comparison is potentially illuminating. After briefly reviewing Pearl's approach to probabilistic networks, I shall sketch the probabilistic interpretation of explanatory coherence and discuss the computational problems that arise. Then a demonstration of how ECHO naturally handles Pearl's central examples will support the conclusion that the theory of explanatory coherence is not obviated by the probabilistic approach.

The point of this chapter, however, is not simply a comparison of two computational models of causal reasoning. Causal reasoning is an essential part of human thinking, so the nature of such reasoning is an important question for cognitive science. Do people use coherence-based or probabilistic inference when they evaluate competing causal accounts in social, legal, medical, engineering, and scientific contexts? Many researchers in AI and philosophy assume that probabilistic approaches are the only ones appropriate for understanding such reasoning, but there is much experimental evidence that human thinking is often not in accord with the prescriptions of probability theory (see, e.g., Kahneman, Slovic, and Tversky 1982; Tversky and Koehler 1994). On the other hand, there is some psychological evidence that explanatory coherence theory captures aspects of human thinking (Read and Marcus-Newhall 1993; Schank and Ranney 1991, 1992; Thagard and Kunda 1998). Moreover, as earlier chapters showed, coherence-based reasoning is pervasive in human thinking, in areas as diverse as perception, decision making, ethical judgments, and emotion. Clarification of the relation between explanatory coherence and probabilistic accounts is thus part of the general psychological project of understanding how human causal reasoning works.

The probabilistic view assumes that the degrees of belief that people have in various propositions can be described by quantities that comply with the principles of the mathematical theory of probability. In contrast, the explanationist approach sees no reason to use probability theory to model degrees of belief. Probability theory is an immensely valuable tool for making statistical inferences about patterns of frequencies in the world, but it is not the appropriate mathematics for understanding human inference in general.

2 PROBABILISTIC NETWORKS

The theory of explanatory coherence employs vague concepts such as explanation and acceptability, and ECHO requires input specifying explanatory relations. It is reasonable to desire a more precise way of understanding causal reasoning, for example, in terms of the mathematical theory of probability. That theory can be stated in straightforward axioms that establish probabilities as quantities between 0 and 1. From the axioms it is trivial to derive Bayes's theorem, which can be written thus:

$$P(H/E) = \frac{P(H) \times P(E/H)}{P(E)}$$

This equation says that the probability of a hypothesis given the evidence is the prior probability of the hypothesis times the probability of the evidence given the hypothesis, divided by the probability of the evidence. Bayes's theorem is very suggestive for causal reasoning, since we can hope to decide what caused an effect by considering which cause has the greatest probability, given the effect. Hence probabilists are often called Bayesians.

In practice, however, application of the probability calculus becomes complicated. Harman (1986, 25) has pointed out that in general probabilistic updating is combinatorially explosive, since we need to know the probabilities of a set of conjunctions whose size grow exponentially with the number of propositions. For example, full probabilistic information about three propositions, A, B, and

C, would require knowing a total of 8 different values: $P(A \& B \& C)$, $P(A \& B \& \text{not } C)$, $P(A \& \text{not } B \& \text{not } C)$, etc. Only 30 propositions would require more than a billion probabilities. As Thagard and Verbeurgt (1998) have shown, coherence maximization is also potentially intractable computationally, but the algorithms described in chapter 2 provide efficient ways of computing coherence, and the semidefinite programming algorithm is guaranteed to accomplish at least 0.878 of the optimal constraint satisfaction.

Probabilistic networks enormously prune the required number of probabilities and probability calculations, since they restrict calculations to a limited set of dependencies. Suppose you know that B depends only on A, and C depends only on B. You then have the simple network $A \rightarrow B \rightarrow C$. This means that A can affect the probability of C only through B, so that the calculation of the probability of C can take into account the probability of B while ignoring that of A.

Probabilistic networks have gone under many different names: causal networks, belief networks, Bayesian networks, influence diagrams, and independence networks. For the sake of precision, I want to concentrate on a particular kind of probabilistic network that uses the elegant and powerful methods of Pearl (1988). Though methods for dealing with probabilistic networks other than his are undoubtedly possible, I will not try to compare ECHO generally with probabilistic networks, but will make the comparison specifically with Pearl networks.

In Pearl networks, each node represents a multivalued variable such as a patient's temperature, which might take three values: high, medium, low. In the simplest cases, the variable can be propositional, with two values, true and false. Already we see a difference between Pearl networks and ECHO networks, since ECHO requires separate nodes

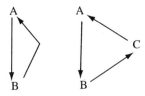

Figure 8.1
Examples of cyclic graphs.

for a proposition and its negation. But translations between Pearl nodes and ECHO nodes are clearly possible and will be discussed below.

More problematic are the edges in the two kinds of networks. Pearl networks are directed, acyclic graphs. Edges are directed, pointing from causes to effects, so that $A \rightarrow B$ indicates that A causes B and not vice versa. In contrast, ECHO's links are all symmetric, befitting the character of coherence and incoherence (principle E1 of chapter 3, section 1), but symmetries are not allowed in Pearl networks. The specification that the graphs be acyclic rules out relations such as those shown in figure 8.1. Since the nodes are variables, a more accurate interpretation of the edge $A \rightarrow B$ would be that the values of B are causally dependent on the values of A.

The structure of Pearl networks is used to localize probability calculations and surmount the combinatorial explosion that can result from considering the probabilities of everything, given everything else. Figure 8.2 shows a fragment of a Pearl network in which the variable D is identified as being dependent on A, B, and C, while E and F are dependent on D. The probabilities that D will take on its various values can then be calculated by looking only at A, B, C, E, and F and ignoring other variables in the network that D is assumed to be conditionally independent of, given the five variables on which it is directly dependent. The

Figure 8.2
Sample Pearl network, in which the variable D is dependent on A, B, and C, while E and F are dependent on D. Lines with arrows indicate dependencies.

probabilities of the values of D can be expressed as a vector corresponding to the set of values. For example, if D is temperature and has values (high, medium, low), the vector (0.5 0.3 0.2) assigned to D means that the probability of high temperature is 0.5, of medium temperature is 0.3, and of low temperature is 0.2. In accord with the axioms of probability theory, the numbers in the vector must sum to 1, since they are the probabilities of all the exclusive values of the variable.

The desired result of computing with a Pearl network is that each node should have a stable vector representing the probabilities of its values, given all the other information in the network. If a measurement determines that the temperature is high, then the vector for D would be (1 0 0). If the temperature is not known, it must be inferred using information gathered from both the variables on which D depends and the ones that depend on D. In terms of Bayes's theorem, we can think of A, B, and C as providing prior probabilities for the values of D, while E and F provide observed evidence for them. The explanatory-coherence interpretation of figure 8.2 is that A, B, and C explain D, while D explains E and F. For each variable X, Pearl uses BEL(x) to indicate the computed degrees of belief (probabilities) that X takes on for each of its values x. BEL(x) is thus a vector with as many entries as X has values, and is calculated using the following equation:

$$\text{BEL}(x) = \alpha \times \lambda(x) \times \pi(x)$$

Here α is a normalizing constant used to ensure that the entries in the vector sum to 1; $\lambda(x)$ is a vector representing the amount of support for particular values of X coming up from below, that is, from variables that depend on X; and $\pi(x)$ is a vector representing the amount of support for particular values of X coming down from above, that is, from variables on which X depends. For a variable V at the very top of the network, the value passed down by V will be a vector of the prior probabilities that V takes on its various values. Ultimately, $\text{BEL}(x)$ should be a function of these prior probabilities and the fixed probabilities at nodes where the value of the variable is known, which produce BEL vectors such as (1 0 0).

Calculating BEL values is nontrivial, because it requires repeatedly updating BEL and other values until the prior probabilities and the known values based on the evidence have propagated throughout the network. It has been shown that the general problem of probabilistic inference in networks is NP-hard (Cooper 1990), so we should not expect there to be a universal efficient algorithm for updating BEL. Pearl presents algorithms for computing BEL in the special case where networks are singly connected, that is, where no more than one path exists between two nodes (Pearl 1988, chap. 4; see also Neapolitain 1990). A loop here is a sequence of edges independent of direction. If there is more than one path between nodes, then the network contains a loop that can interfere with achievement of stable values of BEL, λ, and π. Hence methods have been developed for converting multiply connected networks into singly connected ones by clustering nodes into new nodes with many values. For example, consider the

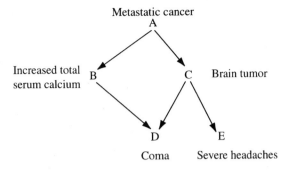

Figure 8.3
Pearl's representation of a multiply connected network that must
be manipulated before probability calculations can be performed.

network shown in figure 8.3 (from Pearl 1988, 196). In
this example, metastatic cancer is a cause of both increased
total serum calcium and brain tumors, either of which can
cause a coma. This is problematic for Pearl because there
are two paths between *A* and *D*. Clustering involves collapsing nodes *B* and *C* into a new node *Z* representing a
variable with values that are all the possible combinations
of the values of *B* and *C*: increased calcium and tumor,
increased calcium and no tumor, no increased calcium and
tumor, and no increased calcium and no tumor. ECHO
deals with cases such as these very differently, using the
principle of competition, as we will see below.

There are other ways of dealing with loops in probabilistic networks besides clustering. Pearl discusses two
approximating alternatives. Lauritzen and Spiegelharter
(1988) have offered a powerful general method for converting any directed acyclic graph into a tree of cliques
of that graph (see also Neapolitain 1990, chap. 7). Hrycej
(1990) shows how approximation by stochastic simulation
can be understood as sampling from the Gibbs distribution
in a random Markov field. Frey (1998) uses graph-based

inference techniques to develop new algorithms for Bayesian networks.

What probabilities must actually be known to compute BEL(x) even in singly connected networks? Consider again figure 8.2, where the BEL values for node D are to be computed from values for A, B, C, E, and F. To simplify, consider only values a, b, c, d, and e of the respective variables. Pearl's algorithms do not simply require knowledge of the conditional probabilities $P(d/a)$, $P(d/b)$, and $P(d/c)$. (Here $P(d/a)$ is shorthand for the probability that D has value d given that A has value a.) Rather, the calculation considers the probabilities of d, given all the possible combinations of values of the variables on which D depends. Consider the simple propositional case where the possible values of D are that it is true (d) or false (not d). Pearl's algorithm requires knowing $P(d/a \ \& \ b \ \& \ c)$, $P(d/a \ \& \ b \ \& \ \text{not } c)$, $P(d/a \ \& \ \text{not } b \ \& \ \text{not } c)$ and five other conditional probabilities. The analogous conditional probabilities for not d can be computed from the ones just given.

More generally, if D depends on n variables with k values each, k^n conditional probabilities will be required for computation. This raises two problems that Pearl discusses. First, if n is large, the calculations become computationally intractable, so that approximation methods must be used. Probabilistic networks nevertheless are computationally much more attractive than the general problem of computing probabilities, since the threat of combinatorial explosion is localized to nodes that we can hope to be dependent on a relatively small number of other nodes. Second, even if n is not so large, there is the problem of obtaining sensible conditional probabilities to plug into the calculations. Pearl acknowledges that it is unreasonable to expect a human or other system to store all this information about conditional probabilities, and he shows

Table 8.1
Comparison of ECHO and Pearl networks

	ECHO	Pearl
Nodes represent	propositions	variables
Edges represent	coherence	dependencies
Directedness	symmetric	directed
Loops	many	must be eliminated
Node quantity updated	activation from -1 to 1	BEL: vector with values having probabilities from 0 to 1
Additional updating	none	λ, π
Additional information used	explanations, data	conditional probabilities, prior probabilities

how it is sometimes possible to use simplified models of particular kinds of causal interactions to avoid having to do many of the calculations that the algorithms would normally require. Table 8.1 summarizes the differences between ECHO and Pearl networks. We now have enough information to begin considering the relation between ECHO and Pearl networks.

3 TRANSLATING ECHO INTO PROBABILISTIC NETWORKS

To see why it is reasonable to consider translating ECHO networks into Pearl networks, let us review some simple examples that illustrate ECHO's capabilities. Given a choice between competing hypotheses, ECHO prefers ones that explain more. A Pearl network can be expected to show a similar preference, since the λ function will send more support up to a value v of a variable from variables whose values v_i are known and where $P(v/v_i)$ is high. ECHO prefers hypotheses that are explained to ones that are not, and a Pearl network will similarly send support down to a value of a variable using the π function. To determine whether Pearl networks can duplicate other aspects of ECHO networks, we will have to consider a possible translation in more detail.

A translation algorithm from ECHO networks to Pearl networks could take either of two forms. The most direct would be an immediate network-to-network translation. Every proposition node in the ECHO network would become a variable in a Pearl network, and every ECHO link would become a Pearl conditional probability between values of variables. This direct translation clearly fails, since ECHO's symmetric links would translate into two-way conditional probabilities, which are not allowed in Pearl networks. Moreover, the translation would produce many cycles, which Pearl networks exclude by definition. (Clarification: In Pearl's terminology, all cycles are loops, but not all loops are cycles. $A \rightarrow B \rightarrow C \rightarrow A$ is a cycle, because the direction of the path is maintained. However, $A \rightarrow B \rightarrow C \leftarrow A$ is a loop, since for loops direction is ignored, but it is not a cycle.) Alternatively, we can bypass the creation of an ECHO network and simply use the input to ECHO to generate a Pearl network directly. We can then try to produce a program that will take ECHO's input and produce an Pearl network suitable for running Pearl's algorithms.

Let us call this program PECHO. First we must worry about creating the appropriate nodes. ECHO creates nodes when it is given input describing a proposition P. Analogously, PECHO would create a variable node with two values, TRUE and FALSE. At this point, PECHO would have to consult ECHO's input concerning contradictions and check whether there is some proposition not P that contradicts *P*. If so, there is no need to construct a new variable node, since not *P* would simply be represented by the FALSE value of the variable node where *P* represents the value TRUE. It becomes more complicated if there are several propositions in ECHO that all contradict each other, but these could all be amalgamated into one variable node with multiple values.

Since the vector representing the BEL values for a variable is required to sum to 1, PECHO will be able to duplicate ECHO's effect that the acceptability of a proposition counts against the acceptability of any proposition that contradicts it. Because we are not directly translating from ECHO networks to Pearl networks, we do not have to worry that ECHO activation values range from -1 to 1, rather than from 0 to 1 like probabilities, but in any case it is possible to normalize ECHO's activations into the range of probabilities. To normalize ECHO in the simplest case, just add 1 to a unit's activation and divide the result by 2. If two units represent contradictory propositions, normalize the resulting values by multiplying each value by 1 divided by the sum of the values.

When a proposition contradicts more than one other proposition, the normalization becomes problematic unless the propositions in question are all mutually contradictory, as when they all represent different values of the same variable. In ECHO networks this is not always the case. Simulation of Copernicus's case against Ptolemy (Nowak and Thagard 1992a) includes the following propositions:

P6   The Earth is always at the center of the heavenly sphere.

P12 The sun moves eastward along a circle about the earth in one year.

C12 The sun is immobile at the center of the universe.

Here Ptolemy's propositions P6 and P12 each contradict Copernicus's C12, but they do not contradict each other.

ECHO uses the range $[-1, 1]$ for both conceptual and computational reasons. Conceptually, ECHO is interpreted in terms of degrees of acceptance (activation > 0) and degrees of rejection (activation < 0), sharing with some expert systems the intuition that attitudes toward hypotheses are better characterized in terms of acceptance versus rejection rather than as degrees of belief, as probabilists hold (see Buchanan and Shortliffe 1984, chap. 10). The computational reason is that activation updating in ECHO has the consequence that if a hypothesis coheres with one that is deactivated, it too will tend to be deactivated. Thus sets of hypotheses (theories) tend to be accepted and rejected as wholes, as is usually the case in the history of science (Thagard 1992b).

Now we get to the crucial question of links. When ECHO reads the input

(explain (P1 P2 P3 P4) Q)

it creates excitatory links between each of the explaining propositions and Q. PECHO correspondingly would note that the variable node whose TRUE value represents Q is causally dependent on the variable node whose TRUE value represents P1, and so on. More problematically, PECHO would have to contrive 4 conditional probabilities: $P(Q/P1)$, $P(Q/\text{not } P1)$, $P(\text{not } Q/P1)$, and $P(\text{not } Q/\text{not } P1)$. The first of these could perhaps be derived approximately from the weight that ECHO puts on the link between the nodes representing P1 and Q, and we could derive the third from the first, since $P(Q/P1)$ and $P(\text{not } Q/P1)$ sum to 1, but ECHO provides no guidance about the other two probabilities.

In fact, the situation is much worse, since Pearl's algorithms actually require 32 different conditional probabilities, for example, $P(Q/P_1 \& \text{ not } P_2 \& P_3 \& \text{ not } P_4)$. In the most complex ECHO network to date, modeling the case of Copernicus against Ptolemy (Nowak and Thagard 1992a), there are 143 propositions. A search through the units created by ECHO that counts the number of explainers shows that the number of conditional probabilities that PECHO would need is 45,348. This is a big improvement over the 2^{143} (more than 10^{43}) probabilities that a full distribution would require, but it is still daunting. Of the 45,348 conditional probabilities, only 469 could be directly derived from the weight on the ECHO link. Does it matter what these probabilities are? Perhaps PECHO could give them all a simple default value and still perform as well as ECHO. We will shortly see that in fact explanatory coherence requires some constraints on the conditional probabilities if PECHO is to duplicate ECHO's judgements.

A derivation of $P(Q/P_1)$ based on the ECHO link between Q and P_1 would effectively implement the simplicity principle, E2 (c) from chapter 3, since it would mean that in updating the Pearl network, P_1 would get less support from Q than it would if P_1 explained Q without the help of other hypotheses. This is because ECHO makes the strength of such links inversely proportional to the number of hypotheses. PECHO is able to get by with a unidirectional link between the node for P and the node for Q, since the contribution of the λ and π functions to the BEL functions of the two nodes effectively spreads support in both directions.

The construction just described would enable PECHO to implement principles E2 (a) and E2 (c) of the theory of explanatory coherence, but what about E2 (b), according to which P_1, P_2, P_3, and P_4 all cohere with each other? Here PECHO encounters serious difficulties. Explanatory-coherence theory assumes that cohypotheses (hypotheses that participate together in an explanation) support each other, but this is impossible in Pearl networks, which have to be acyclic. There is thus a deep difference in the fundamental assumptions of explanatory coherence and probabilistic networks, which gain their relative efficiency by making strong assumptions of independence. In contrast, explanatory coherence assumes that every proposition in a belief system can be affected by every other one, although the effects may be indirect and small. To put it graph-theoretically, ECHO networks are strongly connected, by their symmetric links, but probabilistic networks with directed edges are emphatically not. At first glance, ECHO networks might seem to be similar to the noisy OR gates for which Pearl (1988, 188 ff.) provides an efficient method. However, his method requires assumptions not appropriate for ECHO, such as that an event is presumed false if all conditions listed as its causes are false.

Pearl networks can, however, get the effects of excitatory links between cohypotheses by means of the clustering methods used to eliminate loops. We saw in the last section that Pearl considers collapsing competing nodes into single nodes with multiple values. If H_1 and H_2 together explain E, then instead of creating separate variable nodes for H_1 and H_2, PECHO would create a variable node $\langle H_1\text{-}H_2 \rangle$ with values representing H_1 & H_2, H_1 & not H_2, not H_1 & H_2, and not H_1 & not H_2. To implement explanatory-coherence principle E2 (b), which establishes coherence between H_1 and H_2, PECHO would have to ensure that it has conditional probabilities such that $P(E/H_1 \& H_2)$ is greater than either $P(E/H_1 \& \text{not } H_2)$ or $P(E/\text{not } H_1 \& H_2)$. (I am simplifying the representation here: in the Pearl network, by $P(E/H_1 \& H_2)$ I mean the probability that variable E takes the value TRUE, given that variable $\langle H_1\text{-}H_2 \rangle$ takes the value $\langle H_1 \& H_2 \rangle$.)

A similar method should enable PECHO to deal with the inhibitory links required by ECHO to implement explanatory coherence principle E6, Competition. We saw that PECHO can handle contradictions by constructing complex variables, but it has no direct way of expressing the negative impact of one hypothesis on another when they are competing to explain a piece of evidence. The clustering technique mentioned in the last section shows how this can be done. If an ECHO network has H_1 and H_2 independently explaining E, PECHO will have to replace variable nodes for H_1 and H_2 with a combined node with values for H_1 & H_2, H_1 & not H_2, not H_1 & H_2, and not H_1 & not H_2. PECHO can enforce competition between H_1 and H_2 by requiring that $P(E/H_1$ & $H_2)$ be less than either $P(E/H_1$ & not $H_2)$ or $P(E/\text{not } H_1$ & $H_2)$. In very simple situations, it is possible to enforce competition in probabilistic networks without using clustering. Pearl describes how the effect of one cause *explaining away* another can be modeled in singly connected networks. Often in the examples to which ECHO has been applied, however, two hypotheses compete to explain more than one piece of evidence. Units representing those hypotheses are therefore connected by two different paths, and clustering or some other technique will be necessary to translate the network into one not multiply connected.

The clustering situation gets much more complicated, since H_1 may compete with other hypotheses besides H_2. In the Copernicus versus Ptolemy simulation, ECHO finds 214 pairs of competing hypotheses, and there is an important Copernican hypothesis that competes with more than 20 Ptolemaic hypotheses. In general, if a proposition P has n hypotheses participating in explaining it, either in cooperation or in competition with each other, then a clustered variable node with 2^n values will have to be created.

For example, in the Copernicus versus Ptolemy simulation, there are pieces of evidence explained by 5 Ptolemaic hypotheses working together and by 5 Copernican hypotheses. To handle both support among cohypotheses and competition between conflicting hypotheses, PECHO would need to have a single node with 1,024 values, in place of the 10 nodes corresponding to ECHO units. In fact, the node would have to be still more complicated because these 10 hypotheses compete and cohere with many others, since they participate in additional explanations. Typically, the set of hypotheses formed by collecting all those that either compete with or coexplain with some member of the set will be virtually all the hypotheses that there are. In the Copernicus simulation, there are 80 explaining hypotheses, including Ptolemaic ones, and a search shows that each is connected to every other by chains of coherence or competition. We would thus require a single hypothesis node with 2^{80} values, more than the number of milliseconds in a billion years.

Thus, dealing with competition and cohypotheses in Pearl networks can be combinatorially disastrous, although there may be more efficient methods of clustering. Pearl (1988, 201) considers an alternative method, akin to that of Lauritzen and Spiegelharter (1988), in which the nodes represent cliques in an ECHO network, such as the cluster of H_1, H_2, and E. (Cliques are subgraphs whose nodes are all adjacent to one another.) In the Copernicus simulation, there are more than 4,000 such cliques, so the reconstituted Pearl network would be much larger than the original. More important, it is not at all clear how to assign conditional probabilities in ways that yield the desired results concerning cohypotheses and competitors. Thus in principle ECHO input can be used to drive a Pearl network, but in practice the computational obstacles are formidable.

The input to ECHO also includes information about data and analogies. PECHO can implement something like explanatory-coherence principle E4, Data Priority, by special treatment of variable nodes corresponding to evidence propositions in ECHO. It would be a mistake to instantiate an evidence variable node with a value (1 0), since that would not allow the possibility that the evidence is mistaken. (ECHO can reject evidence if it does not fit with accepted hypotheses.) Pearl (1988, 170) provides a method of dummy variables, which allows a node to represent virtual evidence, an effective solution if updating can lead to low BEL values for such nodes. As for analogy, there is no direct way in a Bayesian network in which a hypothesis H_1 can support an analogous one H_2, but once again dummy nodes might be constructed to favor the hypothesis in question. Analogy is normally used to support a contested hypothesis by analogy with an established one, so little is lost if there is no symmetric link and the contested one is simply viewed as being slightly dependent on the established one. Analogy is thus viewed as contributing to the prior probability of the contested hypothesis.

In sum, the theory of explanatory coherence that is implemented in ECHO by connectionist networks (and by the other coherence algorithms in chapter 2) can also be approximately implemented by probabilistic networks. There is, however, a high computational cost associated with the alternative implementation. A massively greater amount of information in the form of conditional probabilities is needed to run the algorithms for updating probabilistic networks, and the problem of creating a probabilistic network is nontrivial: reconstruction is required to avoid loops, and care must be taken to retain information about cohypotheses and competitors. Combinatorial explosions must also be avoided.

Hence while ECHO's connectionist networks can be abstractly viewed in probabilistic terms, there are potentially great practical gains to be had by not abandoning the explanationist approach for the apparently more general probabilist one. Practically, the probabilist approach must use the explanationist one for guidance in assessing probabilities. We saw that consideration of cohypotheses and competitors puts constraints on the conditional probabilities allowable in probabilistic networks, and explanatory coherence theory can also contribute to setting prior probabilities. One can also think of the principles of analogy and data priority as giving advice on how to set prior probabilities. How far can we go with ECHO alone?

4   TACKLING PROBABILISTIC PROBLEMS WITH ECHO

If ECHO is to qualify as an alternative to probabilistic networks, it must be able to handle cases viewed as prototypical from the probabilist perspective. Consider Pearl's (1988, 49) example of Mr. Holmes at work trying to decide whether to rush home because his neighbor Mr. Watson, a practical joker, has called to say that his alarm at home has sounded. If the alarm has sounded, it may be because of a burglary or because of an earthquake. If he hears a radio report of an earthquake, his degree of confidence that there was a burglary will diminish. Appropriate input to ECHO would be the following:

(explain (BURGLARY) ALARM)

(explain (EARTHQUAKE) ALARM)

(explain (EARTHQUAKE) RADIO-REPORT)

(explain (ALARM) WATSON-CALLED)

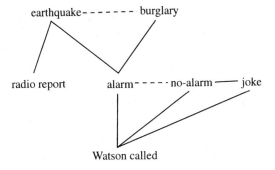

Figure 8.4
The ECHO network created for Pearl's burglary example for input given in the text. Solid lines indicate positive constraints, while dotted lines indicate negative ones.

(explain (JOKE NO-ALARM) WATSON-CALLED)

(contradict ALARM NO-ALARM)

(data (WATSON-CALLED RADIO-REPORT))

The network created by ECHO using this input is shown in figure 8.4. In implementing the competition principle E6, ECHO automatically places inhibitory links between BURGLARY and EARTHQUAKE and between ALARM and JOKE. From the above input, ECHO reaches the conclusion that there was an earthquake rather than a burglary.

This simple qualitative information may give misleading results in cases where statistical information is available. Suppose that Holmes knows that burglaries almost always set off his alarm, but earthquakes do so only rarely. ECHO need not assume that every explanation is equally good; it allows the input to include an indicator of the strength of the explanation. We could, for example, alter the above input to include these statements:

(explain (BURGLARY) ALARM 0.8)

(explain (EARTHQUAKE) ALARM 0.1)

This has the effect of making the excitatory link between BURGLARY and ALARM eight times stronger than the link between EARTHQUAKE and ALARM, so, other things being equal, ECHO will prefer the burglary hypothesis to the earthquake hypothesis.

Statistical information that provides prior probabilities can be used in similar ways. Suppose that an alarm is as likely if there is a burglary as if there is an earthquake, but Mr. Holmes knows that in his neighborhood burglaries are far more common than earthquakes. Without the radio report of the earthquake, Holmes should prefer the burglary hypothesis to the earthquake hypothesis. In Bayesian terms, the burglary base rate is higher. ECHO can implement consideration of such prior probabilities by assuming that the base rates provide a statistical explanation of the occurrences (see Harman 1986, 70). The base rates can be viewed as hypotheses that themselves explain statistical information that has been collected. We could thus have this additional input to ECHO:

(explain (BURGLARY-RATE) BURGLARY 0.1)

(explain (BURGLARY-RATE) BURGLARY-STATISTICS)

(explain (EARTHQUAKE-RATE) EARTHQUAKE-STATISTICS)

(explain (EARTHQUAKE-RATE) EARTHQUAKE 0.01)

(data (BURGLARY-STATISTICS EARTHQUAKE-STATISTICS
    WATSON-CALLED RADIO-REPORT))

The network constructed by ECHO is shown in figure 8.5.

Similar cases in which prior probabilities need to be taken into account often arise in medical diagnosis. Medical students are cautioned to prefer routine diagnoses to exotic ones with the adage, "When you hear hoof beats, think horses, not zebras."

ECHO is also capable of handling the cancer example (figure 8.3) with the prior and conditional probabilities

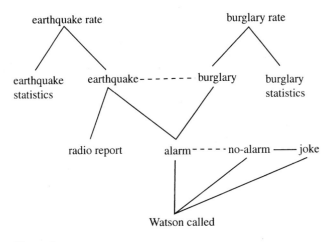

Figure 8.5
An enhanced ECHO network for the burglary example with statistical explanations.

provided by Pearl (1988, 197). Of course, ECHO's final activations are not exactly equivalent to the final probabilities that Pearl calculates, but without recourse to clustering methods, ECHO gets results that are qualitatively very similar. ECHO strongly accepts just the propositions to which Pearl's calculation gives high probability, and strongly rejects just the propositions to which he gives low probability.

ECHO is thus capable of using probabilistic information when it is available, but does not require it. There may well be cases in which a full probability distribution is known and ECHO can be shown to give a defective answer because activation adjustment does not exactly mirror the calculation of posterior probabilities. In such cases where there are few variables and the relevant probabilities are known, it is unnecessary to muddy the clear probabilistic waters with explanatory-coherence considerations. But in most real cases found in science, law, medicine, and ordinary life, the explanationist will not be open to the charge of being probabilistically incoherent, since the probabilities are sparsely available and calculating them is computationally unfeasible. What matters, then, are the qualitative considerations that explanatory coherence theory takes into account, and probabilities are at best epiphenomenal. See Thagard (1999) for further argument that explanatory coherence is crucial to causal reasoning in medicine.

It might be argued that probabilistic approaches are preferable because they provide a clear semantics for numerical assessment of hypotheses. While probability theory undoubtedly has a clear syntax, the meaning or meanings of probability is an unsolved problem. All the available interpretations, in terms of frequencies, propensities, degrees of belief, and possible worlds, can be challenged (for a review, see Cohen 1989). For scientific purposes, statistical inference based on frequencies in observed populations suffices, and we can dispense with the logically problematic and psychologically implausible notion of probabilities as degrees of belief. Frequency views of probability are difficult to apply to individual events such as "Fred has a brain tumor" and to causal hypotheses such as "Fred's headaches are caused by a brain tumor." Whereas probability theory is only a few hundred years old and requires expert calculations, people have been offering and evaluating explanations at least since the pre-Socratic philosophers. Moreover, explanatory reasoning is part of everyday life when people try to understand the behavior of the physical world and other people. Hence, instead of trying to contrive probabilistic accounts of reasoning where frequencies are not available, we should adopt the psychologically plausible and computationally efficient explanationist approach.

At the most general level, this chapter can be understood as offering a reconciliation of explanationism and probabilism. ECHO, the most detailed and comprehensive explanationist model to date, has a probabilistic interpretation. This interpretation should make the theory of explanatory coherence more respectable to probabilists, who should also appreciate how explanatory-coherence issues such as data priority, analogy, cohypotheses, and competition place constraints on probability values.

At a more local level, however, it is an open question whether explanationist or probabilist accounts are superior. Local disputes can be epistemological, psychological, or technological. If one accepts the view of Goldman (1986) that power and speed, as well as reliability, are epistemological goals, then explanationist models can be viewed as desirable ways of proceeding apace with causal inferences, while probabilistic models are still lost in computation. Similarly, the computational cost associated with the probabilistic interpretation of explanatory coherence suggests that such models may be inappropriate as models of human psychology. ECHO and probabilistic networks can be compared as models of human performance, with probabilistic networks apparently predicting that people should be much slower at inference tasks that require the most work to translate into probabilistic terms. We saw such cases arise when there are cohypotheses and competitors. ECHO takes such complications in stride, whereas Pearl networks require computations to realign networks and many more conditional probabilities to handle such cases. It should therefore be possible to present people with examples of increasing complexity and determine whether their reasoning ability declines rapidly, as the complexity of probabilistic computations suggest.

Similarly for technological applications in expert systems, ECHO may perform better than probabilistic networks. If rich probabilistic information is generally not available and if the domains are complex enough with cohypotheses and competitors, then ECHO may be more effective than probabilistic cases. The issue must be decided on a local basis, application by application, just as the psychological issue depends on experiments that have not yet been done. My conjecture is that the psychological and technological applicability of explanationist and probabilist techniques will vary from domain to domain with the following approximate ordering from most appropriate for explanationist to most appropriate for probabilist approaches: social reasoning, scientific reasoning, legal reasoning, medical diagnosis, fault diagnosis, games of chance. The psychological and technological answers need not be the same: diagnosis may well be an enterprise where a nonpsychological probabilistic approach can bring technological gains.

Much remains to be done in the comparative evaluation of the computational and psychological merits of the probabilistic and coherentist approaches to causal reasoning. Following Pearl's seminal 1988 book, there have been improvements in the computational implementation of Bayesian networks, but solutions have not been found for such fundamental problems as the need for many unavailable conditional probabilities and the lack of a frequency interpretation for individual events and causal hypotheses. Since the theory of explanatory coherence has a probabilistic approximation, albeit a computationally expensive one, the analysis in this chapter suggests that probabilism might reign supreme in the epistemology of Eternal Beings.

But explanationism survives in epistemology for the rest of us.

6 SUMMARY

Causal reasoning can be understood qualitatively in terms of explanatory coherence or quantitatively in terms of probability theory. Comparison of these approaches can be done most informatively by looking at computational models, using ECHO's coherence networks and Pearl's probabilistic ones. ECHO can be given a probabilistic interpretation, but there are many conceptual and computational problems that make it difficult to replace coherence networks with probabilistic ones. On the other hand, ECHO provides a psychologically plausible and computationally efficient model of some kinds of probabilistic causal reasoning. Hence coherence theory need not give way to probability theory as the basis for epistemology and decision making.

9

The Future of Coherence

One of the most attractive reasons for putting probability theory at the center of epistemology is that it ties belief closely with decision: combining probabilities with utilities allows us to calculate the expected utilities of different actions and choose the best. This book has presented an alternative approach in which inference concerning what to believe and what to do are both based on coherence. The mathematically exact, computationally feasible, and psychologically plausible account of coherence presented in chapter 2 provided the basis for understanding the development of ordinary, scientific, and metaphysical knowledge (chapters 3 and 4). Adding deliberative coherence into the picture provided a basis for understanding how people make decisions, including judgments about what is right and wrong (chapter 5). Human inference is a matter of emotion as well as cold cognition, and chapter 6 showed how a theory of emotional coherence can be constructed as an extension of the theory of coherence as constraint satisfaction, with applications to understanding diverse judgments ranging from trust to aesthetics. The development of knowledge is a social as well as a cognitive process, and chapter 7 described a theory of consensus based on coherence and communication. In chapter 8, I argued that causal reasoning in many domains is more naturally construed in terms of explanatory coherence than in terms of probability theory.

The results of these inquiries illustrate, I hope, the fecundity of cognitive naturalism, the approach to philosophy in which psychological theories and computational models are combined with philosophical reflection to produce theories of knowledge, reality, ethics, politics, and aesthetics. Cognitive naturalism does not abandon the traditional philosophical concern with epistemological and ethical justification, nor does it try to derive the normative from the descriptive. The aim, rather, is to interweave normative philosophical theories with empirical scientific ones so that they form a coherent whole. Connecting philosophy with empirical and computational investigations does not signal its demise, but rather opens up new possibilities for pursuing answers to its ancient and inescapable questions.

I do not pretend to have answered all these questions in this essay. Although the treatment of coherence in chapter 2 and later is far more comprehensive than previous discussions by philosophers and cognitive scientists, my application of coherence notions to problems in epistemology, metaphysics, ethics, political philosophy, and aesthetics has sometimes devoted only a few pages to important issues that deserve volumes. I have aimed for demonstration of the breadth of the idea of coherence as cognitive and emotional constraint satisfaction, at the expense of depth in many of the suggested applications. It is not circular reasoning to note that one of the great advantages of my version of coherentism is that is highly coherent, applying the same conception of coherence as constraint satisfaction to many diverse kinds of thinking.

Much remains to be done to work out the philosophical and psychological consequences of the hypothesis that a great deal of human thought consists of coherence judgments that maximize constraint satisfaction. The remainder of this chapter suggests a series of research projects that would help to fill in the substantial gaps in the coherentist approach to cognition and philosophy that this book has merely sketched.

In ethics and epistemology, many philosophers have advocated the usefulness of Rawls's notion of reflective equilibrium. According to Elgin (1996, ix), "A system of thought is in reflective equilibrium when its components are reasonable in light of one another, and the account they comprise is reasonable in light of our antecedent convictions about the subject at hand." Elgin sees reflective equilibrium as an alternative to coherence, claiming that a system is coherent if its components mesh but that reflective equilibrium requires in addition reasonableness with respect to antecedent commitments. Obviously, the kind of coherence she rejects is very different from the discriminating and broad coherence that I advocated in chapter 4. In fact, you legitimately reach reflective equilibrium only if your system is maximally coherent, that is, if it maximizes satisfaction of multiple constraints, including ones involving evidence based on observation and experiment. Reflective equilibrium is an attractive metaphor for describing the end state of inquiry, but it depends on well-developed theories of coherence-based inference to provide an explanation of how equilibrium can and should be reached. Coherence as computational constraint satisfaction provides the overall framework for understanding reflective equilibrium in both epistemology and ethics, with specific theories of explanatory, deductive, conceptual, analogical, perceptual, and deliberative coherence providing the details concerning the elements and constraints involved. I agree with Stich (1988) that reflective equilibrium is an insufficient basis for a theory of epistemological and ethical justification.

Still, it would be desirable to have a fuller account of how coherence-based inference dynamically produces reflective equilibrium. The examples discussed in chapter 3 and 4 presume that an individual is presented all at once with an array of elements and coherence relations, with maximization of constraint satisfaction proceeding in a single step. More realistically, people's beliefs develop incrementally, with equilibrium being achieved in smaller steps than one global coherence calculation (Hoadley, Ranney, and Schank 1994). Studying this process psychologically and computationally should provide a better understanding of how people can reach reflective equilibria that are optimal in that they maximize the coherence of all available information, and also a better understanding of how people sometimes reach equilibria that are suboptimal.

A psychologically realistic theory of coherence-based inference should also have practical applications to help people reason better. I often teach an undergraduate class on critical thinking, and do so within the cognitive naturalist framework presented in this book. Most critical-thinking textbooks assume, in line with philosophical orthodoxy, that human inference is and should be based on arguments, with deduction providing the gold standard of what an argument should look like. Although arguments are important for indicating the elements and constraints relevant to making an inference, they give a misleadingly linear picture of how inferences are actually made. If inference is coherence-based, with emotional as well as cognitive constraints contributing, it becomes much easier to see why people are so frequently prone to inferential errors that have nothing to do with deduction. The standard philosophical list of fallacies does not begin to capture the array of common reasoning errors that psychologists have identified (e.g., Gilovich 1991). Cognitive naturalism can draw on research concerning the psychological processes that can lead people to think poorly, while at the same time urging reasoning strategies that encourage assembly of all the information that people need to maximize explanatory and other kinds of coherence. Ranney and Schank (1998) describe an educational program, Convince Me, that uses explanatory-coherence computations to help students develop and revise arguments, but working out how the coherentist understanding of reason and emotion can be used systematically to produce a new approach to critical thinking is a task that remains to be done. It is also possible to derive insights into how people can improve their decision making by drawing lessons from the theories of deliberative and emotional coherence (Thagard, forthcoming). In chapter 5, I rejected the common philosophical view that intuitions contribute to ethical justification, but intuitions can be a valuable part of individual decision making when they provide an emotional summary of tacit judgments about what is most important to a person.

The metaphysical applications of coherence theory also need to be much further developed. I hope, for example, that someone with an interest in theology will work out in much greater detail the explanatory and analogical structure of the case for and against the existence of God. However, I suspect that further analysis along these lines would only account for the attitudes of small numbers of religious believers, with many more asserting that their beliefs rest on faith rather than reason. I would like to see the development of a theory of faith as a kind of emotional coherence, in which belief in God is adopted because of its contribution to satisfaction of personal and social goals that are important to many people. This theory would not provide any further justification of theistic beliefs, but would be valuable for solving the psychological puzzle of why so many people believe in God despite the paucity of good evidence.

For more philosophical purposes, it would also he highly desirable to say more about the connection between coherence and truth. Millgram (2000) raises doubts about whether the constraint-satisfaction characterization of coherence is fully adequate for philosophical purposes. His main objection is that it is not appropriate for epistemology, because it provides no guarantee that the most coherent available theory will be true. In a forthcoming reply, I argue that the constraint-satisfaction account of coherence is not at all flawed in the ways that Millgram describes and in fact satisfies the philosophical, computational, and psychological prerequisites for the development of epistemological and ethical theories (see http://cogsci.uwaterloo.ca/Articles/Pages/coh.price.html). Nevertheless, I would like to see a much fuller account of the conditions under which progressively coherent theories can be said to approximate the truth.

Chapter 5 barely begins the discussion of the applicability of coherentist ideas to ethics and politics. The topics discussed in that chapter—capital punishment, abortion, and the justification of the state—need to receive a much fuller treatment to bring out many more of the elements and constraints that are relevant to reaching conclusions by coherence maximization. Moreover, there are many other ethical and political issues that deserve a full discussion from the perspective of coherence as constraint satisfaction. At the methodological level, more thorough critical analysis is needed of the appropriate contribution of ethical thought experiments to analogical and general coherence. If I am right that political decisions primarily are and should be based on maximizing the three constraints of freedom, flourishing, and fairness, then much more needs to be said about how we can assess the relative importance and appropriate tradeoffs of these constraints.

The theory of emotional coherence developed in chapter 6 is limited by its emphasis on positive and negative valences, and needs to be expanded to take into account the full range of human emotions. Our understanding of the cognitive neuroscience of emotions is increasing rapidly, and I hope that the theory of emotional coherence will expand to take these developments into account. Like other artificial-neural-network models used in cognitive science, my computational models of coherence are enormously simplified in comparison with the complexity of the brain and its neurons. In recent years, dramatic progress has been made in understanding the brain structures and mechanisms involved in emotions (e.g., Panksepp 1998). I plan to make my computational models more neurologically realistic by introducing distributed representations and more complex structures corresponding to brain anatomy.

The current version of HOTCO uses localist representations in which each unit (neuronlike node) represents a whole concept or proposition. Obviously, the brain does not have a single node for representations such as *Clinton*, but somehow distributes the information across numerous neurons. In current work on artificial neural networks, there are two main ways of distributing complex information across multiple nodes: vector coding and neural synchrony. Vector coding represents a complex piece of information such as a proposition by a vector of k real numbers, corresponding to the firing rates of k neurons. Encoding and decoding schemes have been devised to perform variable binding and thus distinguish the proposition *Clinton loves Hillary* from *Hillary loves Clinton*, a distinction that was not possible in early artificial neural networks with simple nodes (Smolensky 1990). Eliasmith and Thagard (forthcoming) employ vector coding to produce distributed representation of complex relational propositions used in analogical mapping.

Within vector-coding schemes, the natural way to attach emotional valences to representations is to treat them as vectors that are algebraically blended with the vector that represents the proposition. Just as the vector representing *Clinton loves Hillary* is built by combining vectors for *Clinton*, *loves*, and *Hillary*, an enhanced vector could combine the proposition vector with an emotion vector representing the emotional attitude toward the proposition. In contrast to HOTCO, which can only associate positive and negative valences with nodes, using vectors to encode emotions would make possible the association of many different emotions with a proposition or other representation. The positive or negative emotions associated with *Clinton*, for example, could include liking, disliking, admiration, disgust, and so on.

The other main method for producing complex distributed representations in artificial neural networks is neural synchrony, which uses time as an additional means of binding information together (e.g., Hummel and Holyoak 1997). Representations such as *Clinton*, *Hillary*, *loves*, *agent*, and *recipient* are each represented by groups of artificial neurons with their own firing patterns, and relations between the representations are modeled by synchronies among those firing patterns, with neurons for related representations all firing or all not firing. Within this system, an emotion could be represented by a group of neurons that fire in synchrony with the neurons corresponding to the object of the emotion. It would be desirable to produce both neural-synchrony and vector-coding models of emotional inference in order to determine which is a more psychologically and neurologically plausible way of combining emotions with distributed representations.

Another way in which artificial-neural-network models such as HOTCO are not neurologically realistic is that they have few neuronal units and lack the high degree of anatomical organization found in the brain. As chapter 6 reported, Damasio and his colleagues have identified regions of the human brain whose damage consistently compromises processes involving connections between reasoning and emotion, which leads to defective reasoning in the personal and social domains (Damasio 1994; Damasio, Damasio, and Christen 1996). The crucial regions include the ventromedial prefrontal cortices, the amygdala, and the somatasensory cortices in the right hemisphere. Contrary to the popular view that emotions interfere with rational thought, Damasio and his colleagues have found that in patients with damage to these regions, the inability to integrate emotional considerations with cognitive planning actually produces inferior decisions. I hope to model the importance of these regions by organizing the units in my artificial neural networks in much more modular fashion.

Another promising area for research is the role of emotions in scientific thinking. Scientists are supposed to be dispassionate, but scientific cognition is often highly emotional. Here is a passage from James Watson's *Double Helix*, describing work leading up to the discovery of the structure of DNA; I have highlighted in boldface the positive emotion words and in italics the negative emotion words.

As the clock went past midnight I was becoming more and more **pleased**. There had been far too many days when Frances and I *worried* that DNA structure might turn out to be superficially very *dull*, suggesting nothing about either its replication or its function in controlling cell biochemistry. But now, to my **delight** and **amazement**, the answer was turning out to be profoundly **interesting**. For over two hours I **happily** lay awake with pairs of adenine residues whirling in front of my closed eyes. Only for brief moments did the *fear* shoot through me that an idea this good could be wrong. (Watson 1969, 118)

Watson's short book contains hundreds of such emotional expressions. Positive emotions involved in mental states such as interest, wonder, and excitement contribute to the pursuit of potentially important scientific ideas, while negative emotions involved in boredom, worry, and fear help to steer scientists away from unpromising pursuits. I hope to extend my theory of emotional coherence and link it to previous computational work on scientific discovery, producing a theory of the role of emotions as inputs and outputs of scientific discoveries.

In addition to helping to motivate problem solving and discovery, emotions attend the evaluation of scientific theories: highly coherent theories are viewed as elegant and beautiful, while ad hoc theories are rejected as ugly. My theory of emotional coherence can be extended to model the positive aesthetic feelings that attend the adoption of a highly coherent theory, as well as the negative feelings involved in the entertainment of unsatisfactory ones. Scientists' decisions to pursue answers to some questions rather than others seem based in part on emotional reactions such as surprise and excitement. I am more interested in the aesthetics of science than in the aesthetics of art, literature, or music, but I hope that philosophers and psychologists more inclined towards those areas will expand on my sketchy account of the role of emotional coherence in aesthetics.

A long-term objective for future work on emotional coherence would be to develop a theory of emotional change. The theory and computational model of emotional coherence are intended to explain why people make the emotional judgments that they do, but the theory and model do not address the question of how such judgments can change over time. Emotion changes can include minor alterations in attitudes (e.g., "I used to like football, but I don't anymore") to major emotional shifts such as occur when people fall in love, turn their lives around through psychotherapy, or undergo religious or political conversions. It should be possible to build onto the theory of emotional coherence to develop a comprehensive theory of the cognitive and affective mechanisms that underlie emotional change, analogous to the theory of conceptual change that I developed to explain scientific revolutions (Thagard 1992b, 1999). We need to be able to answer questions such as the following: How are emotional constraints formed? How do elements acquire new input valences? How do changes in the valences of some elements contribute to dramatic shifts in attitudes towards persons and situations? Computational answers to these questions should help generate a model of both minor and major emotional changes. There is a substantial literature in social psychology on variables that affect attitude changes, but there is very little work on the cognitive-emotional mechanisms that produce such changes.

As chapter 7 stated, my model of consensus as communication plus coherence is highly idealized, and the development of more realistic models would shed further light on how consensus is achieved in science and other enterprises. As I indicated at the end of chapter 8, there is a need for further comparative evaluation of the computational and psychological merits of probabilistic and coherentist approaches to causal reasoning. I would like to see expanded computational experiments in which large ECHO networks are reinterpreted as Bayesian networks and simulated using one of the various programs now available for computing probabilistically (see, for example, the HUGIN system at http://www.hugin.dk/). Such experiments should be done in numerous domains, such as scientific, medical, and legal reasoning. For example, it would be desirable to construct a very large analysis of a legal trial, comparable to that performed by Wigmore (1937), and to determine the comparative feasibility of implementing the causal relations essential to legal inferences in Bayesian networks and the explanatory coherence program ECHO.

I have outlined these projects to indicate that there is much to be done on the coherentist research project in cognitive science, in synchrony with the philosophical movement of cognitive naturalism. Philosophy can go beyond analyzing concepts, conducting a priori investigations, and studying the great philosophers of the past. Borrowing ideas and methods from psychology and other sciences, it can help to develop robust theories of how people do and should think. Computational modeling provides a valuable methodology for working out and testing the feasibility of different theories of how people can increase their empirical and ethical knowledge. The coherentist approach, working within the theory of coherence as constraint satisfaction, is psychologically realistic and computationally feasible, yet it can contribute to the traditional goal of philosophy to be prescriptive as well as descriptive of human thought and action. Philosophy and cognitive science can thrive together in the twenty-first century.

References

Achinstein, P. (1991). *Particles and waves*. Oxford: Oxford University Press.

Allen, R. J. (1994). Factual ambiguity and a theory of evidence. *Northwestern University Law Review* 88: 604–660.

Anderson, N. (1974). Information integration theory: a brief survey. In D. H. Krantz, R. C. Atkinson, R. D. Luce, and P. Suppes (eds.), *Contemporary developments in mathematical psychology* (vol. 2, pp. 236–305). San Francisco: W. H. Freeman.

Anonymous. (1996). *Primary colors*. New York: Random House.

Aristotle. (1984). *The complete works of Aristotle*. Princeton: Princeton University Press.

Arrow, K. J. (1963). *Social choice and individual values*. Second ed. New York: Wiley.

Ash, M. G. (1995). *Gestalt psychology in German culture, 1890–1967*. Cambridge: Cambridge University Press.

Audi, R. (1993). Fallibilist foundationalism and holistic coherentism. In L. P. Pojman (ed.), *The theory of knowledge: classic and contemporary readings* (pp. 263–279). Belmont, Calif.: Wadsworth.

Bacchus, F., and van Beek, P. (1998). On the conversion between non-binary and binary constraint satisfaction problems. *Proceedings of the National Conference on Artificial Intelligence (AAAI-98)* (pp. 311–318). Menlo Park, Calif.: AAAI Press.

Baird, R. M., and Rosenbaum, S. E. (eds.), (1993). *The ethics of abortion*. Buffalo: Prometheus Books.

Baker, G. L., and Gollub, J. P. (1990). *Chaotic dynamics: an introduction*. Cambridge: Cambridge University Press.

Barnes, A. (1998). *Reading other minds*. Unpublished Ph.D. thesis, University of Waterloo, Waterloo, Ontario.

Barnes, A., and Thagard, P. (1997). Empathy and analogy. *Dialogue: Canadian Philosophical Review* 36: 705–720.

Batson, C. D., Sympson, S. C., Hindman, J. L., Decruz, P., Todd, R. M., Weeks, J. L., Jennings, G., and Burris, C. T. (1996). "I've been there, too": effect on empathy of prior experience with a need. *Personality and Social Psychology Bulletin* 22: 474–482.

Beck, A. T. (1976). *Cognitive therapy and the emotional disorders*. New York: International Universities Press.

Beck, A. T., Rush, A. J., Shaw, B. F., and Emery, G. (1979). *Cognitive therapy of depression*. New York: Guilford.

Bender, J. W. (ed.), (1989). *The current state of the coherence theory*. Dordrecht: Kluwer.

Bianco, W. T. (1994). *Trust: representatives and constituents*. Ann Arbor: University of Michigan Press.

Blake, R. (1960). Theory of hypothesis among renaissance astronomers. In R. Blake, C. Ducasse, and E. H. Madden (eds.), *Theories of scientific method* (pp. 22–49). Seattle: University of Washington Press.

Blanchette, I., and Dunbar, K. (1997). Constraints underlying analogy use in a real-world context: politics. In M. G. Shafto, and P. Langley (eds.), *Proceedings of the Nineteenth Annual Conference of the Cognitive Science Society* (pp. 867). Mahwah, N.J.: Erlbaum.

Blanshard, B. (1939). *The nature of thought*. Vol. 2. London: George Allen and Unwin.

Bloor, D. (1991). *Knowledge and social imagery*. Second ed. Chicago: University of Chicago Press.

BonJour, L. (1985). *The structure of empirical knowledge*. Cambridge: Harvard University Press.

Bosanquet, B. (1920). *Implication and linear inference*. London: Macmillan.

Bower, G. H. (1981). Mood and memory. *American Psychologist* 36: 129–148.

Bower, G. H. (1991). Mood congruity of social judgments. In J. P. Forgas (ed.), *Emotion and social judgments* (pp. 31–53). Oxford: Pergamon Press.

Bradley, D. R., and Petry, H. M. (1977). Organizational determinants of subjective contour: the subjective Necker cube. *American Journal of Psychology* 90: 253–262.

Bradley, F. H. (1914). *Essays on truth and reality*. Oxford: Clarendon Press.

Brink, D. O. (1989). *Moral realism and the foundations of ethics*. Cambridge: Cambridge University Press.

Brush, S. G. (1996). *Fruitful encounters: the origin of the solar system and of the moon from Chamberlin to Apollo*. Vol. 3 of *A history of modern planetary physics*. Cambridge: Cambridge University Press.

Buchanan, B., and Shortliffe, E. (eds.), (1984). *Rule-based expert systems*. Reading, Mass.: Addison Wesley.

Byrne, M. D. (1995). The convergence of explanatory coherence and the story model: a case study in juror decision. In J. D. Moore, and J. F. Lehman (eds.), *Proceedings of the Seventeenth Annual Conference of the Cognitive Science Society* (pp. 539–543). Mahwah, N.J.: Erlbaum.

Caputi, M. (1996). National identity in contemporary theory. *Political psychology* 17: 683–694.

Carnap, R. (1950). *Logical foundations of probability*. Chicago: University of Chicago Press.

Cartwright, N. (1983). *How the laws of physics lie*. Oxford: Clarendon Press.

Chalmers, D. J. (1996). *The conscious mind*. Oxford: Oxford University Press.

Charniak, E. (1993). *Statistical language learning*. Cambridge: MIT Press.

Churchland, P. M. (1995). *The engine of reason: the seat of the soul*. Cambridge: MIT Press.

Churchland, P. S. (1986). *Neurophilosophy*. Cambridge: MIT Press.

Cohen, L. J. (1977). *The probable and the provable*. Oxford: Clarendon Press.

Cohen, L. J. (1989). *An introduction to the philosophy of induction and probability*. Oxford: Clarendon.

Collingwood, R. G. (1997). *Outlines of a philosophy of art*. Bristol: Thoemmes Press.

Cooper, G. (1990). The computational complexity of probabilistic inference using Bayesian belief networks. *Artificial Intelligence* 42: 393–405.

Cooper, J., and Fazio, R. H. (1984). A new look at dissonance theory. In L. Berkowitz (ed.), *Advances in experimental social psychology* (vol. 17). New York: Academic Press.

Cottrell, G. W. (1988). A model of lexical acces of ambiguous words. In S. L. Small, G. W. Cottrell, and M. K. Tanenhaus (eds.), *Lexical ambiguity resolution* (pp. 179–194). San Mateo: Morgan Kaufman.

Crick, F. (1994). *The astonishing hypothesis: the scientific search for the soul*. London: Simon and Schuster.

Cummins, R. (1998). Reflection on reflective equilibrium. In M. R. DePaul, and W. Ramsey (eds.), *Rethinking intuition* (pp. 113–127). Lanham: Rowman and Littlefield.

D'Ambrosio, B. (1999). Inference in Bayesian networks. *AI Magazine* 20 (no. 2, Summer): 21–36.

Damasio, A. R. (1994). *Descartes' error*. New York: G. P. Putnam's Sons.

Damasio, A. R., Damasio, H., and Christen, Y. (eds.), (1996). *Neurobiology of decision making*. Berlin: Springer-Verlag.

Daniels, N. (1979). Wide reflective equilibrium and theory acceptance in ethics. *Journal of Philosophy* 76: 256–282.

Daniels, N. (1996). *Justice and justification: reflective equilibrium in theory and practice*. Cambridge: Cambridge University Press.

Davidson, D. (1986). A coherence theory of truth and knowledge. In E. Lepore (ed.), *Truth and interpretation*. Oxford: Basil Blackwell.

Davies, P., and Brown, J. (1988). *Superstrings*. Cambridge: Cambridge University Press.

De Sousa, R. (1988). *The rationality of emotion*. Cambridge: MIT Press.

DeGeorge, R. (1990). Ethics and coherence. *Proceedings and Addresses of the American Philosophical Association* 64 (no. 3): 39–52.

DeMarco, J. P. (1994). *A coherence theory in ethics*. Amsterdam: Rodopi.

Dennett, D. (1991). *Consciousness explained*. Boston: Little, Brown.

Derbyshire, J. D., and Derbyshire, I. (1996). *Political systems of the world.* New York: St. Martin's Press.

Deutsch, M. (1973). *The resolution of conflict.* New Haven: Yale University Press.

Dunn, J. (1993). Trust. In R. E. Goodin, and P. Pettit (eds.), *A companion to contemporary political philosophy* (pp. 638–644). Oxford: Blackwell.

Elgin, C. Z. (1996). *Considered judgment.* Princeton: Princeton University Press.

Eliasmith, C., and Thagard, P. (1997). Waves, particles, and explanatory coherence. *British Journal for the Philosophy of Science* 48: 1–19.

Ellis, A. (1962). *Reason and emotion in psychotherapy.* New York: Lyle Stuart.

Ellis, A. (1971). *Growth through reason.* Palo Alto: Science and Behavior Books.

Ellis, R. E. (1992). *Coherence and verification in ethics.* Lanham, Md.: University Press of America.

Falkenhainer, B., Forbus, K. D., and Gentner, D. (1989). The structure-mapping engine: algorithms and examples. *Artificial Intelligence* 41: 1–63.

Feldman, J. A. (1981). A connectionist model of visual memory. In G. E. Hinton, and J. A. Anderson (eds.), *Parallel models of associative memory* (pp. 49–81). Hillsdale, N.J.: Erlbaum.

Fenno, R. F. (1978). *Home style: house members in their districts.* Boston: Little, Brown.

Festinger, L. (1957). *A theory of cognitive dissonance.* Stanford: Stanford University Press.

Fishbein, M., and Ajzen, I. (1975). *Belief, attitude, intention, and behavior.* Reading, Mass.: Addison-Wesley.

Fiske, S., and Pavelchak, M. (1986). Category-based vs. piecemeal-based affective responses: developments in schema-triggered affect. In R. Sorrentino, and E. Higgins (eds.), *Handbook of motivation and cognition* (vol. 1, pp. 167–203). New York: Guilford.

Flanagan, O. (1996). Ethics naturalized: ethics as human ecology. In L. May, M. Friedman, and A. Clark (eds.), *Mind and morals: essays on ethics and cognitive science* (pp. 19–44). Cambridge: MIT Press.

Frank, R. H. (1988). *Passions within reason.* New York: Norton.

Frege, G. (1964). *The basic laws of arithmetic.* Trans. by M. Furth. Berkeley: University of California Press.

Frey, B. J. (1998). *Graphical models for machine learning and digital communication.* Cambridge: MIT Press.

Frijda, N. H. (1993). Moods, emotion episodes, and emotions. In M. Lewis, and J. M. Haviland (eds.), *Handbook of emotions* (pp. 381–403). New York: Guilford.

Frith, U. (1989). *Autism: explaining the enigma.* Oxford: Basil Blackwell.

Frith, U., and Snowling, M. (1983). Reading for meaning and reading for sound in autistic and dyslexic children. *British Journal of Developmental Psychology* 1: 329–342.

Fukuyama, F. (1995). *Trust: social virtues and the creation of prosperity.* New York: Free Press.

Gambetta, D. (ed.), (1988). *Trust: making and breaking cooperative relations.* Oxford: Basil Blackwell.

Gardner, H. (1985). *The mind's new science.* New York: Basic Books.

Garey, M., and Johnson, D. (1979). *Computers and intractability.* New York: Freeman.

Gibbard, A. (1990). *Wise choices, apt feelings.* Cambridge: Harvard University Press.

Giere, R. (1988). *Explaining science: a cognitive approach.* Chicago: University of Chicago Press.

Giere, R. N. (1999). *Science without laws.* Chicago: University of Chicago Press.

Gilovich, T. (1991). *How we know what isn't so.* New York: Free Press.

Glynn, P. (1997). *God: the evidence.* Rocklin, Calif.: Prima Publishing.

Goemans, M. X., and Williamson, D. P. (1995). Improved approximation algorithms for maximum cut and satisfiability problems using semidefinite programming. *Journal of the Association for Computing Machinery* 42: 1115–1145.

Goldman, A. I. (1986). *Epistemology and cognition.* Cambridge: Harvard University Press.

Goldman, A. I. (1992). *Liaisons: philosophy meets the cognitive and social sciences.* Cambridge: MIT Press.

Goodman, N. (1965). *Fact, fiction, and forecast.* Second ed. Indianapolis: Bobbs-Merrill.

Group for the Advancement of Psychiatry (GAP) (1987). *Us and them: the psychology of ethnonationalism.* New York: Brunner/Mazel.

Gwartney, J., and Lawson, R. (1997). *Economic freedom in the world, 1997.* Vancouver: Fraser Institute.

Gwartney, J., and Lawson, R. (1998). *Economic freedom in the world: 1998/1999 interim report.* Vancouver: Fraser Institute.

Haack, S. (1993). *Evidence and inquiry: towards reconstruction in epistemology.* Oxford: Blackwell.

Hacking, I. (1975). *The emergence of probability.* Cambridge: Cambridge University Press.

Hardwig, J. (1991). The role of trust in knowledge. *Journal of Philosophy* 88: 693–708.

Hardy, G. H. (1967). *A mathematician's apology.* Cambridge: Cambridge University Press.

Harman, G. (1973). *Thought.* Princeton: Princeton University Press.

Harman, G. (1986). *Change in view: principles of reasoning.* Cambridge: MIT Press.

Hartmann, W. K., Phillips, R. J., and Taylor, G. J. (eds.), (1986). *Origin of the moon.* Houston: Lunar and Planetary Institute.

Hegel, G. (1967). *The phenomenology of mind.* Trans. by J. Baillie. New York: Harper and Row. Originally published in 1807.

Heider, U. (1994). *Anarchism: left, right, and green.* San Francisco: City Light Books.

Hesse, M. (1974). *The structure of scientific inference.* Berkeley: University of California Press.

Hoadley, C. M., Ranney, M., and Schank, P. (1994). Wander ECHO: a connectionist simulation of limited coherence. In A. Ram, and K. Eiselt (eds.), *Proceedings of the Sixteenth Annual Conference of the Cognitive Science Society* (pp. 421–426). Hillsdale, N.J.: Erlbaum.

Holland, J. H., Holyoak, K. J., Nisbett, R. E., and Thagard, P. R. (1986). *Induction: processes of inference, learning, and discovery.* Cambridge: MIT Press.

Holmes, J. G. (1991). Trust and the appraisal process in close relationships. In W. H. Jones, and D. Perlman (eds.), *Advances in personal relationships* (vol. 2, pp. 57–104). London: Jessica Kingsley.

Holyoak, K. J., and Spellman, B. A. (1993). Thinking. *Annual Review of Psychology* 44: 265–315.

Holyoak, K. J., and Thagard, P. (1989). Analogical mapping by constraint satisfaction. *Cognitive Science* 13: 295–355.

Holyoak, K. J., and Thagard, P. (1995). *Mental leaps: analogy in creative thought.* Cambridge: MIT Press.

Holyoak, K. J., and Thagard, P. (1997). The analogical mind. *American Psychologist* 52: 35–44.

Horwich, P. (1982). *Probability and evidence.* Cambridge: Cambridge University Press.

Howson, C., and Urbach, P. (1989). *Scientific reasoning: the Bayesian tradition.* Lasalle, Ill.: Open Court.

Hrycej, T. (1990). Gibbs sampling in Bayesian networks. *Artificial Intelligence* 46: 351–363.

Hummel, J. E., and Biederman, I. (1997). Dynamic binding in a neural network for shape recognition. *Psychological Review* 104: 427–466.

Hurley, S. L. (1989). *Natural reasons: personality and polity.* New York: Oxford University Press.

Husserl, E. (1962). *Ideas: general introduction to pure phenomenology.* Trans. by W. R. B. Gibson. New York: Collier.

Hutcheson, F. (1973). *Francis Hutcheson: an inquiry concerning beauty, order, harmony, design.* The Hague: M. Nijhoff.

Ignatieff, M. (1993). *Blood and belonging: journeys into the new nationalism.* Toronto: Viking.

Jeffrey, R. (1983). *The logic of decision.* Second ed. Chicago: University of Chicago Press. First published in 1965.

Johnson, M. L. (1993). *Moral imagination: implications of cognitive science for ethics.* Chicago: University of Chicago Press.

Johnson, M. L. (1996). How moral psychology changes moral theory. In L. May, M. Friedman, and A. Clark (eds.), *Mind and morals: essays on ethics and cognitive science* (pp. 45–68). Cambridge: MIT Press.

Jordan, M. I. (ed.), (1998). *Learning in graphical models.* Dordrecht: Kluwer.

Josephson, J. R., and Josephson, S. G. (eds.), (1994). *Abductive inference: computation, philosophy, technology*. Cambridge: Cambridge University Press.

Kahneman, D., Slovic, P., and Tversky, A. (1982). *Judgment under uncertainty: heuristics and biases*. New York: Cambridge University Press.

Kaplan, M. (1996). *Decision theory as philosophy*. Cambridge: Cambridge University Press.

Kecmanovic, D. (1996). *The mass psychology of ethnonationalism*. New York: Plenum.

Keith-Spiegel, P. (1972). Early conceptions of humor: varieties and issues. In J. H. Goldstein, and P. E. McGhee (eds.), *The psychology of humor* (pp. 3–39). New York: Academic Press.

Keynes, J. M. (1921). *A treatise on probability*. London: Macmillan.

Kintsch, W. (1988). The role of knowledge in discourse comprehension: a construction-integration model. *Psychological Review* 95: 163–182.

Kintsch, W. (1998). *Comprehension: a paradigm for cognition*. Cambridge: Cambridge University Press.

Kitcher, P. (1983). *The nature of mathematical knowledge*. New York: Oxford University Press.

Kitcher, P., and Salmon, W. (eds.), (1989). *Scientific explanation*. Minneapolis: University of Minnesota Press.

Koffka, K. (1935). *Principles of gestalt psychology*. New York: Harcourt Brace.

Kosslyn, S. M. (1994). *Image and brain: the resolution of the imagery debate*. Cambridge: MIT Press.

Kramer, R. M., and Tyler, T. R. (eds.), (1996). *Trust in organizations*. Thousand Oaks, Calif.: Sage.

Kunda, Z. (1987). Motivation and inference: self-serving generation and evaluation of causal theories. *Journal of Personality and Social Psychology* 53: 636–647.

Kunda, Z. (1990). The case for motivated inference. *Psychological Bulletin* 108: 480–498.

Kunda, Z., Miller, D., and Claire, T. (1990). Combining social concepts: the role of causal reasoning. *Cognitive Science* 14: 551–577.

Kunda, Z., and Oleson, K. C. (1995). Maintaining stereotypes in the face of disconfirmation: constructing grounds for subtyping deviants. *Journal of Personality and Social Psychology* 68: 565–579.

Kunda, Z., and Thagard, P. (1996). Forming impressions from stereotypes, traits, and behaviors: a parallel-constraint-satisfaction theory. *Psychological Review* 103: 284–308.

Kusch, M. (1995). *Psychologism*. London: Routledge.

Kyburg, H. (1983). *Epistemology and inference*. Minneapolis: University of Minnesota Press.

Lakoff, G. (1996). *Moral politics: what conservatives know that liberals don't*. Chicago: University of Chicago Press.

Larson, D. W. (1997). Trust and missed opportunities in international relations. *Political Psychology* 18: 701–734.

Latouche, D. (1990). Betrayal and indignation on the Canadian trail. In P. Resnick (ed.), *Letters to a Québécois friend* (pp. 85–119). Montreal: McGill-Queen's University Press.

Latour, B., and Woolgar, S. (1986). *Laboratory life: the construction of scientific facts*. Princeton, N.J.: Princeton University Press.

Laudan, L. (1981). *Science and hypothesis*. Dordrecht: Reidel.

Lauritzen, S., and Spiegelharter, D. (1988). Local computation with probabilities in graphical structures and their applications to expert systems. *Journal of the Royal Statistical Society* B 50: 157–224.

LeDoux, J. (1996). *The emotional brain*. New York: Simon and Schuster.

Lefcourt, H. M., and Martin, R. A. (1986). *Humor and life stress: antidote to adversity*. New York: Springer-Verlag.

Lehrer, K. (1990). *Theory of knowledge*. Boulder: Westview.

Lehrer, K., and Wagner, C. (1981). *Rational consensus in science and society*. Dordrecht: Reidel.

Lempert, R. (1986). The new evidence scholarship: analyzing the process of proof. *Boston University Law Review* 66: 439–477.

Lévesque, R. (1968). *An option for Quebec*. Toronto: McClelland and Stewart.

Levi, I. (1980). *The enterprise of knowledge*. Cambridge: MIT Press.

Lewis, J. D., and Weigert, A. (1985). Trust as a social reality. *Social Forces* 63: 967–985.

Lipton, P. (1991). *Inference to the best explanation.* London: Routledge.

Lodge, M., and Stroh, P. (1993). Inside the mental voting booth: an impression-driven process model of candidate evaluation. In S. Iyengar, and W. J. McGuire (eds.), *Explorations in political psychology* (pp. 225–295). Durham: Duke University Press.

Lycan, W. (1988). *Judgement and justification.* Cambridge: Cambridge University Press.

MacDonald, M. C., Pearlmutter, N. J., and Seidenberg, M. S. (1994). Lexical nature of syntactic ambiguity resolution. *Psychological Review* 101: 676–703.

Maher, P. (1993). *Betting on theories.* Cambridge: Cambridge University Press.

Marr, D., and Poggio, T. (1976). Cooperative computation of stereo disparity. *Science* 194: 283–287.

May, L., Friedman, M., and Clark, A. (eds.), (1996). *Mind and morals: essays on ethics and cognitive science.* Cambridge: MIT Press.

McAllister, J. W. (1996). *Beauty and revolution in science.* Ithaca: Cornell University Press.

McClelland, J. L., and Rumelhart, D. E. (1981). An interactive activation model of context effects in letter perception. Part 1: An account of basic findings. *Psychological Review* 88: 375–407.

McClelland, J. L., and Rumelhart, D. E. (1989). *Explorations in parallel distributed processing.* Cambridge: MIT Press.

Medin, D. L., and Ross, B. H. (1992). *Cognitive psychology.* Fort Worth: Harcourt Brace Jovanovich.

Menzel, W. (1998). Constraint satisfaction for robust parsing of spoken language. *Journal of Experimental and Theoretical Artificial Intelligence* 10: 77–89.

Millgram, E. (1991). Harman's hardness arguments. *Pacific Philosophical Quarterly* 72: 181–202.

Millgram, E. (2000). Coherence: the price of the ticket. *Journal of Philosophy* 97: 82–93.

Millgram, E., and Thagard, P. (1996). Deliberative coherence. *Synthese* 108: 63–88.

Minsky, M. (1997). A framework for representing knowledge. In J. Haugeland (ed.), *Mind design II* (pp. 111–142). Cambridge: MIT Press.

Misztal, B. A. (1996). *Trust in modern societies*. Cambridge: Polity Press.

Neapolitain, R. (1990). *Probabilistic reasoning in expert systems*. New York: John Wiley.

Neurath, O. (1959). Protocol sentences. In A. J. Ayer (ed.), *Logical positivism* (pp. 199–208). Glencoe, Ill.: Free Press.

Nowak, G., and Thagard, P. (1992a). Copernicus, Ptolemy, and explanatory coherence. In R. Giere (ed.), *Cognitive models of science* (vol. 15, pp. 274–309). Minneapolis: University of Minnesota Press.

Nowak, G., and Thagard, P. (1992b). Newton, Descartes, and explanatory coherence. In R. Duschl, and R. Hamilton (eds.), *Philosophy of Science, Cognitive Psychology, and Educational Theory and Practice* (pp. 69–115). Albany: SUNY Press.

O'Laughlin, C., and Thagard, P. (forthcoming). Autism and coherence: a computational model. *Mind and Language*.

Oatley, K. (1992). *Best laid schemes: the psychology of emotions*. Cambridge: Cambridge University Press.

Ortony, A., Clore, G. L., and Collins, A. (1988). *The cognitive structure of emotions*. Cambridge: Cambridge University Press.

Paley, W. (1963). *Natural theology: selections*. Indianapolis: Bobbs-Merrill.

Panksepp, J. (1998). *Affective neuroscience: the foundations of human and animal emotions*. Oxford: Oxford University Press.

Paulos, J. A. (1980). *Mathematics and humor*. Chicago: University of Chicago Press.

Pearl, J. (1988). *Probabilistic reasoning in intelligent systems*. San Mateo: Morgan Kaufman.

Peirce, C. S. (1958). *Charles S. Peirce: selected writings*. New York: Dover.

Peng, Y., and Reggia, J. (1990). *Abductive inference models for diagnostic problem solving*. New York: Springer-Verlag.

Pennington, N., and Hastie, R. (1986). Evidence evaluation in complex decision making. *Journal of Personality and Social Psychology* 51: 242–258.

Pojman, L. P. (ed.), (1993). *The theory of knowledge: classic and contemporary readings*. Belmont, Calif.: Wadsworth.

Polya, G. (1957). *How to solve it*. Princeton, N.J.: Princeton University Press.

Prince, A., and Smolensky, P. (1997). Optimality: from neural networks to universal grammar. *Science* 275: 1604–1610.

Putnam, H. (1983). There is a at least one *a priori* truth. In H. Putnam (ed.), *Realism and reason*, vol. 3 of *Philosophical papers* (pp. 98–114). Cambridge: Cambridge University Press.

Quine, W. V. O. (1960). *Word and object*. Cambridge: MIT Press.

Quine, W. V. O. (1963). *From a logical point of view*. Second ed. New York: Harper Torchbooks.

Railton, P. (1986). Moral realism. *Philosophical Review* 95: 163–207.

Ranney, M., and Schank, P. (1998). Toward an integration of the social and the scientific: observing, modeling, and promoting the explanatory coherence of reasoning. In S. J. Read, and L. C. Miller (eds.), *Connectionist models of social reasoning and social behavior* (pp. 245–274). Mahwah, N.J.: Erlbaum.

Rawls, J. (1971). *A theory of justice*. Cambridge: Harvard University Press.

Rawls, J. (1996). *Political liberalism*. New York: Columbia University Press.

Raz, J. (1992). The relevance of coherence. *Boston University Law Review* 72: 273–321.

Read, S., and Marcus-Newhall, A. (1993). The role of explanatory coherence in the construction of social explanations. *Journal of Personality and Social Psychology* 65: 429–447.

Reed, E. S. (1997). *From soul to mind: the emergence of psychology from Erasmus Darwin to William James*. New Haven: Yale University Press.

Richardson, H. S. (1994). *Practical reasoning about final ends*. Cambridge: Cambridge University Press.

Rock, I. (1983). *The logic of perception*. Cambridge: MIT Press.

Rosen, J. (1975). *Symmetry discovered*. Cambridge: Cambridge University Press.

Rosen, J. (1995). *Symmetry in science: an introduction to the general theory*. New York: Springer-Verlag.

Rumelhart, D., Smolensky, P., Hinton, G., and McClelland, J. (1986). Schemata and sequential thought processes in PDP models. In J. McClelland, and D. Rumelhart (eds.), *Parallel distributed processing: explorations in the microstructure of cognition* (vol. 2, pp. 7–57). Cambridge: MIT Press.

Russell, B. (1973). *Essays in analysis.* London: Allen and Unwin.

Sanders, J. T., and Narveson, J. (eds.), (1996). *For and against the state.* Lanham, Md.: Rowman and Littlefield.

Sayre-McCord, G. (1996). Coherentist epistemology and moral theory. In W. Sinnott-Armstrong, and M. Timmons (eds.), *Moral knowledge? New readings in moral epistemology* (pp. 137–189). Oxford: Oxford University Press.

Schank, P., and Ranney, M. (1991). Modeling an experimental study of explanatory coherence. *Proceedings of the Thirteenth Annual Conference of the Cognitive Science Society* (pp. 892–897). Hillsdale, N.J.: Erlbaum.

Schank, P., and Ranney, M. (1992). Assessing explanatory coherence: a new method for integrating verbal data with models of on-line belief revision, *Proceedings of the Fourteenth Annual Conference of the Cognitive Science Society* (pp. 599–604). Hillsdale, N.J.: Erlbaum.

Sears, D., Huddy, L., and Schaffer, L. (1986). A schematic variant of symbolic politics theory, as applied to racial and gender equality. In R. Lau, and D. Sears (eds.), *Political cognition* (pp. 159–202). Hillsdale, N.J.: Erlbaum.

Selman, B., Levesque, H., and Mitchell, D. (1992). A new method for solving hard satisfiability problems. *Proceedings of the Tenth National Conference on Artificial Intelligence* (pp. 440–446). Menlo Park: AAAI Press.

Shelley, C., Donaldson, T., and Parsons, K. (1996). Humorous analogy: modeling *The Devil's Dictionary.* In J. Hulstijn, and A. Nijholt (eds.), *Proceedings of the Twente Workshop on Language Technology 12: Automatic Interpretation and Generation of Verbal Humor.* Twente: University of Twente.

Shrager, J., and Langley, P. (1990). *Computational models of scientific discovery and theory formation.* San Mateo: Morgan Kaufmann.

Shultz, T. R., and Lepper, M. R. (1996). Cognitive dissonance reduction as constraint satisfaction. *Psychological Review* 103: 219–240.

Sinclair, L., and Kunda, Z. (1999). Reactions to a black professional: motivated inhibition and activation of conflicting stereotypes. *Journal of Personality and Social Psychology* 77: 885–904.

Smolensky, P. (1990). Tensor product variable binding and the representation of symbolic structures in connectionist systems. *Artificial Intelligence* 46: 159–217.

Spivey-Knowlton, M. J., Trueswell, J. C., and Tanenhaus, M. K. (1993). Context effects in syntactic ambiguity resolution: discourse and semantic influences in parsing reduced relative clauses. *Canadian Journal of Experimental Psychology* 47: 276–309.

St. John, M. F., and McClelland, J. L. (1992). Parallel constraint satisfaction as a comprehension mechanism. In R. G. Reilly, and N. E. Sharkey (eds.), *Connectionist approaches to natural language processing* (pp. 97–136). Hillsdale, N.J.: Erlbaum.

Stern, P. C. (1995). Why do people sacrifice for their nations? *Political Psychology* 16: 217–235.

Stich, S. (1988). Reflective equilibrium, analytic epistemology, and the problem of cognitive diversity. *Synthese* 74: 391–413.

Stocker, M., and Hegeman, E. (1996). *Valuing emotions*. Cambridge: Cambridge University Press.

Swanton, C. (1992). *Freedom: a coherence theory*. Indianapolis: Hackett.

Swinburne, R. (1990). *The existence of God*. Second ed. Oxford: Oxford University Press.

Swinburne, R. (1996). *Is there a god?* Oxford: Oxford University Press.

Taylor, G. J. (1994). The scientific legacy of Apollo. *Scientific American*, July, 40–47.

Thagard, P. (1988). *Computational philosophy of science*. Cambridge: MIT Press.

Thagard, P. (1989). Explanatory coherence. *Behavioral and Brain Sciences* 12: 435–467.

Thagard, P. (1991). The dinosaur debate: explanatory coherence and the problem of competing hypotheses. In J. Pollock, and R. Cummins (eds.), *Philosophy and AI: essays at the interface* (pp. 279–300). Cambridge: MIT Press.

Thagard, P. (1992a). Adversarial problem solving: modelling an opponent using explanatory coherence. *Cognitive Science* 16: 123–149.

Thagard, P. (1992b). *Conceptual revolutions.* Princeton: Princeton University Press.

Thagard, P. (1993). Computational tractability and conceptual coherence: why do computer scientists believe that P ≠ NP? *Canadian Journal of Philosophy* 23: 349–364.

Thagard, P. (1996). *Mind: introduction to cognitive science.* Cambridge: MIT Press.

Thagard, P. (1999). *How scientists explain disease.* Princeton: Princeton University Press.

Thagard, P. (forthcoming). How to make decisions: coherence, emotion, and practical inference. In E. Millgram (ed.), *Varieties of practical inference.* Cambridge: MIT Press.

Thagard, P., Eliasmith, C., Rusnock, P., and Shelley, C. P. (forthcoming). Knowledge and coherence. In R. Elio (ed.), *Common sense, reasoning, and rationality* (vol. 11). New York: Oxford University Press.

Thagard, P., Holyoak, K., Nelson, G., and Gochfeld, D. (1990). Analog retrieval by constraint satisfaction. *Artificial Intelligence* 46: 259–310.

Thagard, P., and Kunda, Z. (1998). Making sense of people: coherence mechanisms. In S. J. Read, and L. C. Miller (eds.), *Connectionist models of social reasoning and social behavior* (pp. 3–26). Hillsdale, N.J.: Erlbaum.

Thagard, P., and Millgram, E. (1995). Inference to the best plan: a coherence theory of decision. In A. Ram, and D. B. Leake (eds.), *Goal-driven learning* (pp. 439–454). Cambridge: MIT Press.

Thagard, P., and Shelley, C. P. (forthcoming). Emotional analogies and analogical inference. In D. Gentner, K. H. Holyoak, and B. N. Kokinov (eds.), *The analogical mind: perspectives from cognitive science.* Cambridge: MIT Press.

Thagard, P., and Verbeurgt, K. (1998). Coherence as constraint satisfaction. *Cognitive Science* 22: 1–24.

Thomson, J. J. (1971). A defense of abortion. *Philosophy and Public Affairs* 1: 47–66.

Trabasso, T., and Suh, S. (1994). Understanding text: achieving explanatory coherence through on-line inferences and mental operations in working memory. *Discourse Processes* 16: 3–34.

Tversky, A., and Koehler, D. J. (1994). Support theory: a nonextensional representation of subjective probability. *Psychological Review* 101: 547–567.

Van den Broek, P. (1994). Comprehension and memory of narrative texts: inferences and coherence. In M. A. Gernsbacher (ed.), *Handbook of psycholinguistics* (pp. 539–588). San Diego: Academic Press.

Watson, J. D. (1969). *The double helix*. New York: New American Library.

Westen, D. (2000). Integrative psychotherapy: integrating psychodynamic and cognitive-behavioral theory and technique. In C. R. Snyder, and R. Ingram (eds.), *Handbook of psychotherapy: the processes and practices of psychological change*. New York: Wiley.

Westen, D., and Feit, A. (forthcoming). All the president's women: affective constraint satisfaction in ambiguous social cognition. Unpublished manuscript, Department of Psyclology, Boston University.

Whewell, W. (1967). *The philosophy of the inductive sciences*. New York: Johnson Reprint Corp. Originally published in 1840.

Wigmore, J. H. (1937). *The science of judicial proof as given by logic, psychology, and general experience and illustrated in judicial trials*. Third ed. Boston: Little Brown.

Wilson, D. J. (1990). *Science, community, and the transformation of American philosophy, 1860–1930*. Chicago: University of Chicago Press.

Wood, J. A. (1986). Moon over Mauna Loa: a review of hypotheses of formation of Earth's moon. In W. K. Hartmann, R. J. Phillips, and G. J. Taylor (eds.), *Origin of the moon* (pp. 17–55). Houston: Lunar and Planetary Institute.

Zajonc, R. (1980). Feeling and thinking: preferences need no inferences. *American Psychologist* 35: 151–175.

Zemach, E. M. (1997). *Real beauty*. University Park: Pennsylvania State University Press.

Index

BonJour, L., 5, 49, 76
Bosanquet, B., 5, 76–77
Bower, G., 170, 176
Bradley, D., 57
Bradley, F., 5, 86
Brentano, F., 7
Brink, D., 21, 125
Brown, J., 74
Bruner, J., 10
Brush, S., 237
Buchanan, B., 260
Byrne, M., 48

Campbell, K., 181
Capital punishment, 125, 133, 136–137, 143
Capitalism, 154, 156
Caputi, M., 187
Carnap, R., 11, 247
Carter, J., 165
Cartwright, N., 90
Causal reasoning, 245–249, 270
Cayley, A., 56
CCC, 226–230, 235–237, 240
Chalmers, D., 101
Charniak, E., 247
Chrétien, J., 192
Christen, Y., 283
Churchland, P. M., 10, 162
Churchland, P. S., 10
Circularity, 75–76
Clark, A., 10
Clinton, B., 185, 219
Clore, G., 170
Cognitive dissonance, 23, 25, 197
Cognitive naturalism, 2, 9–12, 162, 220, 276, 278–279
Cognitive science, 2, 9–10
Cognitive therapy, 208–210
Cohen, L., 247, 270
Coherence
  analogical (see Analogical coherence)

conceptual (see Conceptual coherence)
computing, 25–37
conditions, 18, 26, 71
as constraint satisfaction, 15–19, 81
deductive (see Deductive coherence)
deliberative (see Deliberative coherence)
discriminating, 71–73, 227, 277
emotional (see Emotional coherence)
explanatory (see Explanatory coherence)
perceptual (see Perceptual coherence)
in philosophy, 4–6
in psychology, 2–4
measuring, 37–39
problem, 17–18, 37
and truth, 280
Collingwood, R., 199
Collins, A., 170
Communication, 223, 226, 228–229
Competition, 43, 50
Conceptual coherence, 60–65, 81, 168, 179, 213, 215, 277
Conferences, 224–225, 230, 238–241
Connectionism, 30. See *also* Algorithm, connectionist
Consciousness, 97–98, 100–101, 140
Consensus, 142, 223–243, 285
Consequentialist ethics, 130, 147–148
Conservatism, 75
Constraint satisfaction, 15–19, 132
Constraints, 17, 67–68, 140, 170–171